VIRGINIAS
TRAVEL ★ SMART®

ALSO INCLUDES WASHINGTON, D.C.

W9-CKF-335

VIRGINIAS
TRAVEL ✦ SMART®

ALSO INCLUDES WASHINGTON, D.C.

Gail Doyle

John Muir Publications
Santa Fe, New Mexico

Acknowledgments

With special thanks to US Airways, Cindy Harrington, Steve Shaluda, Martha Steger, Anne Atkinson, Lisa Holland, Brian Ball, Gail Lowry, Joanne Mitchell, Bill Arey, Aly Goodwin, Ann Walker, Mary and Gil Willis, Stephen Plescow, Beverly Wellman, Debra Dodson, Pat Kloenne, Suzanne Taylor, Sam Martinette, Mary Calos, William Luebke, Jennifer Mullen, Teresa Fremaux, Ronald Lamers, David Parker, Sheila Harrison, Michelle Menendez, Catherine Fox, Sharon Cavileer, Leslie King, Deb Perry, Sacil Armstrong, Connie New, Sandy Belan, my husband Don, and my daughter Ryan.

John Muir Publications, P.O. Box 613, Santa Fe, New Mexico 87504

Printed in the United States of America.
First printing June 1999.

ISSN: 1099-8705
ISBN: 1-56261-453-3

Editors: Marybeth Griffin, Jane Salodof MacNeil
Graphics Editor: Bunny Wong
Production: Rebecca Cook
Design: Marie J.T. Vigil
Cover Design: Janine Lehmann, Marie J.T. Vigil
Typesetting: Diane Rigoli
Map Style Development: American Custom Maps–Albuquerque, NM
Map Illustration: Michael Hermann, Scott Lockheed, Kathy Sparkes
Printing: Publishers Press
Front Cover Photos: *small*— © Roberto Arakak/Photo Network (United States Capitol)
                  large— © Fridmar Damm/Leo de Wys (Virginia, natural stone bridge)
Back Cover Photo: © Jeff Greenberg/Leo de Wys (Yorktown Victory Center)

Distributed to the book trade by
Publishers Group West
Berkeley, California

VIRGINIAS TRAVEL•SMART: A GUIDE THAT GUIDES

Most guidebooks are basically directories, providing information but very little help in making choices—you have to guess how to make the most of your time and money. *Virginias Travel•Smart* is different: By highlighting the very best of the region it acts like a personal tour guide rather than a directory.

TAKE THE STRESS OUT OF TRAVEL

Sometimes traveling causes more stress than it relieves. Sorting through information, figuring out the best routes, determining what to see and where to eat and stay, scheduling each day in order to get the most out of your time—all of this can make a vacation feel daunting rather than fun. Relax. We've done a lot of the legwork for you. This book will help you plan a trip that suits *you*—whatever your time frame, budget, and interests.

SEE THE BEST OF THE REGION

Author Gail Doyle has lived in Virginia for 32 years. She has hand-picked every listing in this book, and she gives you an insider's perspective on what makes each one worthwhile. So while you will find many of the big tourist attractions listed, you'll also find lots of smaller, lesser known treasures, such as the charming gristmills along the Blue Ridge Parkway in Southwest Virginia or the intriguing National Radio Astronomy Observatory in the West Virginia Highlands.

In selecting the restaurants and accommodations for this book, the author sought out unusual spots with local flavor. While in some areas of the region chains are unavoidable, wherever possible the author directs you to one-of-a-kind places. We also know that you want a range of options: One day you may crave well-bred Virginia venison accompanied by traditional peanut soup, while the next day you would be just as happy (as would your wallet) with country cooking served buffet style. Most of the restaurants and accommodations listed here are moderately priced, but the author also includes budget and splurge options, depending on the destination.

CREATE THE TRIP YOU WANT

We all have different travel styles. Some people like spontaneous weekend jaunts, while others plan longer, more leisurely trips. You may want to cover as much ground as possible, no matter how much time you have. Or maybe you prefer to focus your trip on one part of the state or on some special interest, such as history, nature, or art. We've taken these differences into account.

Though the individual chapters stand on their own, they are organized in a geographically logical sequence, so that you could conceivably fly into Washington/Dulles International Airport in D.C., drive chapter by chapter to each destination in the book, and end up close to where you started. Of course, you don't have to follow that sequence, but it's there if you want a complete picture of the region.

Each destination chapter offers ways of prioritizing when time is limited: In the Perfect Day section, the author suggests what to do if you have only one day to spend in the area. Also, every Sightseeing Highlight is rated, from one to four stars: ★★★★—or "must see"—sights first, followed by ★★★ sights, then ★★ sights, and finally ★—or "see if you have spare time"—sights. At the end of each sight listing is a time recommendation in parentheses. User-friendly maps help you locate the sights, restaurants, and lodgings of your choice.

And if you're in it for the ride, so to speak, you'll want to check out the Scenic Routes described at the end of several chapters. They take you through some of the most scenic parts of the region.

In addition to these special features, the appendix has other useful travel tools:

- The Mileage Chart and Planning Map help you determine your own route and calculate travel time.
- The Special Interest Tours show you how to design your trip around any of 6 favorite interests.
- The Resources guide tells you where to go for more information about national and state parks, individual cities and counties, local bed-and-breakfasts, and more.

HAPPY TRAVELS

With this book in hand, you have many reliable recommendations and travel tools at your fingertips. Use it to make the most of your trip. And have a great time!

WHY VISIT
THE VIRGINIAS?

Undoubtedly, at one time or another, something will draw you to this place. Even if you live a continent away there's something in America's story that touches the very soul. For this is the place where a new democracy was born and men and women fought against tyranny. Here, an idea was born that "all men are created equal, that they are endowed by their Creator with certain unalienable rights, that among these are Life, Liberty and the Pursuit of Happiness." Thomas Jefferson's words often come to mind when traveling around this land where a free nation was born, blood was shed to end slavery, and a revolutionary political system steers the most powerful nation in the modern world.

Imagine what the first European settlers must have thought as they explored this new land with its rolling hills, ancient mountains, and native people. The natives of the region left their marks on the land approximately 11 thousand years ago. Virginia and West Virginia have protected their natural environment so that expansion and technology does not spoil its riches. In the two states alone, there are more than 100 state and national parks, forests, and wildlife management areas as diverse as they are worthwhile.

The coastal area offers variety—from the undisturbed Eastern Shore where wild ponies roam to the resort hotels of Virginia Beach. Out west, the land turns wild with rolling hills and soft-peaked mountains filled with historic and natural surprises down every country back road. Not just another pretty face, this area also offers some of the country's best outdoor activities—hiking, biking, skiing, and white-water rafting, just to name a few.

This region has stored away America's most precious historic and cultural artifacts, and now they're on display for you at some of the world's most famous museums, galleries, and historic sites. Washington, D.C., the grand-daddy of museum cities, showcases an endless array of cavernous museums, monuments, and public buildings for you to tour—most of them at no admission cost. At Mount Vernon, Monticello, and other great historic homes, you can catch a glimpse of the everyday life of the country's founding fathers. In Colonial Williamsburg, an entire city has been brought back to life with costumed interpreters giving tours, making pottery, blowing glass, and driving horse-drawn carriages down its dusty streets.

In essence, great care has been taken to share the country's heritage with visitors here. Those who believe that history is one big yawn will be pleasantly surprised. Here, visitors are encouraged to be actively involved in the presentation and understanding of the nation's history.

THE LAY OF THE LAND

The diverse region stretches from the Coastal Plain to the mountains of the Blue Ridge and Alleghenies. Within a days' drive are rugged mountains, rolling hills, marshlands, beaches, and large metropolitan cities. The Tidewater region itself along the coastline is dramatically different from point to point. The Eastern Shore's quiet shoreline sits across from the busy ports of Norfolk and the resort sands of Virginia Beach. Heading up towards Washington, the Northern Neck region simmers down again with small town peacefulness. The York, Rappahannock, James, and Potomac Rivers slice Virginia into three peninsulas from the coastline.

Moving westward, the Piedmont Plateau extends from the fall line running from the District of Columbia through Richmond. West from here the terrain becomes hilly reaching the Blue Ridge Mountains. The Blue Ridge stretches for more than 100 miles in Virginia. Its highest elevation is Mount Rogers at 5,729 feet. Beyond these mountains lies the Shenandoah Valley (Shenandoah is an Indian word meaning "daughter of the stars"), which stretches from Winchester to Roanoke.

The Alleghenies comprise the entire eastern half of the state and most of West Virginia is considered backcountry. The Alleghenies have a highest peak of 4,861 feet on Spruce Knob. Deep gorges can be found throughout these rugged mountains with wild mountain waters at their base. North and northwest of the mountains are lower-lying regions where more commercial areas and towns exist. The slender regions to the northeast and northwest are called the Eastern and Northern Panhandles.

FLORA AND FAUNA

When the first European settlers arrived in Jamestown, they were at once amazed and beguiled by the beauty of the landscape. Although more than 300 years has done quite a bit to change the region, it is still a lovely site to behold. The Tidewater coast, a combination of wetlands and dense brush, is home to an abundance of wildlife such as cranes, hawks, otters, and water moccasins. The Chesapeake Bay, once threatened by technology, has been passionately guarded by environmentalists. Today, the region is a great comeback story and is a haven for wildlife. Visitors to the area can even take whale-watching expeditions off the coast.

Once in Central Virginia, thick undercover and foliage gives way to rolling hills with evergreens, flowering trees, and towering oaks. Virginia's springtime is characterized by its profusion of color made possible by the region's Bradford pear, crepe myrtle, azaleas, magnolia, and dogwood. Central Virginia's Piedmont region makes up more than half of the state and is also home to a variety of wildlife including fox, rabbit, whitetail deer, black bear, beaver, raccoon, opossum, and eagles.

The misty blue-hued mountains of the Blue Ridge and sharper-edged Alleghenies are lush and resplendent with acres of dense forests, mountain streams, and rocky cliffs. Their valleys are tranquil with unspoiled green meadows sprinkled with small towns, farms, and churches. While the herds of buffalo feasting on tall grasses are long gone, black bear and mountain lion have remained a part of Virginia's mountain wildlife. On the higher elevations in West Virginia, there are even snowshoe hares and rattlesnakes to be found.

HISTORY AND CULTURE

The earliest Native Americans in the Virginia and West Virginia region can be traced to about 9500 B.C. They hunted bear, deer, elk, and moose, and there have even been traces of woolly mammoth and mastodon found in the region.

By the 1400s, the Powhatan tribes were living in permanent villages and farming the lowlands from the James to Potomac Rivers. In the late sixteenth century the Powhatans consolidated about 30 Algonquian groups to form a Powhatan chiefdom numbering more than 13,000 people. In addition to the Powhatan tribe, individual tribes inhabiting the region at this time included

Saponi, Tutelo, Occaneechi, Monacan, Manahoac, Nottoways, Meherrins, Mattaponi, and Pamunkey.

In 1584 Englishman Sir Walter Raleigh named this territory after the "virgin queen," Elizabeth. Although his settlement on Roanoke Island in today's North Carolina perished, a second major expedition was carried out by the London Co. in 1607 which prevailed despite numerous setbacks. By the time the *Susan Constant, Godspeed,* and *Discovery* arrived on the shores of Chesapeake Bay, those aboard had already endured storms, high winds, and illness before they faced the unknowns of this new land. These explorers had heartily volunteered for this adventure for many reasons—riches, political objectives, and religious freedom being the primary ones. As they explored the Virginia coast with its lush foliage and natural beauty, they often came to violent blows with Native Americans. These blood-curdling confrontations lasted for nearly two centuries.

The site of Jamestown, named for King James I, was declared the first permanent settlement on May 13, 1607. One of the most dynamic and fearless leaders of this brave band of settlers was Captain John Smith who played a pivotal role in holding the colony together. It was Smith, you may have heard, who was captured by the natives and brought before the tribe's leader, Powhatan, to be executed, but was saved by a young Indian princess, Pocahontas.

In addition to clashes with the natives, starvation and disease also took their toll on the settlers. Sir Thomas Dale arrived to lead the settlement in 1611 and sent some settlers further upstream on the James River, near present-day Richmond. John Rolfe, later the husband of Pocahontas, was the main influence in cultivating tobacco and making it marketable to England. Tobacco's viability led to the survival of the colony.

The first General Assembly was held in 1619 at Jamestown—the first step in building the new democratic society. That same year, Africans were brought to Virginia—the beginning of the country's legacy of slavery. In 1661 slavery was legalized in Virginia, and by 1671 more than 2,000 slaves were in the colony.

Nearly 8,000 colonists had come to the colony of Virginia since 1607, but by 1624 only 1,095 were still living. Frequent skirmishes between the natives and recent settlers, and other problems such as disease and crop failure, resulted in devastating mortality figures. Nathaniel Bacon became important at this time as a rebel who had taken his fill of the attacks by the Occaneechi and Pamunkey tribes. He led a revolt against the Indians causing a political upheaval in the colony known as Bacon's Rebellion. The Virginia Company survived, however, and more and more settlers began moving westward into the new wilderness despite the dangers of Indians and wild animals. As a matter of fact, the area that is today West Virginia was thought to be too wild for settlement by the Indians. Most natives used the rugged territory as hunting grounds, not as habitat. Eventually, explorers such as Abraham Wood, who discovered and named the New River, crossed wilderness and even the treacherous Allegheny Mountains. Among those who proved they could endure the land were German-Swiss settlers and Scots Irish migrating down from Pennsylvania and Maryland.

At this time, it was decided to move the colonial capital from Jamestown to Williamsburg. Opposition against English rule grew, especially following the French and Indian War. In addition to the everyday concerns in the early 1700s about slave insurrections, pirates off the coast, and westward expansion, there was fiery opposition to British taxation. When England imposed a stamp tax on the colonists without their approval in 1765, a young Virginia lawyer named Patrick Henry led the charge to fight it.

The first engagement of the Revolution is often thought to have occurred in 1774 when Indians were defeated by Virginia militia at the Battle of Point Pleasant in today's West Virginia. The First Virginia Convention met to discuss the problems in Williamsburg that year, with Patrick Henry, George Washington, and Benjamin Harrison among the representatives. In March 1775, the Second Virginia Convention was called in Richmond where Henry shouted his immortal words, "Give me liberty, or give me death!"

By April 1775, the Revolution had begun against the British. In May 1776, after cutting ties with England at another Convention, Virginia established its own constitution with its own code of law. It was the first of the 13 colonies to do so. At this same time, Thomas Jefferson drafted the Declaration of Independence and on July 4, 1776, the document was signed. Patrick Henry was chosen as Virginia's first governor. In 1779, when Thomas Jefferson succeeded Henry as governor, it was voted to move Virginia's capital from Williamsburg to Richmond. Part of the reason for doing this was to distance the governing bodies from British occupation in Tidewater. George Washington led the Continental Army and received much assistance from the Marquis de Lafayette. Cornwallis invaded Virginia in 1781 but was defeated at Yorktown. Peace was declared a year and a half later.

Prior to the Revolution, Colonel Andrew Lewis was ordered to raise 1,000 men to march from the Shenandoah Valley and southwestern Virginia to the Ohio River for a confrontation with Indians due to some recent attacks on settlers. Lewis and his men settled in an area on the site of today's Lewisburg, West Virginia. Here they defeated the Shawnees driving them back across the Ohio River. This victory paved the way for future explorations, including that of George Rogers Clark to the Northwest.

Virginia's George Washington, Patrick Henry, Thomas Jefferson, James

Monroe, James Madison, and others were instrumental in the formative years of the nation. During his presidency, Washington was responsible for shaping many of the ideas concerning expansion in Virginia, including canals, roadways, and railroads. In 1788 the Virginia Convention voted to approve the Constitution under narrow margins—significant because if the populous state had chosen not to ratify, it might have threatened the formation of the Union.

The beginning of the nineteenth century was a tumultuous era. In 1793 the cornerstone of the nation's Capitol building was laid. In 1800 the nation's capital was moved from Philadelphia to Washington, D.C., where a 10-mile tract was laid out and called the District of Columbia. Most of the political leaders were not pleased with this move from luxurious Philadelphia to "wilderness city." During the War of 1812, the British attacked Washington (1814) burning the White House and other public buildings.

Growing controversy also mounted among states as they differed in their opinions regarding slaveholding. Those citizens living in the area that is today West Virginia held few slaves and felt discriminated against on voting issues concerning slaveholding. Although a constitution upholding the right to own slaves was ratified after a Virginia Convention in 1829–30, those in the trans-Allegheny region were against it.

In 1831 Nat Turner's Insurrection in Southampton County brought slavery to the forefront of political issues. John Brown's raid in 1859 and the election of Abraham Lincoln as president in 1860 brought matters to a head. Virginia seceded from the Union on April 17, 1861, and Richmond was chosen as the Capital of the Confederate States. More Civil War battles were fought on Virginia soil than in any other state. The commander of the Confederate Army was eventually Robert E. Lee, who fought tirelessly despite overwhelming odds. Union general Ulysses S. Grant captured Richmond on April 3, 1865, and Lee, followed closely by Grant, was forced to retreat to the west. On April 9, 1865, Lee surrendered at Appomattox Court House ending the conflict.

It would take more than 20 years for Virginia to reestablish its land, economy, and industry. One third of Virginia became West Virginia on June 20, 1863. In 1870, Virginia's statehood was regained and a plan to settle war debts was established. By the turn of the century, industries other than agriculture were increasing. The Tidewater area was vital to World War I and II with its ship-building and the expansion of the Norfolk Naval Base.

In 1954 the U.S. Supreme Court ruled in favor of desegregation in Brown vs. Board of Education. Following that historic ruling, Virginia Governor Harry Byrd and a large contingent of supporters spent years fighting desegregation within the state. A major victory was finally won when the Civil Rights Act of

1964 and the Voting Rights Act of 1965 were passed in Washington. Although change came about slowly in Virginia, as in other Southern states, in 1968 the Supreme Court ruled that localities were required to demonstrate actual progress in desegregation.

Washington, D.C., grew to the city that it is today during this time and Virginia's economy also grew, largely as the government's employment base. Since the turn of the century, Washington has evolved into a cosmopolitan city with diverse cultures and global concerns. West Virginia's coal, logging, and burgeoning outdoor tourism industry have made it a survivor. And in 1989, just a few miles south in what was once the capital of the Confederacy, an enormous sign of change occurred—Virginia elected L. Douglas Wilder as the nation's first African American governor.

THE ARTS

Much of the early pioneer arts and crafts legacy can be found in Virginia and West Virginia. Trades of necessity during those days are treasures to be appreciated today. Native artisans have been passing down the traditions of hand-blowing glass, weaving, quilting, pottery, metal working, and woodworking for more than a century.

Age-old traditions of folk music and performing arts have been handed down in the region as well. Bluegrass was formed as a melding of cultures—fiddles from Ireland and Scotland, banjos from Africa, and guitars from Spain. Events like the Old Time Fiddlers' Convention in Galax, Virginia, celebrate the rich tradition of this music. To accompany the down-home sounds, new types of dancing were created, (e.g. clogging in Virginia and flatfooting in West Virginia). These dances are a combination of Scots Irish stepping with African and Native American influences. Today, see clogging and flatfooting throughout the region at festivals and special events.

The region's diverse infusion of cultures make it a thriving art center offering world-class outlets to display the country's finest works. In Washington alone are more than 125 art museums and galleries, including the National Gallery of American Art, the National Museum of African Art, and the National Portrait Gallery. Truly in Washington there is an enormous wealth of art collections far outreaching its proportions in size. You could spend a full week here viewing masterpieces, and still not see everything. Richmond's Virginia Museum of Fine Arts and Norfolk's Chrysler Museum also hold their own against the nation's most prestigious collections.

Architecturally, the region holds some of the nation's and the world's finest accomplishments. From the stately dome of the U.S. Capitol building to the splendid gothic National Cathedral to the neoclassical lines of Monticello, the capital region is a study in perfection.

And then there are the monuments—from Lincoln sitting solemnly in his chair to Washington's likeness in the Virginia State Capitol—few areas in the country can boast so many recognizable sculptures. Richmond's Monument Avenue is a symbol of a city torn by war and the bronze Iwo Jima Memorial in Northern Virginia is a moving tribute to the brave. Throughout the region, the voluminous history of the nation's beginnings is carved out in stone and marble, or forged in bronze.

CUISINE

While this is the northernmost point of the South, the region still clings to favorite country basics. Even some of the region's finest restaurants serve up their versions of grits and spoonbread. Country ham, biscuits, collard greens, and fried chicken are still Sunday dinner staples. Minced pork barbecue is practically as popular as burgers and fries. For dessert, pecan and sweet potato pies share the list with bread pudding and fruit cobblers. A colonial favorite, peanut soup, can sometimes be found on menus and is quite delicious. The closer you get to Chesapeake Bay, the more seafood is favored. Fresh oysters, crab, and fish are some of the finest catches on the East Coast.

Surprisingly, fine dining in the region is not as conservative as you may imagine. Washington, Northern Virginia, Richmond, and Tidewater, among other areas, have produced some excellent restaurants. Global-minded D.C. has a long list of adventurous opportunities to satisfy their dignified political clientele. Richmond is moving higher and higher up the ranks with talented chefs using fresh, native ingredients (wild game, seafood), great local wines competitive with California, and a decidedly Southern twist. While Virginians and West Virginians are still cautious about trying new styles of cooking, the cosmopolitan flair of D.C. and the northeast are gradually waking up the area's taste buds and creating some pleasant surprises throughout the region.

OUTDOOR ACTIVITIES

Both Virginia and West Virginia have a superb collection of state and national parks/forests. In Virginia, Shenandoah National Park, the George Washington National Forest, and Jefferson National Forest make up nearly two million acres of pristinely preserved forests, mountains, and waterfalls for camping, hiking, and getting back to nature. In West Virginia, the Monongahela National Forest makes up the largest portion of public lands in the state with 909,064 acres. In addition to more than 1.5 million acres of nationally-run parks, there are more than 200,000 acres of state-operated parks/forests. Camping in the region is a one-of-a-kind experience combining natural beauty, wildlife, and history.

Water cravers are able to swim, surf, or boat along the coastline at the resort area of Virginia Beach and several other coastline facilities. Surf and deep-sea fishing are best along the coast and in the lower bay, as these waters are full of bass, bluefish, and flounder among others. Lakes and streams in both states provide excellent freshwater fishing and are regularly stocked with trout and bass by state fish hatcheries.

Hunters will find an abundance of game in virtually all areas of the region including whitetail deer, black bears, wild turkey, ruffed grouse, and more. Check with game officials (Virginia 804/367-1000 and West Virginia 304/558-2771) for hunting seasons in regard to licenses, regions and species, and phone numbers.

Thrill seekers know that West Virginia's Gauley and New Rivers are synonymous with white-water rafting. Expeditions from Class I–VI are available here with an overwhelming choice of qualified outfitters. In Richmond, Virginia, rafters can experience a unique white-water experience, where outfitters offer the only urban white-water rafting in the country. For information on outfitters in West Virginia, contact 888/RAFT WVA, and in Virginia, call the Virginia Tourism Corp. at 800/VISIT VA.

West Virginia offers renowned skiing and snowboarding on its peaks including Snowshoe/Silver Creek, Canaan Valley, Timberline, and Winterplace resorts. The five major ski areas in Virginia are Wintergreen, Massanutten, Bryce, The Homestead, and Cascade Mountain. Many areas also offer cross-country skiing tours, as well as snowshoeing.

Hundreds of the country's best hiking and biking trails can be found throughout the region, and portions of the Appalachian and Allegheny Trails cut through Virginia and West Virginia. Rock climbers know West Virginia for its challenging cliff walls—especially Seneca Rocks with a 900-foot-tall climbing surface.

PLANNING YOUR TRIP

Before you set out on your trip, you'll need to do some planning. Use this chapter in conjunction with the tools in the appendix to answer some basic questions. First of all, when are you going? You may already have specific dates in mind; if not, various factors will probably influence your timing. Either way, you'll want to know about the weather and other seasonal considerations. This chapter discusses all of that.

How much should you expect to spend on your trip? This chapter addresses various regional factors you'll want to consider in estimating your travel expenses. How will you get around? Check out the section on local transportation. If you decide to travel by car, the Planning Map and Mileage Chart in the appendix can help you figure out exact routes and driving times, while the Special Interest Tours provide several focused itineraries. The chapter concludes with some reading recommendations, both fiction and nonfiction, to give you various perspectives on the region. If you want specific information about individual cities or counties, use the Resource guide in the appendix.

HOW MUCH WILL IT COST?

Traveling in the Virginias is quite affordable. Accommodations and food prices are average to below average in both Virginia and West Virginia during most seasons. Virginia Beach's rates are naturally higher June through August, but bargains during the off-months. The same goes for ski areas during the winter months and resort areas during warm weather—prime golfing—months. Although there are high-end luxury hotels throughout the region with prices to match, the average rate for a mid-range hotel in Virginia and West Virginia is $75 to $85 a night.

Washington, D.C.'s lowest-occupancy months are July and August when Congress is in recess and during the holidays around Christmas. Rates during the week compare with other major cities such as New York and Los Angeles at more than $150 per night, with weekends slightly less expensive. One alternative is to check with hotels south of the Potomac in Virginia or north of the city in Maryland for less expensive rates during these peak times. Many hotels also offer special weekend packages.

Budget lodging is available throughout the region at about $30 to $40 per night, except in Washington, D.C., where rates are higher. Bed-and-breakfast and country inns throughout the region are moderate to expensive with prices ranging from $80 to $150 a night. Spa accommodations are priced to include meals and amenities and are pricey at well over $200 a night. Campsites in Virginia and West Virginia range from $10 to $15 a night. Room tax in Virginia and in West Virginia averages 8 to 10 percent depending on the location. D.C. has a room tax of 13 percent with a $1.50 occupancy tax added on.

Virginia and West Virginia restaurants, even the finer ones, can be called bargains compared to those in major American cities. Dinner for two at a good quality dining establishment, with few exceptions, averages less than $65. Travelers watching their food budget will spend approximately $40 per day, per person on meals, taking into account some fast-food and occasional nicer dinners. In Washington, D.C., however, you will probably spend in excess of $60 per day, per person on food.

You can save on admission prices at certain D.C. attractions by contacting your congressman or senator's office at least two weeks prior to visiting. Free tickets are available for early-morning guided tours of the White House, U.S. Capitol, F.B.I., and Bureau of Printing and Engraving.

Overall, a week's vacation in the Virginias and D.C. will cost between $800 and $1,200. Staying solely in the D.C. area for one week will cost more than $1,500. Both totals include five nights' accommodations at a mid-priced hotel or bed-and-breakfast inn, meals, souvenirs, attraction admission, and transportation costs for two people.

For luxury travelers who only want the best, a vacation in the Virginias and D.C. could easily cost more than $2,500 for the week. In other words, the Virginias and D.C. offer a little bit of everything for every kind of traveler.

CLIMATE

East of the mountains, the Virginia region is primarily temperate with delightful springs and autumns, and mild winters. During the summer, temperatures can climb frequently to the 100-degree mark with humidity to match. Although this area does get occasional snowfall, especially Washington, D.C. and west of Richmond, there is little annual accumulation overall.

When you enter the mountains, however, winters are much more pronounced. Snowfall averages 9.67 inches annually in the Alleghenies of West Virginia from October through April. The rest of the year in West Virginia and the mountain region is unbelievably mild with low humidity and cooler temperatures than the east. Some areas in the higher elevations average only 60 degrees during summer months.

WHEN TO GO

The best time to visit the Virginias and D.C. region is in spring or fall when the temperatures are mild and the foliage is either in full bloom or orange-hued. In D.C., if you don't mind crowds, the cherry blossoms are in full bloom in mid-April. In Virginia, Historic Garden Week is the last week of April and is a good indicator that there will be a spectacular floral backdrop for your visit. The autumn leaves are most dramatic in early November in the Piedmont area and early to mid-October in the mountains and West Virginia. The beach area is not as steamy during the spring and post-Labor Day if you don't mind more frigid water temperatures.

As for D.C., the least crowded times to visit the city's famous museums is during the holidays in December. During this time, most of the congressional folks are on vacation and school groups have taken a rest. Another great time to visit minus throngs is during off-peak hours. Call ahead to the attraction in question for more information.

Although skiing is a principal attraction in the West Virginia mountains, the winter months in the Alleghenies can be harsh. Although locals are very much accustomed to driving along icy and steep mountain roads with hairpin curves and no guardrail reflectors, the average visitor may not be able to navigate as well. Make sure you understand road conditions before heading up a mountain.

ORIENTATION AND TRANSPORTATION

Travel throughout the region is easily navigable due to an abundance of well-cared for roadways. Interstate 95 bisects Virginia through Washington, D.C.

It is the main artery on which to connect to other thoroughfares in the area. I-95 is notoriously busy as the East Coast's main north/south highway. In Northern Virginia, your travel companions will be anxious D.C. commuters, bold truck drivers, and the New England–to–Florida travelers who frequent the roadway. From Washington, D.C., south to Dale City near Potomac Mills Mall, traffic is bumper to bumper from 6:30 until 9:30 a.m. and again from 3:30 until 6:30 p.m. Plan your travels around these key gridlock periods. In Richmond, rush hour on I-95 is milder, but can also come to a standstill. South of Petersburg, there's often construction on the highway (especially just north of the North Carolina border).

Interstate 64 intersects east/west with I-95 at Richmond and extends eastward to the coast and westward into West Virginia. When taking I-64 east to Williamsburg and Tidewater, traffic often builds up west of Norfolk at the tunnel and into the beach area. Westward, there are few hold-ups, except for during inclement weather on Afton Mountain west of Charlottesville. I-64 briefly connects with I-81 from Staunton to Lexington and then continues on into West Virginia where it merges with I-77.

Interstate 81 enters Virginia north of Winchester on the state's northern boundary and travels west through the Shenandoah Valley to Harrisonburg, Staunton, Lexington, Roanoke, and Bristol through Virginia's southern border. Another major thoroughfare is I-77 in West Virginia connecting Bluefield to Charleston and Parkersburg. There are some spectacular scenic back roads off the major interstates in both West Virginia and Virginia, but remember to be cautious in icy or foggy weather. A four-wheel-drive vehicle is recommended in higher elevations during the winter months.

Scenic mountain views can be enjoyed on Virginia's Blue Ridge Parkway/Skyline Drive and the West Virginia's Highlands Scenic Highway. The Colonial Parkway connects key elements of Virginia's historic triangle—Williamsburg, Jamestown, and Yorktown.

In D.C. it is best to park your car and use the city's clean, modern Metro rail and bus system for transportation. This will save you valuable time, money, and frustration trying to understand the geometric street layout. Besides, D.C.'s Metro is one of the nicest in this country. If you just can't stand being away from your car for long, get on the George Washington Memorial Parkway for great views of the area near Arlington.

The three major airports in the region are—Baltimore/Washington International Airport, Washington/Dulles International Airport, and the Ronald Reagan International Airport (formerly Washington National Airport). Richmond International Airport and Norfolk International Airport are also heavily trafficked, although not hubs. In West Virginia, small commercial airports include those at Charleston, Lewisburg, Clarksburg, and Huntington. In Virginia, Roanoke and Charlottesville have mentionable small airports.

The D.C. area airports offer a full range of domestic and international flights from most major carriers. Taxi fare to the city from Washington International or Dulles averages $40; from nearby Washington National, $15. Washington National is also on the Metro's yellow and blue lines. If you are not limited to just visiting D.C., the airport in Richmond may be a way to escape the size and bustle of the D.C. facilities. Airfare prices, however, will be more expensive.

Amtrak trains service the D.C. area at the gorgeous Union Station or the Alexandria, Virginia, station. The Beaux Arts Union Station has been restored to its original splendor and contains a 125-store mall, great restaurants, and other amenities. In Richmond, the spectacular Main Street Station is being revived and is slated for rail stops by 1999. Amtrak stops in every corner of Virginia and also has stops in West Virginia in the Eastern Panhandle, Charleston, and Greenbrier Valley regions. The Cardinal offers regular rail service that stops directly outside the Greenbrier Resort's front gates. This makes Greenbrier a convenient weekend getaway for Washingtonians. For a complete list of scheduled stops call, 800/USA RAIL.

Washington's Metrorail/Metrobus is one of the finest intracity transportation services in the country. Metro stops are convenient to virtually all of the city's attractions, restaurants, and hotels. Entrances to the stations are marked by large columns marked with the letter M. The base fare is $1.10 per person, and children under age four travel free. Farecards are used instead of tokens and are available at machines at each station entrance. One-day passes are available for unlimited riding for $5. Buses are used where there is no rail service such as Georgetown. For a schedule and list of routes, call, 202/637-7000 or 888/METRO INFO.

A few Virginia/West Virginia cities have intracity transportation. Richmond, Norfolk, Virginia Beach, Hampton, Roanoke, and Charleston have bus service used mainly by commuters. Richmond, Virginia Beach, and Charleston offer downtown trolley service between hotels and attractions.

CAMPING, LODGING, AND DINING

Virginia and West Virginia, laden with acres of parkland, offer a wide variety of commercial, state, and national campgrounds. Sites at state and national parks and forests are great values at less than $20 and often are located in spectacular spots. Many parks, especially those in West Virginia, have unbelievable cabin accommodations that are rustic but charming, and often at bargain prices. Even during the heaviest travel seasons, often these campsites and cabins have availability. In D.C., there is a small number of commercial campgrounds available. Definitely call ahead to reserve spots at one of these if you are interested.

Lodging in the region ranges from lavish big city hotels with room service to quaint log cabins hidden among hundreds of acres of forest. In rural areas, as well as in the cities, there are some fine bed-and-breakfast inns located in restored homes in a variety of periods and decor. Be adventurous! Seek out extraordinary accommodations. Try a homey bed-and-breakfast inn one night and a rustic cabin with wraparound porch the next. Treat yourself to a stay at a pampering spa in the mountains of Virginia or West Virginia. There are so may unique lodgings, there's little excuse to settle for the ordinary.

Reservations are recommended at most accommodations, but many properties still take walk-ins regularly. Most properties highlighted in this book will expect reservations. Although some major chains and basic accommodations are noted in the book, most lodgings listed are those that are unique, have special amenities, historical significance, or good quality for the area. If you prefer a particular chain or property, consult their directory for locations nearby. Some toll-free reservation numbers have been included in the Resources section of the book.

Dining in the region is a good value with many above-par restaurants serving regional cuisine and fresh seafood. Although dinner prices average $30 for two at most mid-level establishments, plan to dine at a superior restaurant occasionally. The restaurants listed in the book are those that are superior in quality for the area and are primarily lunch and dinner spots. A number of great local spots are also included in the guide. Dress at fancier restaurants and more urbane locales is jacket and tie for men and nice pants or a dress for women; rural restaurants, like those located near ski resorts or the beach, usually require tasteful casual attire.

RECOMMENDED READING

By touring the Capital Region, you might also feel obligated to brush up on a little American history. Leave the textbooks alone; instead skim a number of expertly crafted volumes that will leave you wanting to know more and eager to see sites for yourself. The definitive compilation of Virginia history told in a lively fashion is Virginius Dabney's, *Virginia: The New Dominion*. Dabney weaves little-known facts and personal stories into the stuff we've all heard in history class. Other great choices include, *The Virginia Adventure* and *Here Lies Virginia*, by Ivor Noel Hurne, which provide wonderful historical and archaeological views of Virginia's history.

In similar fashion, *West Virginia: A History* by Otis K. Rice and Stephen W.

Brown is one of the most current historic resources on West Virginia. You'll get swept into the drama and anguish of the Civil War when you read *To the Gates of Richmond: The Peninsula Campaign* by Stephen W. Sears. It is considered one of the finest works on the most written about campaign of the Civil War and makes for great reading. A different sort of history chronology is *Child of the Bay* by Mary Ellen Olcese. The author takes readers on a trip from colonial settlement on the Chesapeake Bay until present time. To get a real flavor of the region and its people you'll enjoy *Virginia Folk Legends* by Thomas E. Borden, which is a compilation of stories passed down by rural Virginians.

A number of great travel companion books provide detailed information to even the most remote attractions. Keep a copy of, *The Hornbook of Virginia History* by Emily Salmon and Edward D.C. Campbell Jr. handy while traveling around the state. The book is a well-researched and well-organized inventory of historic places, people, and events. While traveling along Virginia's back roads, *A Guidebook to Virginia's Historical Markers* by John Salmon is a fantastic car companion. To help you grasp the overwhelming amount of Civil War sites in the region, *Civil War Sites in Virginia: A Tour Guide* by James Robertson Jr. provides a comprehensive list of attractions.

If you just can't make it through history volumes—however well-written— try reading one of many fiction selections. One person who seems to know how to bring the past to life in gripping detail is James Michener. His *Chesapeake*, is a classic saga about America's great bay which takes readers from the Bay's Native American roots until modern times in masterful style. *Cold Mountain* by Charles Frazier is a recent best-selling Civil War novel set against the backdrop of the Blue Ridge Mountains.

If unforgettable photography is what you need to get you in the right frame of mind, you'll appreciate a number of pictorial volumes available. *Bringing Back the Bay* by Marion Warren is an emotionally charged photo album depicting the Chesapeake Bay community. *Washington, D.C.: A Smithsonian Book on the Nation's Capital,* edited by Patricia Gallagher, offers spectacular photographs along with expert information. If you've always dreamed of seeing the rooms and exteriors of bed-and-breakfast inns before you get there, *Bed and Breakfasts and Unique Inns of Virginia*, third edition, by Lynn Matthews Davis, has full-color photos and detailed descriptions of many of Virginia's bed-and-breakfast inns.

Those planning to spend time outdoors will find several books on the subject helpful. *National Washington* by Richard L. Berman and Deborah Gerhard is an easy-to-use guide to hiking, biking, birds, and lovers of nature in the nation's capital. One of the best resources for outdoor travel in West Virginia's wild frontier is *West Virginia, A Guide to Backcountry Travel & Adventure* by James Brannon. This guide to the wilds of West Virginia has great maps and expert tips.

1
WASHINGTON, D.C.

Washington, D.C., is one of the world's great cities, with splendid architecture, famous monuments, prestigious museums, and great parks and waterways. The city's patriotic fervor is almost overwhelmed by an infusion of cultures, which creates an all-around international ambiance. Having the world's most powerful government as its chief resident has also definitely shaped the cynical civic climate here.

In addition, the clean modern Metro subway system makes navigating the confusing maze of streets a breeze. Where else can you view the mysterious Hope Diamond, be moved to tears by reminders of the Nazi Holocaust, or read from original documents that established America as a free nation?

A PERFECT DAY IN WASHINGTON, D.C.

Taking an early morning tour of the White House is a wonderful way to set the tone for the day. Walk five blocks east to the Federal Bureau of Investigation for a fascinating tour of the country's premier law enforcement organization. Work your way through The National Mall to visit the various museums at the Smithsonian Institution. Be focused and decide ahead of time which museums you wish to visit and for how long. It is very easy to lose track of time and find yourself in one museum for four hours. End your day along the Potomac at the Lincoln, Jefferson, and FDR Memorials.

WASHINGTON, D.C.

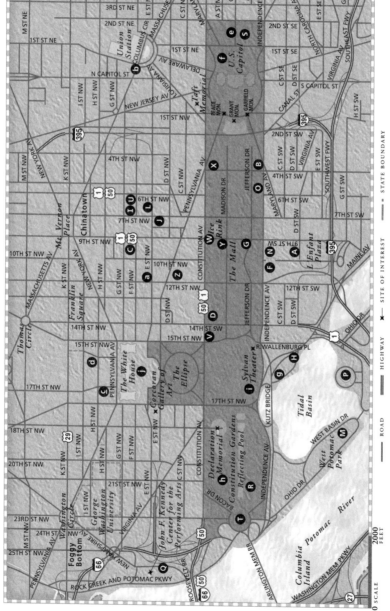

To K

To E N

6TH ST NE
5TH ST NE
K ST NE
H ST NE
4TH ST NE
3RD ST NE
2ND ST NE
1ST ST NE
M ST NE
Union Station
COLUMBUS CIR
N CAPITOL ST
1ST ST NW
H ST NW
G ST NW
395
NEW JERSEY AV
4TH ST NW
D ST NW
C ST NW
MASSACHUSETTS AV
LOUISIANA AV
DELAWARE AV
NEW YORK AV
MASSACHUSETTS AV
M ST NW
K ST NW

6TH ST NE
5TH ST NE
A ST NE
CAPITOL
A ST SE
PENNSYLVANIA AV
4TH ST SE
E ST SE
G ST SE

C ST NE
MARYLAND AV
A ST NE
INDEPENDENCE AV
2ND ST NE
e
S
f
U.S. Capitol
1ST ST NE
C ST SE
D ST SE
S CAPITOL ST
Taft Memorial
PEACE MON.
GRANT MON.
GARFIELD MON.
CANAL ST
395
2ND ST SW
VIRGINIA AV
SOUTHEAST FWY
H ST SW

1ST ST NW

X
MADISON DR
JEFFERSON DR
B
O
C ST SW
D ST SW
VIRGINIA AV
SOUTHWEST FWY
F ST SW
G ST SW
4TH ST SW
MARYLAND AV
6TH ST SW
7TH ST SW

1 50
6TH ST NW
U
L
7TH ST NW
J
9TH ST NW
1 50
C
A ST NW
Z
10TH ST NW
a
G ST NW
F ST NW
12TH ST NW
50 1
D ST NW
14TH ST NW
15TH ST NW

Chinatown
Mt. Vernon Place
Franklin Square
Thomas Circle
10TH ST NW
17TH ST NW
18TH ST NW
29
20TH ST NW
21ST ST NW
23RD ST NW
24TH ST NW
25TH ST NW
M ST NW

PENNSYLVANIA AV
CONSTITUTION AV
Ice Rink
Y
The Mall
G
N
F
A
L'Enfant Plaza
395
D ST SW

V
15TH ST NW
d
The White House
f
c
Corcoran Gallery of Art
Art of the Ellipse
17TH ST NW

R. WALLENBURG PL
H
g
i
Sylvan Theater
KUTZ BRIDGE
Tidal Basin
P
WEST BASIN DR
M
West Potomac Park
Columbia Island

Declaration Memorial
h
Constitution Gardens Reflecting Pool
CONSTITUTION AV
R
INDEPENDENCE AV
OHIO DR
1

Foggy Bottom
George Washington University
Washington Circle
66
NEW HAMPSHIRE AV
John F. Kennedy Center for the Performing Arts
Q
ROCK CREEK AND POTOMAC PKWY
50
66
ARLINGTON MEM BR
ROOSEVELT BR
BACON DR
T
50
Potomac River
WASHINGTON MEM PKWY
27

SCALE
0   2000
        FEET

ROAD   HIGHWAY   SITE OF INTEREST
★ SITE OF INTEREST   STATE BOUNDARY

GETTING AROUND

Washington's central location on the East Coast makes it easily accessible via car, plane, or train. The three major airports in the area (Dulles, Washington National, and Washington International) are all busy and bustling. Cab fare to downtown D.C. from Washington International or Dulles averages a whopping $40. Washington National has the luxury of being located near the city with an average cab fare of $15. Washington National is also on the Metro's yellow and blue lines. Train arrivals to beautiful Union Station also have the benefit of access to the super-convenient Metro.

Getting around the nation's capital is even a challenge to the folks who live and work in the city. The city is shaped like a diamond with the Capitol as its centerpoint. It is divided into four sections (NW, NE, SW, SE), which are used to decipher addresses. Throughout the city there are numerous traffic circles and dead ends leading to frustration when trying to navigate. Parking can also be difficult downtown and garages are notoriously expensive. Therefore, even if you normally prefer driving over public transportation, I suggest you swallow your pride and take the Metro subway and buses. The

SIGHTS

- **A** African Art Museum, National
- **B** Air and Space Museum, National
- **C** American Art Museum, National
- **D** American History Museum, National
- **E** Anacostia Museum
- **F** Arthur M. Sackler Gallery
- **G** Arts and Industries Building
- **H** Bureau of Engraving and Printing
- **I** Discovery Channel: *Destination D.C.*
- **J** Federal Bureau of Investigation
- **K** Folger Shakespeare Library
- **L** Ford's Theatre and Lincoln Museum/ Petersen House
- **M** Franklin D. Roosevelt Memorial
- **N** Freer Gallery of Art
- **O** Hirshborn Museum and Sculpture Garden
- **P** Jefferson Memorial
- **Q** John F. Kennedy Center for the Performing Arts
- **R** Korean War Veterans Memorial
- **S** Library of Congress
- **T** Lincoln Memorial
- **U** MCI National Sports Gallery
- **V** National Aquarium
- **W** National Archives and Records Administration
- **X** National Gallery of Art
- **Y** Natural History Museum, National
- **Z** Old Post Office Pavilion
- **a** Portrait Gallery, National
- **b** Postal Museum, National
- **c** Renwick Gallery
- **d** St. John's Church
- **e** Supreme Court of the United States
- **f** United States Capitol
- **g** United States Holocaust Memorial Museum
- **h** Vietnam Veterans Memorial/Vietnam Women's Memorial
- **i** Washington Monument
- **j** White House and White House Visitor Center

system is easy to understand, clean, and well-lit. Take advantage of it! The stations are open at 5:30 a.m. on weekdays and at 8 a.m. on weekends. The Metro closes at midnight. The base fare is $1.10 and children four and under travel free. One-Day Passes are $5 and are well worth it if you plan to visit many destinations throughout the city.

SIGHTSEEING HIGHLIGHTS

★★★★ BUREAU OF ENGRAVING AND PRINTING
U.S. Treasury Dept., 14th and C Sts., SW, Metro Stop: Smithsonian, 202/874-3019

There's just something fascinating about watching money being printed. The enormous presses at the Bureau of Engraving and Printing print bills at a rate of 7,000 sheets an hour—more than $100 billion a year. Today, modern science and technology have to be three steps ahead of would-be counterfeiters the world over. Self-guided tours of the Bureau of Engraving and Printing take you through the entire money-making process—from design to printing to destruction of old bills. As you walk along the tour you'll see exhibits showing everything from pieces of eight to a $1 million note. The Bureau also prints postage stamps, Treasury bonds, and White House invitations.

Details: Mon–Fri 9–2. Free. (There is a big demand for tours; tickets are bought on a first-come, first-serve basis May–Aug. Ticket booth opens at 7:30 a.m. Also, large crowds during the summer require the Treasury to cut off the ticket lines at noon.) (30 minutes)

★★★★ DISCOVERY CHANNEL: DESTINATION D.C.
MCI Center, 601 F St., NW, Metro Stop: Gallery Place-Chinatown, 202/639-0908

The Discovery Channel's new four-story store is more attraction than retailer with its ominous 42-foot *T.rex* skeleton looming overhead and an elevator straight out of a Jules Verne novel. Unbelievable artifacts can be seen around every turn, educational interactives are scattered throughout the store and you will stop more than a few times to watch provocative films on everything from bears to ancient cultures.

There are 15 interactive stations exploring earth science, aviation, and oceanography. Visitors can see a fuselage of a real World War II bomber, view a Hubble observatory, and be mesmerized by a 36-screen gallery showing Discovery Channel documentaries. On the

Robert Baum/Unicorn Stock Photos

fourth floor you'll find an 80-seat theater showing *Destination D.C.*, a fun and offbeat 15-minute tour of D.C. Merchandise includes toy dinosaurs, crystals, volcano stuff, tribal masks, toys, art, ceramics, telescopes, bomber jackets, model planes, and rockets. Got more than a couple of bucks to spend? You can choose from an Ice Age cave bear skeleton ($75,000) or a dinosaur tooth ($200), among other pricey items.

Details: Mon–Sat 10–10, Sun 10–6. Free. Destination D.C. film every half hour beginning at 10:30 a.m.; admission for film is $2.50 adults, $1.50 children/seniors. (1–2 hours)

★★★★ FEDERAL BUREAU OF INVESTIGATION
Ninth and Pennsylvania Ave., Metro Stop: Metro Center 202/324-3447

Who hasn't ever wanted to wander into a real-life crime lab? By touring the FBI's central headquarters in D.C., not only can you see working crime and DNA labs, but you can also watch sharpshooter demonstrations and glimpse the Bureau's vast computer system. You'll see weapons used by Al Capone, John Dillinger, and Bonnie and Clyde among others. Tours give visitors a lesson in Crime 101 with information on the FBI's fight against organized crime, white-collar crime, violent crime, and foreign counterintelligence. Stop by the exhibit of the 10 most-wanted fugitives and see if there's anyone you recognize.

Details: Mon–Fri 8:45–4:15. Free. (1 hour 15 minutes)

★★★★ JEFFERSON MEMORIAL
E. Potomac Park, Metro Stop: Smithsonian, 202/426-6822

John Russell Pope designed the graceful neoclassical marble monument to the third president and primary author of the Declaration of Independence. The colonnade and dome reflect Jefferson's love of the architectural style. Inside, there is a 19-foot bronze statue, and excerpts from Jefferson's inspirational writings are etched into the monument walls. This is truly a breathtaking memorial—one of the most beautifully conceived in the world. Paddle boats are available for rent at the body of water surrounding the memorial.

Details: Park ranger available 8 a.m.–midnight. Free. (30 minutes)

★★★★ KOREAN WAR VETERANS MEMORIAL
Lincoln Memorial Reflecting Pool, Metro Stop: Foggy

Bottom, 202/619-7222

This memorial is adjacent to the Lincoln Memorial. Built with $18 million in donated funds, it features a column of 19-foot soldiers and a 164-foot mural with 2,500 photos of nurses, chaplains, crew chiefs, mechanics, and other people involved in the war effort. The inscribed message, "Freedom Is Not Free," is a reminder of the sacrifices of war. **Details:** *Daily 8 a.m.–midnight. Free. (30 minutes)*

★★★★ LIBRARY OF CONGRESS
101 Independence Ave., SE, Metro Stop: Capitol South
202/707-8000

The country's national library is the largest in the world, containing more than 111 million items in three buildings. Its collection includes some impressive documents: the contents of Lincoln's pockets the night he died, and one of the world's three perfect copies of the Gutenberg Bible. The spectacular Italian Renaissance Jefferson Building (1897), has recently been restored and contains the permanent rotating exhibit, American Treasures of the Library of Congress. The Adams Building is open only for research and the James Madison Building houses special exhibits including the Gutenberg Bible. There is a 12-minute film shown continuously in the visitor center (accessible through the West Front ground floor entrance at 10 First Street, SE).

Details: *Recording of current exhibits 202/707-4604, reading rooms 202/707-6400, reference info. 202/707-5522. Jefferson Building Mon–Sat 10–5:30, public tours at 11:30, 1, 2:30, and 4. Madison Building Mon–Fri 8:30–6, Sat 8:30–6:30. Free. (1–2 hours)*

★★★★ LINCOLN MEMORIAL
West end of the Mall at 23rd St., NW, Metro Stop: Foggy Bottom, 202/426-6895 or 202/426-6842

The most famous of the three presidential monuments is the one dedicated to the sixteenth president. The monument has been the site of several of history's greatest moments and a focal point for many city festivities. The neoclassical monument overlooks the Reflecting Pool, Washington Monument, and U.S. Capitol. Inside the memorial is a 19-foot marble statue of Lincoln solemnly looking toward the Capitol building. The limestone walls on either side of the monument bear inscriptions of his Second Inaugural Address and the Gettysburg Address. The 60-foot murals on the north and south walls are spectacular, as is the view from here.

Details: *Park ranger in attendance 24 hours, Visitor Center 8 a.m.–midnight. Free. (30 minutes)*

★★★★ NATIONAL ARCHIVES AND RECORDS ADMINISTRATION
Constitution Ave. and Eighth St., NW, Metro Stop: Archives-Navy Memorial, 202/501-5000

This is where America stores its most valuable records and documents (more than 3 billion). You can gaze upon original copies of the Declaration of Independence, the Constitution of the United States, the Bill of Rights, the 1297 Magna Carta, and other documents.

Details: *Mon–Sat 10–9, guided tours by appt. Mon–Fri 10:15 and 1:15. Genealogy library Mon & Wed 8:45–5, Tue, Thu, Fri 8:45–9, Sat 8:45–4:45. Free. (30 minutes–1 hour)*

★★★★ NATIONAL GALLERY OF ART
Fourth and Constitution Ave., NW Metro Stop: Archives-Navy Memorial, 202/737-4215

This fine art museum contains a permanent collection of European (thirteenth to nineteenth centuries) and American paintings, sculpture, decorative arts, and works on paper. Works are exhibited in chronological order beginning in the west wing on the main floor. The museum features a superior collection of Renaissance paintings, Dutch masterworks, French impressionism, and abstract expressionism. Just a sampling of the recognizable names include da Vinci, El Greco, Renoir, Monet, and Whistler. There is always a great changing exhibition as well.

Details: *Guided tour reservations 202/842-6246. Mon–Sat 10–5, Sun 11–6, guided tours available in five languages. Free. (2 hours)*

★★★★ FRANKLIN D. ROOSEVELT MEMORIAL
West Potomac Park at West Basin and Ohio Dr. Metro Stop: Foggy Bottom, Smithsonian, or Arlington Cemetery, 202/619-7222

The new memorial to our 32nd president is one of the most poignant monuments in the city. FDR is paid homage in a new 7.5-acre park with splashing waterfalls and artwork that depicts a tide of change following the Great Depression. The memorial is divided into four galleries representing each of FDR's terms as president. During his 12 years in the White House, Roosevelt introduced the New Deal to bring the country out of the Depression and led the nation during World War II. The open-air rooms of the monument contain bronze sculptures of Roosevelt. One statue of Roosevelt depicts him seated in a chair wearing a long cape with his dog, Fala, at his feet and First Lady Eleanor standing before the United Nations. The other sculptures will have a unique meaning to virtually everyone who lived during those four event-filled presidential terms.

Details: Grounds are open 24 hours a day, park ranger in attendance 8 a.m.–midnight. Wheelchair accessible. Free. (30 minutes)

★★★★ SUPREME COURT OF THE UNITED STATES
First Street and Maryland Ave., NE, Metro Stop: Capitol South, 202/479-3211

Get here early to view sessions at the nation's highest court. Oral arguments are heard October through April and decisions are read May through June. Those wishing to hear arguments can choose from a three-minute or regular line during busy times. (The three-minute line allows visitors to listen for a short period to get a glimpse of proceedings, while the regular line is for those who wish to stay for a while.) The ground floor houses an exhibit on the history of the court and a film explaining court proceedings.

Details: Mon–Fri 9–4:30. Court sessions 10–noon, 1–3. Public lectures given by tour guides every hour on the ½ hour 9:30–3:30. Free. (1 hour)

★★★★ UNITED STATES CAPITOL
Metro Stop: Capitol South, 202/737-2300 or 800/723-3557

One of the world's most beautiful and recognized landmarks houses the legislative branches of the U.S. government. The stunning white-domed building was designed to be the focal point for D.C., dividing the city into four sectors and organizing the street numbers. The cornerstone for the Capitol was laid in 1793, with Dr. William Thornton as designer; however, noted architect Benjamin Latrobe was hired by Thomas Jefferson in 1799 to continue work on the building. After the partially completed building was burned during the War of 1812, the first Capitol building was completed in 1827 and increased in size in 1859. The building contains fine marble, wrought iron, woodwork, and state-of-the-art engineering (for that time). Artist Constantino Brumidi spent 20 years painting the fresco that adorns the inside of the 180-foot

A limited number of free passes to the House and Senate galleries are available by contacting your representative's office, or better yet, stop by their offices across the street from the Capitol building.

dome. Check the calendar listing in the *Washington Post* for times that Congress is in session and the issues to be debated that day.

Details: *Daily 9:30–4:30, Memorial Day–Labor Day daily 9:30–8, free guided tours of the building leave every 15 minutes from the Rotunda, Mon–Sat 9:30–3:45. Free. (1–2 hours)*

★★★★ UNITED STATES HOLOCAUST MEMORIAL MUSEUM
100 Raoul Wallenberg Pl., SW, Metro Stop: Smithsonian
202/488-0400

The nation's only national memorial to victims of the Holocaust features emotionally charged exhibits where you are led along a controlled pathway. While on the elevator to the first exhibits, you will see video footage showing soldiers who have just discovered the horrors of genocide. When the elevator doors open, you step out into Ohrdruf Camp, face-to-face with images of dazed survivors and smoldering bodies. On the third floor you walk through a freight car that carried people to death camps and exit the car beside a cast of the gate at Auschwitz. Once there, you will find living quarters, ration bowls, Zyklon-B cans used in the gas chambers, evidence of the crematoria with reproductions of the ovens and tables for extracting gold fillings.

Finally, on the second floor, exhibits chronicle the Allied victory and the liberation of the prisoners. These permanent exhibits are not recommended for children under 12 years old.

Details: *Daily 10–5:30. Free. Timed tickets are required to view the permanent collection with an allotment of 2,000 same-day tickets (limit 4/person) given out each day and usually depleted by noon, advance tickets may be reserved by calling ProTix at 800/400-9373. (2–3 hours)*

★★★★ VIETNAM VETERANS MEMORIAL/VIETNAM WOMEN'S MEMORIAL
Constitution Gardens and Henry Bacon Dr., NW, Metro Stop: Foggy Bottom, 202/634-1568

This memorial, erected in 1982, is dedicated to the men and women who became missing or lost their lives in the Vietnam War. The long,

V-shaped wall of black granite contains the names of 58,191 soldiers. A steady stream of visitors come prepared with paper to trace their loved ones' names from the wall. Many leave flowers as a tribute at its base—their faces reflected in the shiny surface of the monument as they do so. Maya Ying Lin designed the solemn tribute and Frederick Hart sculpted a moving statue of three young servicemen. Although names are listed chronologically by platoon, there are directories to aid in finding names. The Vietnam Women's Memorial, located across from the Vietnam Veterans Memorial, is a moving bronze sculpture created by Glenna Goodacre depicting three servicewomen with one wounded soldier.

Details: Open 24 hours, park ranger on site 8 a.m.–midnight. Free. (30 minutes–1 hour)

★★★★ WASHINGTON MONUMENT
15th and Constitution Ave., NW, Metro Stop: Smithsonian, 202/426-6841

The 70-second elevator ride to the top of the Washington Monument carries you to panoramic views of the city and is a great way to get a general lay of the land. The 555-foot-tall obelisk is made of marble and is the tallest free-standing masonry structure in the world. Construction of the monument began in 1848, but halted and didn't begin again until 1878. Visitors will notice the color change in the marble from the two construction periods. It was finally open to the public in 1888. The immense structure is a reminder of the immensity of George Washington's contribution to the republic.

Details: Daily 8–5, Apr–Labor Day 8 a.m.–11:45 p.m. Free. Free timed passes required; to reserve passes ahead of time (for a $1.50 fee) call TicketMaster, 800/505-5040. Due to renovations, Washington Monument is closed to the public until the year 2000. (1 hour)

★★★★ WHITE HOUSE AND WHITE HOUSE VISITOR CENTER
1600 Pennsylvania Ave., NW, Metro Stop: Federal Triangle, 24-hour info. line 202/456-7041, 202/208-1631 or 800/717-1450

The private residence of America's president is also the business office for the commander in chief. Here, the president holds meetings, signs new legislation, carries out the majority of his duties, and entertains guests. The elegant, white-columned building has been home to every president, except George Washington. During the twentieth century, administrations have made it a priority to make the house a showcase of fine American furnishings and art.

Tours begin at the visitor center, where exhibits focus on the history of the White House. Your self-guided tour takes you across the grounds to the house where you'll notice the Rose Garden used for formal ceremonies and the Jacqueline Kennedy Garden. The tour takes you through the Library, the State Dining Room, the Vermeil Room, the Green Room, the Blue Room, the Red Room, and the China Room among others.

You'll also see the East Room which is the largest room in the White House and is used for large receptions, ceremonies, press conferences, and other events. This is also the room where bodies of presidents have lain in state.

Details: *Self-guided tours daily 10 a.m.–noon. Free. Tickets (limit of four/person) issued from the Visitors Center (southeast corner of 15th and E Sts., look for three American flags and a blue awning) on the morning of the tour only, first-come, first-serve starting at 7:30 a.m. Congressional guided tours Tue–Sat 8:15–9. Limited tickets can be obtained in advance from your representative or senator. The easiest way to reach them is to call the Capital Switchboard, 202/224-3121, and ask for them by name. (2 hours)*

★★★ FORD'S THEATRE AND LINCOLN MUSEUM/ PETERSEN HOUSE
511 10th St., NW, Metro Stop: Metro Center, 202/426-6924

This historic theater is the place where Abraham Lincoln was assassinated by John Wilkes Booth on April 14, 1865. The bunting-draped presidential box has been preserved to look as it did at the time of the event. Lincoln was shot while watching a performance of *Our American Cousin*. He was carried across the street to the Petersen House, where he died at 7:22 the next morning. There is a museum downstairs, operated by the National Park Service, that contains artifacts from the assassination. The theater is currently one of D.C.'s most popular small playhouses as well.

Details: *Daily 9–5 (park rangers are usually available to talk with visitors except between noon–2 p.m. when there is a break for lunch). Free. (30 minutes)*

★★★ JOHN F. KENNEDY CENTER FOR THE PERFORMING ARTS

New Hampshire Ave., NW, at Rock Creek Parkway
Metro Stop: Foggy Bottom, 202/467-4600
This modern facility is totally independent and privately supported. It contains five gorgeous theaters presenting symphony, opera, dance performances, films, concerts, Broadway shows, and theater. Located on the Potomac River in the Foggy Bottom district, the Kennedy Center is home to the National Symphony Orchestra, the Washington Opera, and the American Film Institute. Free concerts that vary from jazz to gospel are presented on the Millennium Stages every night of the week at 6 p.m., so there's always something going on. The theater also has gift shops, restaurants, a cafeteria, and exquisite views of the river from its terrace.
Details: Daily 10 a.m.–midnight, guided tours 10–1. Free. (45 minutes)

★★★ OLD POST OFFICE PAVILION
1100 Pennsylvania Ave., NW, Metro Stop: Federal Triangle
202/289-4224
Views from the observation deck of the beautiful 1899 Post Office are quite spectacular. A great alternative for panoramic views during the renovation of the Washington Monument. The clock tower is home to the Congressional Bells, a Bicentennial gift from Great Britain to the U.S. Inside, a 10-story atrium features shops and a popular food court.
Details: Mon–Sat 10–9, Sun noon–7 p.m. Free for observation deck and tours of the clock tower. (1 hour)

★★ FOLGER SHAKESPEARE LIBRARY
201 E. Capitol St., SE, Metro Stop: Capitol South
202/544-7077
This building houses the world's largest collection of items pertaining to William Shakespeare. There is even a replica of the famous Globe Theatre; it is used for a variety of purposes. Items and artifacts include more than 250,000 early printings of his plays, rare books, and playbills.
Details: Mon–Sat 10–4. Free. (30 minutes)

★★ NATIONAL AQUARIUM
Commerce Dept. Bldg., Pennsylvania Ave. and 14th St.,
NW, Metro Stop: Federal Triangle, 202/482-2825
The National Aquarium here is much smaller than the internationally acclaimed National Aquarium in Baltimore, but still features more than

270 species of native and exotic fish, reptiles, amphibians, and invertebrates. Founded in 1873, the institution was the nation's first public aquarium. The aquarium features a touch tank, videos, and children's programs. There's always a surge in visitors around 2 p.m.—feeding time for the sharks (Saturday, Monday, and Wednesday) and piranhas (Sunday, Tuesday, and Thursday).

Details: Daily 9–5. $2 adults, $.75 children/seniors. (45 minutes)

★ **MCI NATIONAL SPORTS GALLERY**
MCI Center, 601 F St., NW, Metro Stop: Gallery Place-Chinatown, 202/661-5133

This new 25,000-square-foot interactive sports museum showcases American sports history through memorabilia and sports-themed exhibits. Among the prized artifacts are a 1909 Honus Wagner baseball card, Ty Cobb's uniform, and "Shoeless" Joe Jackson's only known autographed bat. The big draw here, however, is the various interactive exhibits, where you can join in the fun and play with the big boys. The virtual reality games allow you to get in a Redskins huddle and receive play calls from Joe Theismann or pitch a baseball to Jim Thorne.

Details: Daily 10–10. $4 general admission (free with ticket to same day's event at MCI Center), $9 pass to play all the games. (30 minutes–1 hour)

★ **ST. JOHN'S CHURCH**
Lafayette Sq., Metro Stop: McPherson Sq., 202/347-8766

Every president since James Madison has worshipped at this church, built in 1816, across from the White House. The pale yellow Episcopal Church's Pew 54 has been the seat at one time or another for each of the presidents.

Details: Office is open Mon–Thu 9–5. Tours are available, but you need to make an appt. Services Mon–Fri 12:10, Sun 8 a.m., 9 a.m., and 11 a.m. Free. (15 minutes)

SMITHSONIAN INSTITUTION SIGHTSEEING HIGHLIGHTS

Fifteen museums and educational areas make up the Smithsonian Institution—most of them in and around the National Mall. The museums house more than 140 million artifacts and collectively constitute the world's largest museum complex. From the signature castle to the world famous Air and Space Museum, the Smithsonian is a destination in itself. You could spend a full week here and not see everything in each museum. The visitors center is located at the castle, 202/357-2700.

★★★★ NATIONAL AIR AND SPACE MUSEUM
Sixth and Independence Ave., SW, Metro Stop: L'Enfant Plaza, 202/357-1686

This is the most visited museum in the world with more than 9 million visitors every year. The Smithsonian's largest museum, it houses some of the world's most precious artifacts relating to air and space. From Charles Lindbergh's *Spirit of St. Louis* to the *Apollo 11* lunar command module, there is something here to inspire awe in everyone. See how it all started with the Wright Brothers' *1903 Flyer*, then view the latest in space technology by entering a Skylab Workshop. There are changing exhibits (from *Star Wars* film props to interactive displays) and great space-related films at the Langley IMAX Theater. Also on site are daily planetarium shows every 40 minutes, a cafeteria, restaurant, and flight-related gift shops.

Details: *Daily 9:45–5; guided tours 10:15 and 1; IMAX films $5 adults, $3.75 children/seniors. Free. (2–3 hours)*

★★★★ NATIONAL AMERICAN ART MUSEUM
Eighth and G Sts., Metro Stop: Gallery Place–Chinatown 202/357-2700

Inside the opulent nineteenth-century Greek Revival building at the corner of Eighth and G Streets are more than 35,000 works of American art. The paintings, sculptures, folk art, photos, and graphics featured here offer viewers a sweeping look at American art since the eighteenth century. A gift shop and café are inside.

Details: *Daily 10–5:30, group tours available by appt. only. Free. (2 hours)*

★★★★ NATIONAL AMERICAN HISTORY MUSEUM
14th St. and Constitution Ave., Metro Stop: Smithsonian 202/357-2700

The American History Museum is so unfailingly special, that it is one of the most repeated museums on the Smithsonian's line-up. Crowds clamor around the bullet-ridden flag that inspired Francis Scott Key to write the "Star Spangled Banner." Women remember the elegance of Jackie Kennedy as they gaze at her ball gown. Children smile at the antique toys and trains. Pop culture fans never miss seeing Archie

Bunker's chair or the ruby slippers from *The Wizard of Oz*. From stirring to amusing, the museum is a tribute to the people, the ideals, and the imagination of America. A great bookstore, gift shop, and ice-cream parlor are inside.

Details: *Daily 10–5:30, guided highlights tours Mon–Sat 10 and 1. Free. (2 hours)*

★★★★ NATIONAL NATURAL HISTORY MUSEUM
10th and Constitution Ave., NW, Metro Stop: Smithsonian, 202/357-2747

For millions of Americans, the Museum of Natural History is their first exposure to giant dinosaur skeletons. A favorite of kids, both young and old, the museum houses a vast collection of earth-oriented artifacts from prehistoric times to the present. More than 120 million objects are displayed throughout the museum, which includes a gallery of gems and minerals, (the world-famous Hope Diamond and Star of Asia), fossils and animal exhibits, a marine zoology area, dioramas of now-extinct animals, a live insect zoo, and a hands-on Discovery Room that allows kids to throw the "look but don't touch" philosophy right out the window.

Details: *Daily 10–5:30. Free. (2–3 hours)*

★★★ ARTHUR M. SACKLER GALLERY
1050 Independence Ave., SW, Metro Stop: Smithsonian
202/357-2700

The Sackler Gallery contains some of the world's most exotic art from China, the Ancient Near East and Japan, Southeast Asia, and Islamic Iran. The artwork's mediums range from jades, bronzes, lacquerware, furniture, and paintings. The building features an unusual architectural design and connects with the Freer Gallery of Art. There is also a great gift shop here.

Details: *Daily 10–5:30. Free. (1 hour)*

★★★ ARTS AND INDUSTRIES BUILDING
900 Jefferson Dr., SW, Metro Stop: Smithsonian
202/357-2700

The 1876 centennial exhibition in Philadelphia has been recreated in this museum. An antique steam engine is a favorite item in the world's largest collection of Victorian Americana and memorabilia. There are changing exhibits on African American and Native American cultures as well. Children's performances are housed in the museum's Discovery Theater.

Details: Daily 10–5:30, guided tours by appt. only. Free. (45 minutes)

★★★ FREER GALLERY OF ART
12th and Jefferson Dr., SW, Metro Stop: Smithsonian 202/357-4880, ext. 245

This outstanding art museum features an extensive collection of Asian artwork that includes Chinese paintings and ancient bronzes; Japanese screens and scrolls; and Japanese, Chinese, and Near Eastern ceramics. The museum also has a fine collection of American nineteenth- and twentieth-century artists. James McNeill Whistler's famous Peacock Room remains the only surviving example of his interior design work.

Details: Daily 10–5:30, guided tours. Free. (45 minutes)

★★★ HIRSHBORN MUSEUM AND SCULPTURE GARDEN
Seventh and Independence Ave., SW, Metro Stop: L'Enfant Plaza, 202/357-2700

Matisse, Rodin, Eakins, and Moore are only some of the artists whose works are on display at this highly modern museum. Shaped like a cylinder and filled with natural light, the Hirshborn contains the nineteenth- and twentieth-century collection of Joseph H. Hirshborn and new acquisitions focusing on the latest trends in modern art. There is also a sculpture garden.

Details: Tours Mon–Sat 10:30, noon, and 1:30, Sun 12:30, 1:30, and 2:30. Free. (1 hour)

★★★ NATIONAL PORTRAIT GALLERY
Eighth and F Sts., NW, Metro Stop: Gallery Place Chinatown, 202/357-2700

The faces of America are displayed in this gallery of portraiture, which contains hundreds of paintings of the famous and historically significant. The Hall of Presidents features the official portraits of all the U.S. Presidents. Other famous faces are drawn from political, scientific, sports, literary, stage, and screen arenas.

Details: Daily 10–5:30. Free. (45 minutes)

★★★ NATIONAL POSTAL MUSEUM
2 Massachusetts Ave., NE, Metro Stop: Union Station

202/357-2700

Neither wind nor rain could keep the nation's mail-carrying story from coming to life at this museum dedicated to the postal service. Featured artifacts include a Ford Model A mail truck, a WWI bomber–turned–mail carrier, stagecoaches, rare stamps, and items relating to the Pony Express. Dramatic and poignant letters from American pioneers, slaves, and Native Americans are especially affective. The gift shop features a stamp collectors' shop, postal service memorabilia, and, of course, a post office.

Details: Daily 10–5:30. Free. (45 minutes)

★★ ANACOSTIA MUSEUM
1901 Fort Pl., SE, Metro Stop: Anacostia, then take Ft. Staunton bus #W1 or #W2, 202/357-1300

This museum chronicles African American history in the region. Featured exhibits include photographs, artifacts, and documents that deal with the history, art, and culture in D.C., Maryland, Virginia, Georgia, and the Carolinas. The museum is currently under renovation.

Details: Daily 10–5:30. Free. (1 hour)

★★ NATIONAL AFRICAN ART MUSEUM
950 Independence Ave., SW, Metro Stop: Smithsonian 202/357-2700

This extensive collection of African art is the only national museum of its kind. Artifacts date from ancient to contemporary times. You'll see clothing, altars, masks, paintings, and sculptures. A gift shop on site sells reproductions, books, and souvenirs.

Details: Daily 10–5:30, tours Mon–Fri 10:30 a.m.–1:30 p.m., Sat–Sun 11 a.m., 1 a.m., and 3 p.m. Free. (1 hour)

★★ RENWICK GALLERY
17th and Pennsylvania Ave., NW, Metro Stop: Farragut West, 202/357-2700

American crafts and decorative arts are the focus at this gallery, which is part of the National Museum of American Art. The gallery, located in an elegant French Revival building near the White House, contains eighteenth- and nineteenth-century works. Visit the Grand Salon and the Octagon Room—two rooms decorated in grand nineteenth-century style.

Details: Tour reservations 202/357-2531. Daily 10–5:30, guided tours by appt. only. Free. (45 minutes)

GUIDED TOURS

One of the best ways to see the city's highlights is aboard the **Old Town Trolley Tours**, 202/832-9800. These daily two-hour tours are narrated by knowledgeable guides and leave every 30 minutes beginning at 9 a.m. Other fine tours are offered by **Gray Line Tours**, 301/386-8300, **Double Decker Bus Tours**, 212/944-9700, and **Tourmobile Sightseeing**, 202/554-5100.

See Washington, D.C. by water aboard the **Washington Water Buses**, 800/288-7925, **Spirit Cruises**, 202/554-8000, **Potomac Riverboat Co.**, 703/684-0580, **Capitol River Cruises**, 301/460-7447, the **Dandy**, 703/683-6076, and the **C&O Canal Barge Rides**, 301/739-4200.

Washington After Hours, 202/832-9800, offers nighttime tours of the city. They are a wonderful way to view the spectacularly lit city after dark.

Other ways for you to tour D.C. include **Bike the Sites**, 202/966-8662, which offers guided bike tours; **Liberty Helicopter Tours and Charter**, 202/484-8484, and **Capital Helicopters**, 703/417-2150, which offer tours by air; and **D.C. Ducks**, 301/294-9514, which give tours aboard a refurbished 1946 "duck"—a vehicle that goes from water to land.

Living history interpreters also give walking tours to bring D.C.'s historic sites to life. An amusing and sobering sign of the times is the hilarious **Scandal Tours** operated by the **Gross National Product** comedy troupe, 703/218-6500. Tours led by costumed guides posing as political personalities, (e.g. Janet Reno), take you past scandalous sites around Washington, D.C., and poke fun at today's headlines.

FITNESS AND RECREATION

Washington, D.C., is a lush, green city with gorgeous natural and man-made waterways. Hiking and biking trails can be found in virtually every corner of the city. While visiting the monuments and memorials surrounding the Tidal Basin you may want to take a pedal boat, 202/484-0206, out for a spin. Boats can be rented from the base of the Jefferson Memorial. You can also rent canoes, rowing shells, and kayaks at the **Thompson Boat Center**, 2900 Virginia Avenue, NW, 202/333-9543. The **Washington Sailing Marina**, 1 Marina Drive, 703/548-9027, has all-terrain and 15-speed vehicles available.

Events at **RFK Stadium**, 2400 E. Capitol Street, SE, include NFL football with the Washington Redskins, 202/546-2222, and soccer with D.C. United,

WASHINGTON, D.C.

N

6TH ST NE
5TH ST NE
K ST NE
H ST NE
G ST NE
4TH ST NE
F ST NE
3RD ST NE
2ND ST NE
M ST NE
1ST ST NE
CAPITOL
A ST NE
A ST SE
4TH ST SE
G ST SE
E ST NE
E ST SE
MASSACHUSETTS AV
COLUMBUS CIR
E ST NE
C ST NE
PENNSYLVANIA AV
INDEPENDENCE AV
2ND ST SE

Union Station
N CAPITOL ST
MARYLAND AV
U.S. Capitol
1ST ST NE
1ST ST SE
1ST ST NW
H ST NW
G ST NW
1ST ST NW
LOUISIANA AV
DELAWARE AV
NEW JERSEY AV
Taft Memorial
C ST SE
D ST SE
S CAPITOL ST
CANAL ST
PEACE MON.
GRANT MON.
GARFIELD MON.
1ST ST NW
2ND ST SW
VIRGINIA AV
H ST SW
SOUTHEAST FWY
M ST NW
NEW YORK AV
K ST NW
4TH ST NW
D ST NW
C ST NW
PENNSYLVANIA AV
JEFFERSON DR
MADISON DR
C ST SW
D ST SW
VIRGINIA AV
SOUTHWEST FWY
G ST SW
4TH ST SW
6TH ST NW
Mt. Vernon Place
Chinatown
MARYLAND AV
6TH ST SW
7TH ST SW
7TH ST NW
Ice Rink
9TH ST SW
L'Enfant Plaza
9TH ST NW
CONSTITUTION AV
E ST NW
D ST NW
10TH ST NW
The Mall
MAINE AV
10TH ST NW ST NW
O
D
L
12TH ST NW
12TH ST SW
Franklin Square
H ST NW
G ST NW
F ST NW
D ST NW
JEFFERSON DR
C ST SW
D ST SW
OHIO DR
Thomas Circle
V
S
14TH ST NW
14TH ST SW
INDEPENDENCE AV
15TH ST NW
15TH ST NW
R. WALLENBERG PL
N
P
PENNSYLVANIA AV
The White House
Corcoran Gallery of Art
The Ellipse
Sylvan Theater
Tidal Basin
17TH ST NW
17TH ST NW
KUTZ BRIDGE
To Q
I
H ST NW
G ST NW
F ST NW
E ST NW
CONSTITUTION AV
WEST BASIN DR
18TH ST NW
E
K
29
R
Declaration Memorial
Constitution Gardens Reflecting Pool
West Potomac Park
20TH ST NW
B
K ST NW
21ST ST NW
INDEPENDENCE AV
OHIO DR
George Washington University
VIRGINIA AV
John F. Kennedy Center for the Performing Arts
BACON DR
Potomac River
A
C
23RD ST NW
Washington Circle
U
24TH ST NW
NEW HAMPSHIRE AV
50
ARLINGTON MEM. BR
Columbia Island
Foggy Bottom
25TH ST NW
66
ROCK CREEK AND POTOMAC PKWY
ROOSEVELT BR
50
66
WASHINGTON MEM PKWY
27

M ST NE
3RD ST NE
2ND ST NE
1ST ST NE

STATE BOUNDARY
SITE OF INTEREST
HIGHWAY
ROAD

0   SCALE   2000 FEET

703/478-6600. The gleaming new **MCI Center**, 601 F Street, NW, features spectator sports which include NHL hockey with the Washington Capitals, 301/336-CAPS, and NBA basketball with the Washington Wizards, 301/NBA-DUNK.

FOOD

There are so many great restaurants in the D.C. area, it could almost be called an excess. This is an advantage for visitors who will have no problem finding unique and delicious dining experiences in the city.

The ethnic diversity of the city has created a whole slew of restaurants offering everything from Ethiopian to Brazilian food. One great Italian restaurant in Foggy Bottom is **Galileo**, 1110 21st Street, NW, 202/293-7191. The four-star Galileo features northern Italian dishes paired with fine Italian wines in a formal atmosphere.

Nearby, at **Goldoni Ristorante**, 11113 23rd Street, NW, 202/293-1511, the chef serves up liver with onion, risotto with luganesa sausage, and fresh fish dishes. The restaurant has won critical acclaim from a wide variety of distinguished sources including *Esquire Magazine,* which named Goldoni one of the "Best New Restaurants in America." Entering **I Ricchi**, 1220 19th Street, NW, 202/835-0459, is like being invited into a fine country villa. Tuscan classics are prepared in fine Italian style with fresh pastas, oak-grilled sausages, and homemade bread.

If you are craving steaks and other carnivorous selections, a wonderful restaurant is the **Prime Rib**, 2020 K Street, NW, 202/466-8811, in Foggy Bottom. The elegant restaurant serves aged prime beef, thick chops, jumbo crab cakes, Crab Imperial, seafood, and superb rack of lamb.

One of the city's finest French restaurants is **La Colline**, 400 N. Capitol Street, NW, 202/737-0400, near the Capitol. Exquisitely prepared French

---

FOOD
- Ⓐ Chicago Pizzeria
- Ⓑ Galileo
- Ⓒ Goldoni Ristorante
- Ⓓ Hard Rock Café
- Ⓔ I Ricchi
- Ⓕ Kinkhead's
- Ⓖ La Colline
- Ⓗ Marrakesh
- Ⓘ Morton's of Chicago
- Ⓙ Provence

FOOD (continued)
- Ⓚ Prime Rib
- Ⓛ Planet Hollywood

LODGING
- Ⓜ Best Western Downtown Capitol Hill
- Ⓝ The Carlton
- Ⓞ Grand Hyatt

LODGING (continued)
- Ⓟ Hay-Adams Hotel
- Ⓠ Holiday Inn Central
- Ⓡ Hotel Lombardy
- Ⓢ JW Marriott
- Ⓣ Red Roof Inn
- Ⓤ St. James Hotel
- Ⓥ Willard Inter-Continental Hotel

dishes and baked goods are made fresh daily. Another fine French offering is **Provence**, 2401 Pennsylvania Avenue, NW, 202/296-1166, serving elegant dishes like lobster with white truffle olive oil and loin of rabbit. The restaurant is decorated in country French style, with weathered shutters and pretty wrought-iron chandeliers.

At **Marrakesh**, 617 New York Avenue, NW, 202/393-9393, you are seated on traditional cushioned banquettes, served a seven-course Moroccan feast to be eaten with your fingers, and entertained by belly dancers.

Kinkhead's, 2000 Pennsylvania Avenue, NW, 202/296-7700, is one of Washington, D.C.'s most popular restaurants for modern, American cuisine. The inventive food features the freshest seafood presented with artistry and delicious style. If you are looking for serious beef, potato, and salad, you won't be disappointed at **Morton's of Chicago**, 1050 Connecticut Avenue, NW, #1210, 202/955-5889—a favorite nationwide with its USDA prime aged beef, fresh seafood, and award-winning wine list.

In Capitol Hill, families have long been lining up in droves for Armand's **Chicago Pizzeria**, 226 Massachusetts Avenue, NE, 202/547-6600. The D.C. landmark serves up great deep dish pizza, traditional Chicago-style pie, and sandwiches. There are also the requisite tourism town spots that kids don't seem to resist, such as the **Hard Rock Café**, 999 E. Street, NW, 202/737-7625, and **Planet Hollywood**, 1101 Pennsylvania Avenue, NW, 202/783-7827.

LODGING

Those looking for every amenity will appreciate the long list of luxury hotels in Washington, D.C.—both grand and intimate. The most famous is probably the **Willard Inter-Continental Hotel**, 1401 Pennsylvania Avenue, NW, 202/628-9100 or 800/327-0200, just two blocks from the White House. The Beaux Arts grand hotel is a historic landmark and has been restored to its former grandeur. All elegantly detailed rooms feature modern amenities such as minibars and in-room movies. The service-oriented hotel offers 24-hour room service, laundry service, valet, twice-daily maid service, one of the city's finest restaurants, a lounge, and a fitness room. Rates are $179 to $239.

Smaller, but loaded with elegance, is the landmark **Hay-Adams Hotel**, 16th and H Streets, NW, 202/638-6600, across from the White House. The hotel has beautiful guest rooms with minibars, hair dryers, and bathrobes. Services include 24-hour room service, restaurant, and health club privileges. Rates are $145 to $265.

The Carlton, 923 16th Street, NW, 202/638-2626 or 800/325-3535, is a member of the "Leading Hotels of the World," and is located two blocks from the White House. Rooms feature in-room safes, fully stocked bars, and bathrobes. Services include 24-hour room service, coffee/tea with wake up call, afternoon tea, restaurant, lounge, and fitness center. Rates are $159 to $195.

Modern luxury hotels include the Grand Hyatt and the JW Marriott, both downtown. The **Grand Hyatt**, 1000 H Street, NW, 202/582-1234, contains an airy 12-story atrium with lagoon and waterfalls. In the rooms are minibars, voice mail, and hair dryers. The 900-room hotel has room service, dry cleaning, four restaurants, lounge, parking garage, health club, and swimming pool. Rates are $119 to $139. For die-hard shoppers, the **JW Marriott**, 1331 Pennsylvania Avenue, NW, 202/393-2000, has a complete shopping mall connected with its lobby. The sleek hotel also contains a restaurant, bar, lounge, valet parking, business center, health club, and indoor pool. Rooms are small and sometimes noisy, but nicely appointed. Rates are $119 to $159.

The **Holiday Inn Central**, 1501 Rhode Island Avenue, NW, 202/483-2000, is located near the White House and the museums. It features a restaurant, lounge, laundry facilities, indoor pool, fitness and game room. Rates are $75 to $105. Another reasonably priced hotel is the **Best Western Downtown Capitol Hill**, 724 N. Third Street, NW, 202/842-4466. The older, European-feel property has rooms decorated with antique reproductions of various European styles; in addition, a full-service restaurant is located on site. Rates are $100 to $124. The **Red Roof Inn** near the convention center, 500 H Street, NW, 202/289-5959, has a modern appearance and rooms offer Nintendo. Rates are $99 to $119. The **Hotel Lombardy**, 2019 I Street, NW, 202/828-2600, is a lovely old hotel with ornate woodwork and guest rooms that are all individually decorated. The hotel offers a full-service restaurant and a new lounge. Rates are $89 to $209.

In Foggy Bottom, the **St. James Hotel**, 24th and K Streets, NW, 202/457-0500, was built in 1986 and offers large, nicely appointed rooms; many include kitchenettes. The hotel features a swimming pool and a free continental breakfast. Rates are $115 to $200 with lower weekend rates.

NIGHTLIFE

Most of the hottest dance clubs are located in D.C.'s neighborhoods; however, there are a few places near the museum district to let loose. For a 1970s flashback, **Polly Esther's**, 605 12th Street, NW, 202/737-1970, has the requisite strobe-lit dance floor and groovy seventies decor. **The Bank**, 915 F Street, NW, 202/737-3177, located in a long-gone savings and loan building, is one of the hottest dance spots of the moment.

A couple of great bars and brew pubs are downtown as well. At **The Dubliner**, 520 N. Capitol Street, NW, 202/737-3773, the atmosphere is olde-time Celtic with dark wood paneling, pints of Irish brews, and live folk music. The D.C. mainstay, **Bullfeathers**, 410 First Street, SE, 202/543-5005, near Capitol Hill, has been around for nearly a quarter of a century. It is a hangout for congressional staff members and a great place to overhear an interesting conversation. **John Harvard's Brew House**, located downstairs in the Warner Theater, 13th and E Streets, NW, 202/783-2739, makes some tasty liquid concoctions on premises and serves up hearty fare. Give its Nut Brown Ale a try!

On Capitol Hill, the **Capitol City Brewing Company**, 2 Massachusetts Avenue, NE, 202/842-2337, also has great microbrews with views of the Capitol dome. One of D.C.'s largest and most popular sports bars is located near the White House at **Fanatic's**, 1520 K Street, NW, 202/638-6800. Here you can watch a game on any of the 30 TVs or play pool, darts, or trivia games.

PERFORMING ARTS

Performing arts in the nation's capital are world-class, with acclaimed ballet, opera, and symphony. The **John F. Kennedy Center for the Performing Arts**, New Hampshire Avenue NW at Rock Creek Parkway, 202/467-4600, is home to the **Washington Opera**, **National Symphony Orchestra**, and **American Film Institute**.

In addition, the Kennedy Center contains six gorgeous theaters presenting drama, ballet, live concerts, and free nightly concerts at 6 p.m. Tickets for performances can be charged by phone, 202/467-4600, for pick-up at the box office.

The **Washington Ballet** presents performances at various locations during its season, including the Kennedy Center and the Warner Theatre. For tickets and a schedule, call 202/362-3606.

Places to see plays include the three-theater **Arena Stage** near the waterfront (the first regional theater to win a Tony Award); the **National Theatre** on Pennsylvania Avenue; the historic **Ford's Theater**, 10th Street between E and F Streets, 202/347-4833; the **Lincoln Theater**, 1215 U Street NW, 202/328-6000; the **Shakespeare Theater**, 450 Seventh Street NW, between D and E Streets, 202/547-1122; and the gorgeous **Warner Theatre**, 13th Street NW, between E and F Streets, 202/783-4000.

For major sporting events, concerts, dance, and other special events, **TicketMaster** is the prime outlet for tickets. To charge by phone, call

202/432-7328, or purchase tickets (cash only) at Tower Records, 2000 Pennsylvania Avenue, NW, or any Hecht's department store. Discounted day-of-show tickets to plays and concerts are available at the **Old Post Office Pavilion**, 12th and Pennsylvania Avenue, NW, 202/842-5387.

SHOPPING

Such a cosmopolitan city does indeed have a wealth of shopping venues—from cheap to chic. Wonderful malls/shopping areas in downtown D.C. include **Union Station**, located in the restored train station include between Pennsylvania and G Streets, 800/872-7245; the **Shops at National Place**, Connecticut Avenue shopping district, 202/783-9090; **Friendship Heights** and the **Old Post Office Pavilion**, 1100 Pennsylvania Avenue, NW, 202/289-4224. Don't forget the dizzying array of museum gift shops, which offer unique gifts and goods you don't see every day. Antique shops of varying levels are scattered throughout the city, and 20 dealers are under one roof at the **Washington Antiques Center**, 6708 Wisconsin Avenue, 301/654-3798.

2
CAPITAL CITY NEIGHBORHOODS

The majority of visitors to D.C. are so overwhelmed by the sheer volume of sites in and around the National Mall that they never bother to venture out into the surrounding neighborhoods. Dare to leave the camera-toting crowds and begin exploring the rest of the city. You'll find a bustling big city with a high-paced business atmosphere and many pockets of internationally diverse neighborhoods.

Remember, Mr. L'Enfant planned the city to jut out from the Capitol and the city is divided into four quadrants for addresses (NE, NW, SE, SW). To avoid driving around in continual confusion, your best bet is to take the Metro transportation system. No matter what the locals tell you, it is a confusing city to navigate. Some areas are prime strolling spots, like the Waterfront and Georgetown. Others are great people-watching locales, like Adams-Morgan and Dupont Circle. Relax at a local coffeehouse and take in the atmosphere. You'll feel like a real Washington insider.

A PERFECT DAY IN THE CAPITAL CITY NEIGHBORHOODS

Start the day along D.C.'s waterfront; take in grand views of the Potomac and watch the flurry of activity at the Maine Avenue Fish Market. Then head north via Metro to Dupont Circle where you can visit the Phillips Collection's

CAPITAL CITY NEIGHBORHOODS

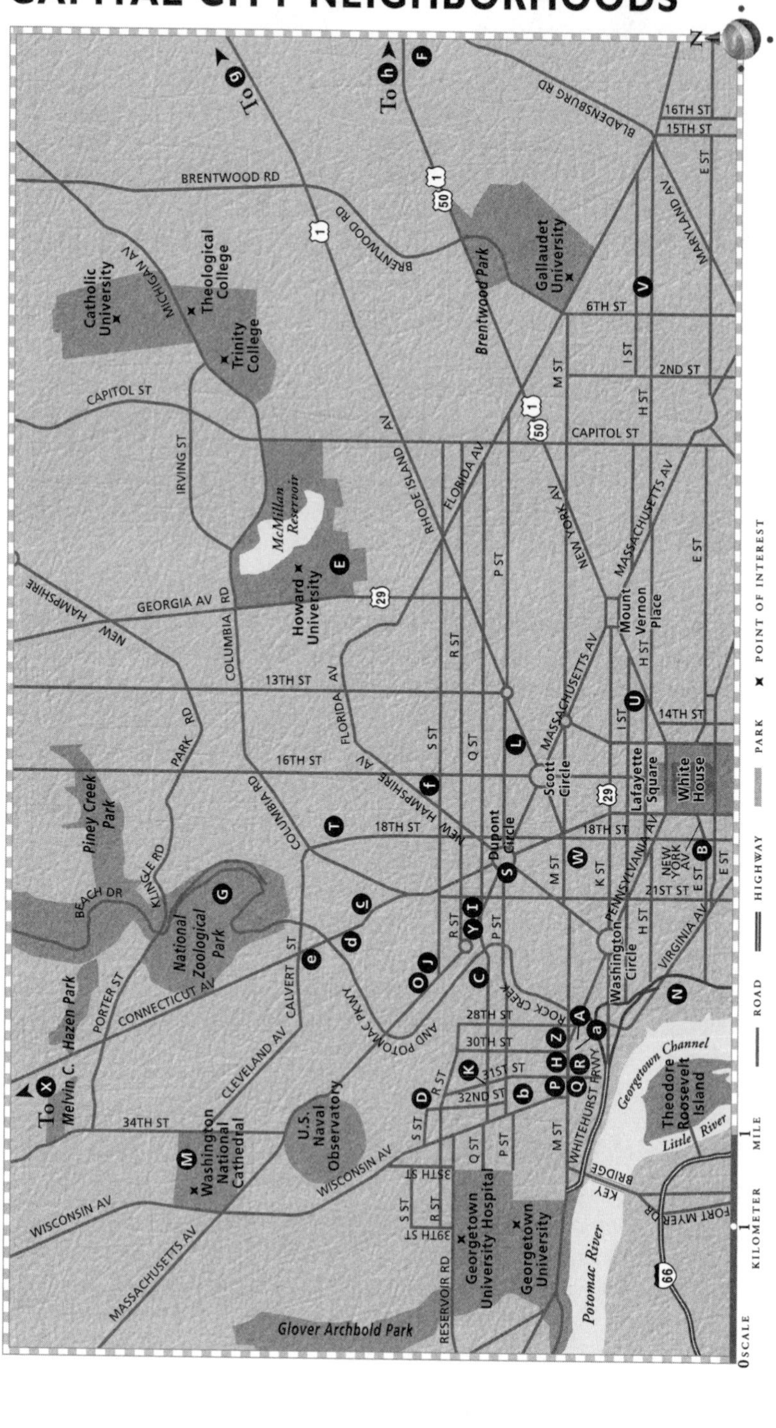

museum of nineteenth- and twentieth-century art or the Textile Museum's fantastic display of historic and handmade frocks. Eat lunch at a sidewalk café before traveling a few blocks north to Adams-Morgan. Wander through some unique shops that sell everything from kitschy antiques to herbs and potions. When you're done here, visit the Washington National Cathedral in Friendship Heights. Then go directly to Georgetown for some serious power shopping. Have dinner at one of the many restaurants overlooking the picturesque C&O Canal.

D.C. NEIGHBORHOODS

Adams-Morgan is similar to Greenwich or SoHo in New York. This eclectic and funky neighborhood is located north of Dupont Circle. Primarily a residential area for D.C.'s coolest residents, Adams-Morgan contains street after street of townhouses from the early 1900s. At 18th Street and Columbia Road, NW, a Saturday morning market is a major draw with vendors offering everything from fresh flowers to home-cooked goodies. There is also an unusually high concentration of ethnic restaurants, and a number of the city's hippest nightclubs, ranging from salsa to jazz to grunge, are located here. Adams-Morgan runs along Columbia Road between 18th and Kalorama Park, NW.

Dupont Circle is a colorful lively neighborhood, located along Connecticut Avenue from N to T Streets, NW. It is home to art galleries and museums, shops, lovely restored townhouses, and restaurants. The area centers around

SIGHTS

- **A** C&O Canal
- **B** Congressional Cemetery
- **C** Dumbarton House
- **D** Dumbarton Oaks
- **E** Howard University
- **F** National Arboretum
- **G** National Zoological Park
- **H** Old Stone House
- **I** The Phillips Collection
- **J** Textile Museum
- **K** Tudor Place
- **L** St. Matthew's Cathedral
- **M** Washington National Cathedral

SIGHTS (continued)

- **N** Washington Navy Yard
- **O** Woodrow Wilson House

FOOD

- **P** Aditi
- **Q** Clyde's
- **R** Filamina Ristorante
- **S** Pesce Fish Market and Bistro Café
- **T** Red Sea
- **U** Taberna del Alabardero
- **V** Tony Cheng's Seafood Restaurant
- **W** Vidalia

LODGING

- **X** Days Inn Uptown
- **Y** Embassy Row Hilton
- **Z** Four Seasons Hotel
- **a** Georgetown Dutch Inn
- **b** Georgetown Inn
- **c** Hotel Sofitel
- **d** Normandy Inn
- **e** Omni Shoreham Hotel
- **f** Swann House

CAMPING

- **g** Cherry Hill Park
- **h** Duncan's Family Campground

the traffic circle/park with its lovely Beaux-Arts fountain called Dupont Circle. West of the circle, you'll find many commercial galleries with a diverse selection of paintings, sculptures, prints, and drawings.

Georgetown is perhaps the icon of the D.C. neighborhood scene. The spire of Georgetown University looms over the maze of eighteenth- and nineteenth-century brick homes and buildings. Boats glide quietly along the Potomac and busy lunchers keep up with the D.C. buzz overlooking the C&O Canal. At night, music emanates from the doorways of dance clubs and neighborhood bars. It is this *St. Elmo's Fire* image of Georgetown that brings thousands of visitors to this charming neighborhood.

During colonial times, the waterfront served as an important port. Later, Georgetown was an important point on the Underground Railroad. The district is also home to George Washington University.

Howard University is located in the African American community of **Shaw**. The area was the business hub of D.C.'s African American community until desegregation laws were passed in the 1950s. The historic district is home to such landmarks as the O Street Market, Bethune Museum and Archives, and the Lincoln Theatre. Shaw is located between North Capitol Street and 15th Street, north of M Street.

Brookland is the second oldest African American neighborhood in D.C. and has been home to singer Pearl Bailey, poet Sterling Brown, and Nobel Peace Prize winner Ralph Bunche. Brookland is located along 12th Street, Michigan Avenue, and South Dakota Avenue, NE.

Just north of Penn Quarter downtown, **Chinatown** contains many Asian restaurants and shops and is the site of the annual Chinese New Year's Day parade. The neighborhood's most identifiable landmark is the much-photographed Friendship Arch at Seventh and H Streets, NW. Chinatown is located between Sixth and Eighth Streets at G and H Streets, NW.

Most of the city's beautiful foreign embassies can be spotted on **Embassy Row**, along Massachusetts Avenue, NW. Although not an embassy, one of the highlights is the Society of the Cincinnati at Anderson House, located at 2118 Massachusetts Avenue.

The historic area known as **LaDroit Park** features some wonderful nineteenth-century houses and has been home to a bevy of historical and literary figures. Its famous residents have included Jesse Jackson; the city's first African American mayor, Walter Washington; African American poet Paul Laurence Dunbar; and author and educator Anna J. Cooper. LaDroit Park runs between Second and Fifth Streets, NW, south of Florida Avenue, NW.

South of Capitol Square, where the Washington Channel of the Potomac River flows into the Anacostia River, is perhaps one of the district's most hidden away tourist attractions—the **Waterfront** district. The southwest portion is where you'll find the lively Maine Avenue Fish Market and a high concentration of D.C.'s tourboats. This is also where you'll find the Arena Stage, which has won countless awards for excellence over the years. Benjamin Banneker Circle and Fountain is located here in L'Enfant Plaza (Maine and Water Streets, SW). Banneker was a noted African American mathematician and astronomer who assisted L'Enfant with the design of the city in 1791. The Waterfront is located south of the National Mall, east to the Anacostia River.

The southeast portion of the Waterfront contains many maritime and naval attractions (see the Washington Navy Yard).

SIGHTSEEING HIGHLIGHTS

★★★★ C&O CANAL
Foundry Mall, 30th and Jefferson Sts., NW, Georgetown
202/472-4376
This historic canal stretches for 184.5 miles from the mouth of Rock Creek in Georgetown to Cumberland, Maryland. The waterway provided commercial transportation during the eighteenth and nineteenth centuries. Today, the towpath along the canal is traversed by bikers, hikers, and strollers. The waterway is used by canoeists, fishermen, and mule-towed canal boats which operate from Georgetown and Great Falls during the warm weather months.
Details: Apr–Sep. $7.50 adults, $6 seniors, $4 children. (1 hour) (See Fitness and Recreation for more waterway outfitters/tours.)

★★★★ NATIONAL ZOOLOGICAL PARK
3001 Connecticut Ave., NW, Metro Stop: Woodley Park-Zoo, 202/673-4717
This large, nicely landscaped zoo is often rated, "One of the Country's Best," with more than 5,000 exotic animals, birds, and reptiles. The recently opened Amazonia Science Gallery is designed to look like what might be found in a modern research facility on the fringe of the Brazilian rain forest. The new Think Tank exhibit allows you to examine the thinking capability of primates and other animals through tool use, language, and society skills.

Other favorites are Hsing-Hsing, (the country's only giant panda, a gift from the People's Republic of China, is best seen around feeding times at 11 a.m. and 3 p.m.), and rare blue-eyed Bengal tigers. The

Visitors must be savvy to make the most of their zoo experience. In general, the best time to spot the animals is early in the morning when they are more active.

exhibit of invertebrates is the only one of its kind in the country with starfish, insects, and other spineless creatures. The park is spread over 163 acres of very hilly terrain so it is important to plan your route (i.e. where you park), for the least amount of wear and tear.

Details: *Tour reservations 202/673-4955. Grounds Oct–Apr 8–6, Apr–Oct 8–8; animal buildings 9–4:30; guided tours by appt. only. Admission is free, but parking is $2–$7 (2–4 hours)*

★★★★ WASHINGTON NATIONAL CATHEDRAL
Massachusetts and Wisconsin Aves., NW, Metro Stop: Tenleytown Station, then take Bus 30, 32, 34 or 36 202/537-6200

This breathtaking gothic cathedral is the second largest church of its kind in the U.S. and the sixth largest in the world. From the moment you enter the National Cathedral your eyes are guided upward to Heaven by the sheer enormousness and grandeur of this building. Begun in 1907 and completed in 1990, the cathedral is built completely of Indiana limestone; no structural steel holds up the ceiling, which is designed with flying buttresses. The cathedral's most remarkable details include the fantastic stained-glass windows—one depicts the Creation and another is of the space flight of *Apollo XI.* Other attractions include a children's chapel featuring tapestries of baby animals, an ornate high altar, and fanciful exterior gargoyles depicting everything from traditional figures to Darth Vader. Don't just wander around, but take a guided tour. There is so much to see, it is easy to miss the details.

Details: *Daily 10–4:30, guided tours Mon–Sat 10–3:15, Sun 12:45–2:45. Free. (1–2 hours)*

★★★ DUMBARTON OAKS
1703 32nd St., NW, Georgetown, 202/339-6400

This is an opulent nineteenth-century mansion with 10 acres of formal gardens. The original federal-period home was bought by Mr. and Mrs. Robert Woods Bliss in 1920. They gave the house, gardens, and collections to Harvard University in 1940. A wing was added in 1963 to display the Bliss's collection of pre-Columbian art and a collection of rare and modern books.

Details: Apr–Oct Tue–Sun 2–5 p.m., gardens daily 2–5 p.m. Donations requested. (30 minutes)

★★ CONGRESSIONAL CEMETERY
1801 E St., SE, Metro Stop: Stadium-Armory
202/543-0539
The nation's first national cemetery dates back to 1807. The burial ground contains the graves of composer John Philip Sousa, F.B.I. chief J. Edgar Hoover, photographer Matthew Brady, two Native American chiefs, senators, Revolutionary War heroes, and other prominent individuals.

Details: Daily 9–5, guided tours by appt. only. Free. (30 minutes)

★★ DUMBARTON HOUSE
2715 Q St., NW, Georgetown, 202/337-2288
Today Dumbarton is the headquarters for the National Society of Colonial Dames of America. A federal-period home, it was once the abode of Joseph Nourse, first registrar of the U.S. treasury.

Details: Tue–Sat 10 a.m.–1 p.m. (last tour at 12:15). $2.50 adults, students free. (30 minutes)

★★ HOWARD UNIVERSITY
2400 Sixth St., NW, Shaw, 202/806-6100
Howard University is one of the most prestigious, historically black universities in the country. The Moorland-Springarn Research Center contains the nation's largest collection of materials documenting the history and culture of African Americans. There is also an excellent art gallery on campus.

Details: Mon–Thu 9–4:45, Fri 9–4:30, Sat 9–5. Free. (1–2+ hours)

★★ NATIONAL ARBORETUM
3501 New York Ave., NE, Metro Stop: Stadium, then take Bus B2, B4, or B5, 202/245-2726
Like an oasis in the center of concrete and marble, the National Arboretum contains more than 400 acres of trees, shrubs, flowering plants, picnic grounds, and herb garden. Favorite spots in the serene expanse include the famous Bonsai collection, English knot garden, and antique rose garden.

Details: Daily 8–5; Bonsai Pavilion daily 10–3:30; tram tours Sat–Sun 11:30 a.m., 1 p.m., 2 p.m., 3 p.m., 4 p.m.; guided tours: by appt. only. $3 adults, $2 children. (30 minutes–1 hour)

★★ THE PHILLIPS COLLECTION
1600 21st St., NW, Dupont Circle, 202/387-2151

This collection contains nineteenth- and twentieth-century art master-pieces by Renoir, Picasso, Matisse, Manet, O'Keeffe, El Greco, Cézanne, Bonnard, and others. The museum is located in the home of Duncan Phillips.

Details: Mon–Sat 10–5, Sun noon–7. $6.50 adults, $3.25 students. (1–2 hours)

★★ ST. MATTHEW'S CATHEDRAL
1725 Rhode Island Ave., NW, Metro Stop: Farragut North or Dupont Circle, 202/347-3215

St. Matthew's Cathedral was established in 1840. Many people who were alive during the Kennedy assassination remember St. Matthew's as the site of this beloved president's funeral mass in 1963. Masses are available to the public.

Details: Mon–Fri 6:30 a.m.–6:15 p.m., Sat 7:30 a.m.–8:30 p.m., Sun 6:30 a.m.–6:30 p.m.; guided tours Sun between 2:30–4:30 p.m. Free. (15 minutes)

★★ TUDOR PLACE
1644 31st St., NW, Georgetown, 202/965-0400

Martha Washington's granddaughter, Martha Parke Custis Peter, once called Tudor Place home. The federal-period mansion contains won-derful furnishings and lovely gardens.

Details: Tue–Fri 10, 11:30, 1, and 2:30, Sat hourly 10–3. $6 adults, $5 seniors, $3 students. (45 minutes)

★★ WASHINGTON NAVY YARD
901 M St., SE, Waterfront

This Waterfront navy yard is one of the oldest in the country (1799) and contains a number of significant museums, as well as a decom-missioned destroyer, the U.S.S. *Barry*.

The Navy Museum, 202/433-4882, is housed in an old Naval Gun Factory and contains model ships, weapons, and more. Highlights include the foremast fighting top of the U.S.S. *Constitution* and hands-on exhibits for kids. The adjacent Marine Corps Museum features exhibits on major ocean battles.

Details: Mon–Fri 9–4, Sat–Sun 10–5. Free. (1 hour)

★★ WOODROW WILSON HOUSE
2340 S St., SW, Dupont Circle, 202/387-4062

Washington, D.C.'s only presidential museum is worth a visit if you are interested in seeing the home that Woodrow Wilson resided in following his presidential years. The house contains the original furnishings and artifacts, as well as presidential memorabilia and changing exhibits.

Details: Tue–Sun 10–4. $5 adults, $2.50 students. (45 minutes)

★ OLD STONE HOUSE
3051 M St., Georgetown, NW, 202/426-6851

Built in 1765 by a cabinet maker, this house is the oldest dwelling in Washington, D.C.

Details: Wed–Sun 8–4:30. Free. (20 minutes)

★ TEXTILE MUSEUM
2320 S St., NW, Dupont Circle, 202/667-0441

Fine textiles of historical and artistic significance are displayed at this museum. Begun in 1925 with the collection of George Hewitt Myers, the museum is housed in a fabulous John Russell Pope mansion.

Details: Mon–Sat 10–5, Sun 1–5. $5 adults. (45 minutes)

FITNESS AND RECREATION

Washington, D.C., offers beautiful, lush foliage and an abundance of waterways and gardens. **Theodore Roosevelt Island** is a favorite for joggers and includes a wildlife refuge and memorial to the former president. Other parks include **Rock Creek Park**, located along Rock Creek which extends through Georgetown, and the **George Washington Carver Nature Trail**, in Anacostia, which are great places to enjoy the scenery.

Enjoy the waterways near Georgetown and the C&O Canal by renting a canoe, a boat, or bicycles. Outfitters in the area include **Thompson's Boat Center**, 2900 Virginia Avenue, NW, 202/333-9543; **Fletcher's Boathouse**, George Washington Parkway on the Virginia side of the Potomac, Key Bridge exit, 202/244-0461; and **Swain's Lock**, 301/299-9006, located just above Great Falls.

Golf courses can be found in the city at the **Langston Golf Course**, 20600

Benning Road, NE, 202/397-8638, and **Rock Creek Golf Course**, 16th and Rittenhouse Street, NW, 202/882-7332. Both locations feature 18-hole courses.

FOOD

One good choice for a special evening out is **Filamina Ristorante** at 1063 Wisconsin Avenue, NW, 202/338-8800. As you enter the Georgetown bistro, you see Italian women stuffing homemade ravioli and making pasta.

A taste of Madrid can be experienced in downtown D.C. at **Taberna del Alabardero**, 1776 I Street, NW, 202/429-2200. The acclaimed restaurant offers traditional Spanish tapas, paella, *angulas,* and a huge selection of Spanish wines. *Condé Nast Traveler* called this restaurant one of the "Top 50 Restaurants in America."

Superior Indian cuisine can be found at **Aditi** in Georgetown at 3299 M Street, NW, 202/625-6825. The restaurant features traditional tandoori, vegetarian, chicken, and seafood dishes in authentic Indian style.

Vidalia, 1990 M Street, NW, 202/659-1990, offers up Southern cooking with French influences, e.g. sautéed shrimp with grits and mushroom ragout—the result is delicious. It is one of the most popular dining choices in the district.

For great dining, but with more reasonable prices, try the **Pesce Fish Market and Bistro Café**, 2016 P Street, NW, 202/466-3474. Pesce serves up fresh fish and seafood with Italian and French influences. The atmosphere is festive and lively.

In Chinatown, reasonably priced Chinese food and seafood can be found at **Tony Cheng's Seafood Restaurant**, 619 H Street, NW, 202/842-8669. The food is great, especially upstairs where Tony Cheng's features seafood on the menu. (There is a different ambiance and menu on the two floors.) In Adams-Morgan, the **Red Sea**, 2463 18th Street, NW, 202/483-5000, is a taste explosion for a small price. This inventive restaurant offers dishes with exciting twists and includes a fantastic vegetarian menu. Try the *Yetekilt Kilikil* dish, which is a delicious mixture of carrots, potatoes, collards, and cabbage. Each vegetable is lightly seasoned with garlic, ginger root, and pepper.

Families will appreciate **Clyde's**, 3236 M Street, NW, Georgetown, 202/333-9180, and various locations throughout the city. These American-cuisine restaurants feature breakfast all day, kids' menus, burgers, pizza, and much more. Clyde's is reliable and very comfortable if you have a whole crew to please.

LODGING

As its name implies, the **Georgetown Inn**, 1310 Wisconsin Avenue, NW, 202/333-8900 or 800/424-2979, is more inn than hotel with an inviting brick front and fewer rooms than the standard luxury hotel. Amenities at this Georgetown district hotel include restaurant, lounge, room service, valet parking, turndown service, complimentary newspapers, and fitness center. Rates are $105 to $139. Also in Georgetown, those who accept only the best will find the **Four Seasons Hotel**, 2800 Pennsylvania Avenue, NW, 202/342-0444, quite pleasing. The luxurious property has elegantly decorated rooms with down pillows and thick terry cloth robes. Amenities include a state-of-the-art health club and spa, restaurant, and 24-hour room service. Rates are steep at $245 to $355. The **Georgetown Dutch Inn**, 1075 Thomas Jefferson Street, NW, 202/337-0900, has very comfortable, tastefully decorated suites and offers a complimentary continental breakfast. Rates are $85 to $130.

Comfortable yet economical lodging can be found at the **Days Inn Uptown**, 4400 Connecticut Avenue, NW, 202/244-5600, not far from the, National Zoo. The rooms are nicely appointed and feature in-room safes, cable television, and voice mail. The hotel has on-site parking. Rates are $65 to $85. Also near the zoo is the **Omni Shoreham Hotel**, 2500 Calvert Street, NW, 202/234-0700, which is a large 770-room property with very comfortable rooms that are complete with robes, iron and ironing board, and two or more phones. The hotel has four restaurants/lounges, an outdoor swimming pool, tennis courts, jogging trails, fitness center, and golf nearby. Rates are $125 to $175.

Located in a beautiful mansion, **Swann House**, 1808 New Hampshire Avenue, NW, 202/265-4414, is truly a gem of a bed-and-breakfast in a city with so many enormous hotels. Like a quiet sanctuary in the center of the bustling city, the Swann House is elegantly decorated with luxurious rooms and wonderful food. Rates range from $125 to $225 and include an extended continental breakfast.

In Dupont Circle, the **Hotel Sofitel**, 1914 Connecticut Avenue, NW, 202/797-2000, has the feel of a small European hotel. The hotel rooms are enormous compared to other D.C. overnights and amenities include a full-service restaurant, bar, and room service. Rates are $145 to $190.

The **Normandy Inn**, 2118 Wyoming Avenue, NW, 202/483-1350, is located in the lovely Embassy area of the city. The small, European-style hotel has basic, but comfortable rooms. Rates are under $100. Also in Embassy Row, the **Embassy Row Hilton**, 2015 Massachusetts Avenue, NW, 202/265-1600, has standard rooms with amenities such as a rooftop pool and a full-service restaurant. Rates are $105 to $125.

CAMPING

Because Washington is such an urban setting, there are only a few camping options available. The largest campground in the D.C. area is **Cherry Hill Park** at 9800 Cherry Hill Road, College Park, Maryland, 301/937-7116 or 800/801-6449. The 400 tent and RV campsites have amenities such as full hookups, cable television capability, camp store, Laundromat, heated pool, hot tub, sauna, game room, TV lounge, playground, miniature golf, and a café. As well as being conveniently located across from the Metro Greenbelt subway line, this campground offers tours of D.C., special charters, and Metro bus service.

Duncan's Family Campground at 5381 Sands Road, Lothian, Maryland, 410/741-9558, is smaller and located in a quiet wooded area. Guests will appreciate the van to the Metro subway, free cable TV, coin-operated laundry, outdoor pool, and gift shop.

NIGHTLIFE

The **Georgetown** district is nationally known as a haven for interesting bars/pubs, dance clubs, and general after-dark merriment. However, a host of nightclubs throughout the D.C. area offers everything from jazz to comedy to country and western. Most clubs begin receiving night crawlers at 9 or 10 p.m. and are open until 2 or 3 a.m.

For live blues, try **Blues Alley**, rear of 1073 Wisconsin Avenue, 202/337-4141. For live comedy (in addition to **Gross National Product**, see p. 34), try the nationally recognized **Improv**, 1140 Connecticut Avenue, between L and M Streets, 202/296-7008, for the hottest stand-up comics. Or **Capitol Steps**, 1055 Thomas Jefferson Street, NW, 202/298-8222, for razor-sharp political satire.

For dancing, **Polly Esther's**, 12th Street beween F and G, NW, 202/737-1970, is a seventies throwback experience, and **Club Zei**, Zei Alley, NW, between 14th and 15th, 202/842-2445, is sleek and sophisticated. Always wanted to hang out at a 1940s club, sipping martinis while Sinatra croons? *L.A. Confidential* fans will appreciate **Felix**, 2406 18th Street, NW, 202/483-3549, in the Adams-Morgan district. There are also numerous microbreweries, cigar clubs, reggae spots, Irish pubs, beatnik clubs, piano lounges, and sports bars. You have no excuse for staying in your hotel room.

PERFORMING ARTS

Near Shaw in the U Street district, the **Lincoln Theater** (1921), 1215 U Street, NW, 202/328-9177, is a former vaudeville/movie house which now turns out touring stage shows, comedy performances, and music and dance. The **Arena Stage** on the Waterfront, Sixth and Maine Avenue, SW, 202/488-3300, is the only theater outside New York to win a Tony Award. Two dinner theater venues include the wonderful **Burn Brae Dinner Theatre**, Burtonsville, Maryland, 301/384-5800, and the **Mystery Menu on the Menu Theater**, 1728 Wisconsin Avenue, NW, 202/333-6875, which shows whodunits.

SHOPPING

Georgetown contains a large number of specialty shops, galleries, and a fabulous upscale mall, the **Shops at Georgetown Park**, 3222 M Street, NW, 202/298-5577. The site on which Georgetown Park is located was built in the 1800s to house horse-drawn omnibuses. Inside the glittering multilevel mall, you'll find only the best boutiques and department stores including **Polo/Ralph Lauren**, **J. Crew**, **Ann Taylor**, **Williams and Sonoma**, **Abercrombie and Fitch**, and **Talbots**. (New Yorkers will feel right at home when they see the Dean and Deluca gourmet food store next to the mall.) Georgetown Park is open Monday through Saturday 10 a.m. to 9 p.m., Sunday noon to 6 p.m.

3
NORTHERN VIRGINIA

So much of this region's history is connected with the nation's capital. The Metro subway service that connects the two areas makes Northern Virginia a viable alternative for lodging and dining while in the area. The region has become a suburb to D.C., but offers a variety of other delights in addition to its conglomeration of shopping malls, office buildings, and townhouses. Here you'll find George Washington's historic estate, Mount Vernon, perched along the Potomac. Directly across from D.C., Arlington National Cemetery and the Iwo Jima Marine Corps memorial are reminders of lives given to protect freedom in America. Combine all this with the region's location, a high concentration of superb restaurants, and a dizzying array of shopping opportunities, and Northern Virginia becomes a destination in itself.

A PERFECT DAY IN NORTHERN VIRGINIA

Begin your diverse journey at Mount Vernon, then travel along the George Washington Memorial Parkway to Arlington National Cemetery. After reflecting on the Tomb of the Unknowns and the eternal flame at John F. Kennedy's gravesite, visit the Iwo Jima Marine Corps Memorial—one of the most recognizable statue groups in the world. Then take a tour of the world's largest office building, the Pentagon, and see the center of American defense. End your day in Old Town Alexandria for dinner at one of the atmospheric restaurants in a historic setting. Many of the Old Town shops are also open late, offering a perfect way to walk off your dinner.

ALEXANDRIA SIGHTSEEING HIGHLIGHTS

The city of Alexandria was named for Scotsman John Alexander who purchased the site in 1669. The city was established in 1749 and was home to many prominent people including George Washington. Old Town Alexandria reflects Alexandria during its early days and has been meticulously restored.

★★★ CARLYLE HOUSE
121 N. Fairfax St., 703/549-2997
The house, built in 1753, hosted a pivotal meeting to discuss the French and Indian War. This meeting resulted in the Stamp Act of 1765. This Georgian-style mansion was once the home of a wealthy merchant and landowner and contains gorgeous gardens to the rear.
Details: *Tue–Sat 10–5, Sun noon–5. $4 adults. (1 hour)*

ALEXANDRIA

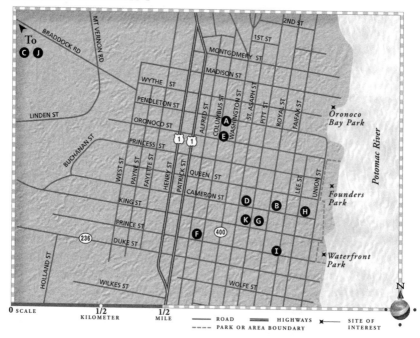

★★★ TORPEDO FACTORY ART CENTER
105 N. Union St., 703/838-4565

The building was used to manufacture torpedoes during World War II. Today it is an art center where you can watch artists at work and purchase a little something for your home. Goods available include everything from ceramics to metalworks. The art center overlooks the water and is adjacent to several waterfront restaurants and a food court.

Details: Daily 10–5. Free. (1 hour)

★★ BOYHOOD HOME OF ROBERT E. LEE
607 Oronoco St., 703/548-8454

Lee lived in this home from the ages of five through 18. Tours include information on the Lee family history, and the house features a charming boxwood garden.

Details: Mon–Sat 10–4, Sun 1–4. $4 adults. (30 minutes)

★★ FORT WARD MUSEUM AND HISTORIC SITE
4301 Braddock Rd., 703/838-4848

The Fort Ward Museum and Historic Site is a restored Union fort. The fort was used to protect the capital from a potential Confederate invasion during the Civil War.

Details: Tue–Sat 9–5, Sun noon–5. $4 adults. (45 minutes)

★★ GADSBY'S TAVERN MUSEUM
134 N. Royal St., 703/838-4242

Gadsby's was once the city's main locale for food and lodging. George Washington once met with patriots here. Today, you can enjoy great food and glimpse at what Alexandria was like during colonial times.

Details: Tue–Sat 10–5, Sun 1–5. $4 adults, $2 students. (1 hour)

SIGHTS
- Ⓐ Boyhood Home of Robert E. Lee
- Ⓑ Carlyle House
- Ⓒ Fort Ward Museum and Historic Site
- Ⓓ Gadsby's Tavern Museum
- Ⓔ Lee-Fendall House Museum
- Ⓕ The Lyceum
- Ⓖ Stabler Leadbeater Apothecary Museum
- Ⓗ Torpedo Factory Art Center

FOOD
- Ⓘ La Bergerie

LODGING
- Ⓙ Doubletree
- Ⓚ Holiday Inn Select

★★ LEE-FENDALL HOUSE MUSEUM
429 N. Washington St., 703/548-1789
The clapboard Lee-Fendall House Museum is where Robert E. Lee's family lived in 1785 and contains many personal objects belonging to the family. It also has an interesting collection of dollhouses.

Details: Tue–Sat 10–4, Sun noon–4. Free. (30 minutes)

★★ THE LYCEUM
201 S. Washington St., 703/838-4994
The Lyceum is the museum of Alexandria's history. The Greek Revival hall was built in 1829 and used as a hospital during the Civil War. The building houses a travel information center, as well as artifacts, documents, paintings, and photographs of the town's history. Some of the artifacts include a slave sale receipt, uniforms, and weapons.

Details: Mon–Sat 10–5, Sun 1–5. Free. (30–45 minutes)

★★ STABLER LEADBEATER APOTHECARY MUSEUM
105 S. Fairfax St., 703/836-3713
Between 1792 and 1933 this apothecary shop was fully operating; today, it is a museum that houses more than 8,000 artifacts. There are hand-blown glass containers, thermometers, and records of pills.

Details: Mon–Sat 10–4, Sun 1–5. $2.50 adults. (30 minutes)

ARLINGTON SIGHTSEEING HIGHLIGHTS

★★★★ ARLINGTON NATIONAL CEMETERY
Southern end of Memorial Bridge, Metro Stop: Arlington Cemetery, 703/979-4886
The largest national cemetery, this 600-acre burial ground is a shrine to men and women who died defending the United States. More than 200,000 soldiers are buried here. Much of the cemetery is located on land that was once owned by Robert E. Lee. His former home, Arlington House (or the Custis-Lee Mansion), is located in the cemetery and is open for tours.

The most visited gravesite at the cemetery is that of John F. Kennedy. Former First Lady Jacqueline Bouvier Kennedy Onassis and Robert Kennedy are buried nearby. Other notable persons buried here are Supreme Court Justice Thurgood Marshall, boxer Joe Louis, and D.C. city-designer Pierre L'Enfant.

Also located here is the Tomb of the Unknowns memorial where unidentified soldiers from World War I, World War II, the Korean War, and the Vietnam War are interred. A new memorial, Women in Military Service for America, is located near the entrance at the western side of Memorial Bridge.

William Ramsay House, 221 King Street, 703/838-4200, is the site of the Alexandria Visitors Center. Here you can find brochures, maps, and shopping and dining information for the area.

Details: *Daily 8–5. Free. Tourmobile tours $4.75 with tickets available at the Visitor Center. (1–2 hours)*

★★★★ IWO JIMA MARINE CORPS MEMORIAL
Marshall Dr. next to Arlington Cemetery, 703/285-2601

This famous monument is dedicated to Marines who have given their lives since 1775. Felis W. deWeldon created this 78-foot cast bronze statue—the largest in the world. It depicts a famous photograph, taken by Joe Rosenthal, of Marines raising the American flag on Mount Suribachi during World War II.

Details: *Open 24 hours. Free. (20 minutes)*

★★★★ THE NEWSEUM
1101 Wilson Blvd., Metro Stop: Rosslyn Station
703/284-3544 or 888/NEWSEUM

Truly unlike any museum you've ever visited, The Newseum is a 50 million dollar, 72,000-square-foot museum that features interactive exhibits, multimedia presentations, and historic artifacts.

A 126-foot-long video news wall features live news broadcasts from around the world. Throughout the room you can go before a camera and present your own live news, weather, or sports report. There are also soundproof studios where you can become a sports announcer, interview professional journalists, and pose for the cover of your favorite magazine. Video terminals located throughout the museum allow you to test your skills as an investigative reporter or editor.

The top level contains memorabilia and photography that pertain to the history of the news. Artifacts range from Sumerian cuneiform tablets (2176–562 B.C.) to the first newspapers (1500–1720) to the rise of television (1950–1960) to digital news. Throughout the exhibit are theaters where you can watch a variety of films and newsreels of famous news footage (assassination attempt on President Reagan, disaster coverage, etc.).

Outside, in Freedom Park, items honor journalists who have died while trying to report the news. Artifacts include segments of the Berlin Wall, a statue of Lenin, a South African ballot box, and a Cuban refugee kayak.

Details: Wed–Sun 10–5. Free. (2 hours)

★★★★ PENTAGON
I-395 South to Boundary Channel Dr. exit, Metro Stop: Pentagon, 703/695-1776

This military pulse-point contains 3.7 million square feet of space and covers 583 acres. The building was constructed in 1943 at a cost of $83 million; it consolidated 17 buildings of the War Department. The unusual shape was designed for efficiency—despite 17½ miles of corridors, it takes no more than seven minutes to walk between any two points in the building.

Tour highlights include the Pentagon Prayer Room, the Air Force Art Collection depicting the evolution of the Air Force, and a Hall of Heroes dedicated to the 3,401 recipients of the Medal of Honor.

Details: Daily 9:30–3:30, tours leave every half hour, a photo I.D. is required for the tour. Free. (1–2 hours)

FAIRFAX COUNTY SIGHTSEEING HIGHLIGHTS

This southern neighbor to Washington, D.C., has been one of the fastest growing communities of the past 20 years. Huge malls, office complexes, and residential areas make up a large percentage of the land area in the county. Several great historic attractions are in the area, however.

★★★★ MOUNT VERNON
George Washington Memorial Hwy., 703/780-2000

George Washington's home is the second most visited historic home in America with nearly 100,000 visitors every year. In 1761 Washington officially inherited the house and grounds, where he lived with his family until his death in 1799. Washington, although a superb politician and statesman, was first and foremost a farmer. Objects in the house create a respectfully touching image of Washington.

Living-history interpreters explain how Washington worked to improve agricultural techniques for the country. The grounds also contain groves of fruit trees, a vineyard, and beautiful formal gardens. Washington's tomb is also located on the property. A small museum along the lane north of the mansion contains a number of personal items.

Cruises aboard a thoroughly modern tour boat are available from Mount Vernon along the Potomac River. The tours aboard the Potomac Spirit take 45 minutes and detail the history of the river. Cruises depart every morning at 11:15 from the wharf area located near the Pioneer Farmer exhibits.

Details: *Daily 8–5. $8 adults, $7.50 seniors, $4 children. (2+ hours)*

★★★ GUNSTON HALL
10709 Gunston Rd., Mason Neck, 703/550-9220

Just 14 miles south of Mount Vernon, Gunston Hall is the former home of George Mason, father of the Bill of Rights and framer of the U.S. Constitution. The brick Georgian-style house was built in 1755 and sits along the Potomac River in Fairfax County. The estate contains original boxwood gardens, a reconstructed kitchen yard, wooded nature trails, elaborate woodwork (the finest in Colonial Virginia), and fine eighteenth-century English and American antiques.

Details: *Daily 9:30–5. $5 adults, $1.50 students. (2 hours)*

★★ WOODLAWN PLANTATION/POPE-LEIGHEY HOUSE
9000 Richmond Hwy., Alexandria, 703/780-4000

Near Mount Vernon, George Washington gave Woodlawn as a wedding gift to his step-granddaughter, Nelly Custis Lewis. The pretty Georgian-style home features many family furnishings, oil paintings, and federal-period needlework. The grounds also contain a home, (the Pope-Leighey House) and furnishings designed by Frank Lloyd Wright.

Details: *Mar–Dec daily 9:30–4:30, Jan–Feb Sat–Sun 9:30–4:30. $6 adults, $4 children. Pope-Leighey House, 703/780-4000, Mar–Dec 9:30–4:30, Jan–Feb Sat–Sun 9:30–4:30. $5 adults, $3.50 students. (2 hours)*

FREDERICKSBURG SIGHTSEEING HIGHLIGHTS
Founded in 1723, the historic town of Fredericksburg quickly became a successful port due to its location at the head of the Rappahannock River. Today Fredericksburg

has one of the finest restored districts in the region and some of the most significant sites pertaining to the Civil War, with block after block of preserved homes, bed-and-breakfasts, shops, galleries, and historic buildings.

★★★★ FREDERICKSBURG AND SPOTSYLVANIA NATIONAL MILITARY PARK
Chancellorsville, Rte. 3 West, 703/786-2880, 1013 Lafayette Blvd., 703/373-6122

Some of the most intense fighting of the Civil War occurred in the area. The park contains nearly 8,000 acres of battlefields and was the site of four major battles—Fredericksburg, Chancellorsville, Spotsylvania Court House, and the Wilderness. The blood that was shed during these battles resulted in the deaths of more than 70,000 Union soldiers and 35,000 Confederates.

The house in which "Stonewall" Jackson died in nearby Caroline County is one of the most important sites in the park. After being wounded at Chancellorsville by his own men, Jackson was brought to this house where he developed pneumonia and died on May 10, 1863. The drive to the site will take you past many Civil War–era forms and homes. Also notable is Chatham, an eighteenth-century restored mansion used by Union troops as a headquarters and hospital.

The Fredericksburg Visitor Center, 706 Caroline Street, Fredericksburg, 800/678-4748, sells block tickets for $19.75 that include most attractions in the historic district.

Details: Daily 9–5. $3 for adult 7-day National Park passes, annual passes are $15. (2 hours)

★★★ KENMORE
1201 Washington Ave., 703/373-3381

Washington's sister, Betty, lived in this colonial house. It is furnished with eighteenth-century antiques and is recognized for the elaborate plasterwork in the house. A bedroom has been hailed by several major preservation and architectural publications as one of the most beautiful rooms in America. During the Civil War the house was used as a hospital.

Details: Mar–Dec Mon–Sat 10–5, Sun noon–5, Jan–Feb Mon–Fri by reservation only. $6 adults, $3 ages 6–18. (1 hour)

★★ FERRY FARM
Rte. 3 East at Ferry Rd., 703/373-3381

George Washington's boyhood home has recently been preserved, and you can view the archaeological work being undertaken on the site. *Details: Mon–Sat 10–5 p.m., Sun noon-5, tours by reservation only. (1 hour)*

★★ JAMES MONROE MUSEUM
908 Charles St., 703/899-4559

In 1876 James Monroe set up his law practice in Fredericksburg. A museum is located on the site of his law office. Also on site are many of Monroe's personal belongings including some of the furnishings he purchased while he was Minister to France.
Details: Mar–Nov daily 9–5. $4 adults, $1.40 children ages 6–18. (30 minutes)

★★ MARY WASHINGTON HOUSE
Charles and Lewis Sts., 703/373-1569

Fredericksburg was also the last home of Washington's mother, Mary. The Mary Washington House contains many of her possessions and some very fine boxwood gardens.
Details: Mar–Nov daily 9–5, Dec–Feb daily 10–4. $4 adults, $1.50 children ages 6–18. (45 minutes)

PRINCE WILLIAM COUNTY/MANASSAS SIGHTSEEING HIGHLIGHTS

Prince William County was formed in 1730 and named after King George II's son. The county is home to one of the most significant Civil War sites (Manassas), the world's largest outlet mall, and some historic sites and museums. Prince William Visitors Center is located at 200 Mill Street in Occoquan, 703/491-4045.

★★★★ MANASSAS NATIONAL BATTLEFIELD PARK
Visitor Center is located off I-66 (Exit 47B) or off I-95 (Exit 152) to Rte. 234 North, 703/361-1339

This 5,000-acre park preserves the site of two bloody Civil War battles. Manassas' location near the nation's capital and a key railroad junction made the site an important strategic location for both the Northern and Southern armies. It was at Manassas that General Thomas "Stonewall" Jackson was observed standing "like a stone wall." The First Battle of Manassas occurred on July 21, 1861 on Henry

Hill. And on August 28, 1862, the Second Battle of Manassas occurred. You can take a walking tour, a driving tour, and even a horse-back equestrian tour of the site.

Details: *Visitor Center open daily 8:30–5; park dawn–dusk. Free. (1+ hour)*

★★★ MANASSAS MUSEUM
9101 Prince William St., Manassas, 703/368-1873

The Manassas Museum features a substantial collection of historic arti-facts and photographs including uniforms, furnishings, and personal items. It is dedicated to the history of the area, especially the events surrounding the Civil War battles.

A wonderful video featured at the museum, *A Community at War*, focuses on the area's role in the Civil War. Another video, *A Place of Passages*, describes the settlement of the area. Walking tour brochures for the downtown historic district are available at the visitors center.

Details: *Tue–Sun 10–5. $2.50 adults, $1.50 seniors and children ages 6–17. (45 minutes)*

★★ QUANTICO MARINE CORPS BASE/MARINE CORPS AIR-GROUND MUSEUM
Base, 703/784-2121; museum, 703/784-2606

Prince William County is home to Quantico Marine Corps Base where America's fiercest soldiers and government agents are trained. The base is beautiful as well as impressive. The Marine Corps Air–Ground Museum gives you an overview of the history of the Marines. Housed in vintage aircraft hangars, the on-base museum focuses on combat operations, air and ground tactics, technology, aircraft, weapons, and vehicles.

Details: *Museum open Tue–Sat 10–5, Sun noon–5. Free. (1–2 hours)*

BOAT TOURS

The **Admiral Tip Tourboat**, 703/684-0580, conducts 40-minute tours of the Alexandria waterfront, and the **Potomac Riverboat Company**, 703/548-9000, takes visitors to Mount Vernon aboard the *Miss Christin* Tourboat. **Dandy Restaurant Cruises**, 703/683-6076, offers fine dining aboard an elegant boat with romantic views of D.C.'s monuments and historic sites.

FITNESS AND RECREATION

One hiking trail of note is the **Mount Vernon Trail** which winds along the Virginia side of the Potomac between Theodore Roosevelt Island and Mount Vernon and offers scenic views of Old Town Alexandria. If you are interested in renting bikes, the **Washington Sailing Marina**, 1 Marina Drive, Alexandria, 703/548-9027, boasts an impressive selection.

Parks in the region include **Cameron Run Regional Park**, 4001 Eisenhower Avenue, Alexandria, 703/960-0767; **Fountainhead Regional Park**, 10875 Hampton Road, Fairfax, 703/250-9124; **Lake Anna State Park**, 6800 Lawyers Road, Spotsylvania, 540/555-1212; Meadowlark Gardens Regional Park, 9750 Meadowlark Gardens Court, Vienna, 703/255-3631; **Potomac Overlook Regional Park**, 2845 Marcey Road, Arlington, 703/528-5406; and **Upton Hill Regional Park**, 6060 Wilson Boulevard, Arlington, 703/534-3437.

The best place in the region to get in a round of golf is Fredericksburg's highly acclaimed **Augustine Course**, Stafford, 540/720-7374.

FOOD

One of the highest rated restaurants in the country is located in Old Town Alexandria at **La Bergerie**, 218 Lee Street, 703/683-1007. The restaurant serves classic French cuisine. Steak lovers will be relieved to find a **Morton's of Chicago**, 703/883-0800, at Tyson's Corner where prime aged beef and chops can be devoured in abundance. The **Evans Farm Inn**, 1696 Chain Bridge Road, Fairfax, 703/356-8000, has a menu that includes spoon bread, prime rib, seafood, and mint juleps. The fanciest of the American/continental offerings is the **Bailiwick Inn** at 4023 Chain Bridge Road, Fairfax, 703/691-2266. The elegant formal restaurant has a prix-fixe, four-course menu with entrée items that include tenderloin with classic bordelaise sauce, rockfish in bouillabaisse broth, and stuffed saddle of rabbit.

For more moderately priced and less formal dining options, there is also a long list of great spots. Tex-Mex fans line up for the food at the **Austin Grill** Rolling and Old Kingmill Roads, Springfield, 703/644-3111, and 801 King Street, Alexandria, 703/684-8969—still another location can be found in D.C. The restaurants offer serious Southwestern dishes such as wood-grilled fajitas, hand-rolled enchiladas, an authentic Texas chili cowboy brunch, and freshly prepared lime margaritas.

Artie's is a family favorite, 3260 Old Lee Highway, Fairfax, 703/273-7600, with huge chicken and seafood salads, great burgers, fresh pecan-crusted trout, and yummy mashed potatoes.

NORTHERN VIRGINIA

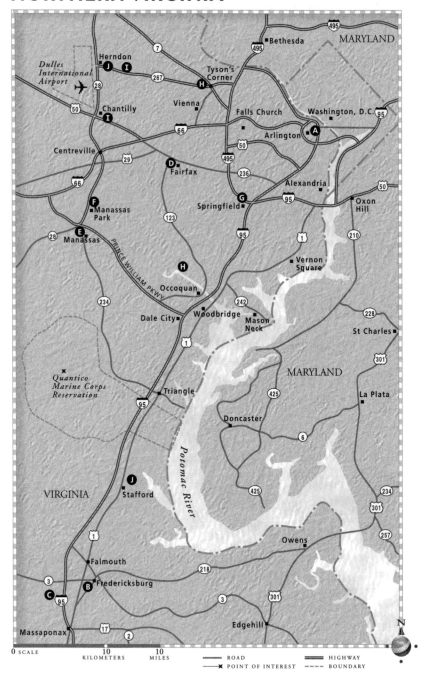

MARYLAND

Bethesda

Dulles International Airport

Herndon

Tyson's Corner

Vienna

Falls Church

Washington, D.C.

Arlington

Chantilly

Centreville

Fairfax

Alexandria

Oxon Hill

Manassas Park

Springfield

Manassas

PRINCE WILLIAM PKWY

Vernon Square

Occoquan

St Charles

Dale City

Woodbridge

Mason Neck

MARYLAND

Quantico Marine Corps Reservation

Triangle

Doncaster

La Plata

VIRGINIA

Stafford

Potomac River

Owens

Falmouth

Fredericksburg

Massaponax

Edgehill

N

0 SCALE	
10 KILOMETERS	10 MILES

ROAD ——— HIGHWAY ═══
✕ POINT OF INTEREST ----- BOUNDARY

Ristorante Renato, 422 Williams Street, 703/371-8228, in Fredericksburg, has wonderfully authentic northern Italian cuisine and is located in Old Town. A great spot for lunch in Old Town is **Sammy T's**, 801 Caroline Street, 703/371-2008, serving wonderful fresh salads, sandwiches, and homemade soups.

LODGING

Northern Virginia boasts two **Ritz Carlton** hotels. One is located at **Pentagon City** at 1250 S. Hayes Street, Arlington, 703/415-5000, and the other at **Tyson's Corner**, 1700 Tysons Boulevard, McLean, 703/506-4300. Both locations offer the best in pampering and are conveniently located near two of the region's largest and most upscale malls. The Pentagon City Ritz is located above a Metro subway station. Rates for both hotels range from $135 to $180.

Also in the fancy category, **Westfields Resort and Conference Center**, 14750 Conference Center Drive, Chantilly, 703/818-0300, is primarily a conference center with upscale amenities. The four-story Georgian-style hotel features multiline phones, refrigerators, room service, on-call physicians, restaurant, pub, lounge, pro shop, free valet parking, indoor heated pool, out-

SIGHTS

- Ⓐ Arlington National Cemetery
- Ⓑ Ferry Farm
- Ⓒ Fredericksburg and Spotsylvania National Military Park
- Ⓓ Gunston Hall
- Ⓐ Iwo Jima Marine Corps Memorial
- Ⓑ James Monroe Museum
- Ⓑ Kenmore
- Ⓔ Manassas Museum
- Ⓕ Manassas National Battlefield Park
- Ⓐ Mary Washington House
- Ⓐ Mount Vernon
- Ⓐ The Newseum

SIGHTS *(continued)*

- Ⓐ Pentagon
- Ⓔ Quantico Marine Corps Base/Marine Corps Air-Ground Museum
- Ⓐ Woodlawn Plantation/ Pope-Leighey House

FOOD

- Ⓓ Artie's
- Ⓖ Austin Grill
- Ⓓ Bailiwick Inn
- Ⓓ Evans Farm Inn
- Ⓗ Morton's of Chicago
- Ⓑ Ristorante Renato
- Ⓑ Sammy T's

LODGING

- Ⓐ Crystal City Marriott
- Ⓘ Hyatt Regency
- Ⓙ Marriott Suites Washington Dulles at Worldgate
- Ⓑ Richard Johnston Inn
- Ⓐ Ritz Carlton Pentagon City
- Ⓗ Ritz Carlton Tyson's Corner
- Ⓘ Westfields Resort and Conference Center

CAMPING

- Ⓙ Aquia Pines Camp Resort
- Ⓑ Fredericksburg KOA
- Ⓓ Lake Fairfax and Burke Lake Parks

Note: Items with the same letter are located in the same place.

door pool, health club, sauna, steam bath, tennis courts, and a championship golf course nearby. Rates are $74 to $99.

Located near Dulles International Airport and a shopping area, the **Hyatt Regency**, 1800 Presidents Street, Reston, 703/709-1234, is a four-star property. The amenities include an indoor pool, room service, airport shuttle, restaurant, lounge, health club, and sauna. Rates are $119 to $149. Also located near the airport, the **Marriott Suites Washington Dulles at Worldgate**, 13101 Worldgate Drive, Herndon, 703/709-0400, has comfortable rooms, restaurant, free parking, health club, and indoor and outdoor pools. Rates are $64 to $85.

In Alexandria, the **Holiday Inn Select**, 480 King Street, 703/549-6080, has been rated one of the top 25 Holiday Inns worldwide. The conveniently located property has colonial-style furnishings, hair dryers, minibars, in-room safes, in-room coffeemakers, voice mail, video check out, shuttles to airport and Metro subway stations, restaurants, indoor parking, indoor pool, and fitness room. Rates are $139 to $189. Families and other travelers looking for suite accommodations (refrigerators, microwaves, etc.) will appreciate the **Doubletree**, 7801 Leesburg Pike, 703/893-1340. The hotel offers a free shuttle to the Metro and a continental breakfast. Rates are $89 to $185.

In Arlington, the **Crystal City Marriott** at 1999 Jefferson Davis Highway, 703/413-5500, is located near a Metro stop, National Airport, and the Pentagon. The hotel offers in-room coffeemakers, irons and ironing boards, restaurant, lounge, indoor pool, and health club. Rates are $75 to $159.

In Fredericksburg, the eighteenth-century **Richard Johnston Inn**, 711 Caroline Street, 540/899-7606, is a restored home featuring elegant surroundings with nine guest rooms.

CAMPING

Quite a few good commercial campgrounds are in the region. In Fairfax, **Lake Fairfax and Burke Lake Parks**, 12055 Government Center Parkway, 703/324-8599, offer a park setting for camping, with recreational facilities for children and adults. In Fredericksburg, the **Fredericksburg KOA**, 7400 Brookside Lane, 540/898-7252 or 800/KOA-1889, also has a long list of amenities. In Stafford, the **Aquia Pines Camp Resort**, 3071 Jefferson Davis Highway, 800/726-1710, offers tours/shuttle service to Washington, D.C.

NIGHTLIFE

One of the most delightful after-hours spots in Virginia is **Old Town Alexandria**. Here, a soft breeze carries live music along the historic streets illuminated by the glow of restaurants and flickering gas lanterns. Brew pub fans will enjoy the **Virginia Beverage Company**, 607 King Street, 703/684-5397, for its selection of made-on-the-premises ales, bitters, and stouts. Attractions at other popular clubs include piano lounge music at **The Grille**, 116 South Alfred, 703/838-8000, and acoustic guitar at the **Seaport Inn**, 6 King Street, 703/549-2341.

PERFORMING ARTS

At the **Wolf Trap Foundation for the Performing Arts**, 1624 Trap Road, Vienna, 703/255-1868, tickets 703/218-6500, a centuries-old barn is the unique setting for live concerts and plays from the world's finest entertainers. The **Nissan Pavilion**, 7800 Cellar Door Drive, Bristow, 703/754-6400, is a modern outdoor concert hall offering live entertainment.

SHOPPING

Landmark shopping areas near D.C. include the glitzy **Fashion Centre at Pentagon City**, 15th Street South, Pentagon City, 703/415-2400, and **Crystal City Shops**, 1755 Jeff Davis Highway, 703/922-4636. **Tysons Corner**, another ritzy shopping center, has grown into the East Coast's largest concentration of retail stores outside of New York City with department stores such as Neiman Marcus, Nordstrom, Saks Fifth Avenue, Macy's, and Bloomingdales, and upscale boutiques such as Tiffany & Co. and Gucci.

Old Town Alexandria offers unique shopping at more than 200 shops carrying goods you don't see everyday. **Why Not**, 200 King Street, 703/548-4420, is a children's boutique with a fantastic selection of clothing and toys.

Virginia's Hunt Country

Traveling westward away from the commercial mecca of the D.C. area, Virginia's Hunt Country is an endless landscape of rolling hills, charming towns, and prestigious horse farms. Begin in **Leesburg**, a kind of hub for the horsey set. Take Route 15 north for miles of white fences, swanky mansions, and gorgeous horse farms. You'll pass **Morven Park**, 703/777-2414, a 1,500-acre estate with a fox hunting museum. Continue to Route 665 to the historic town of **Waterford** which appears much as it did in the eighteenth century.

Take Route 665 south to Route 704 past **Oatlands**, 703/777-3174, a white Greek Revival plantation house. Take 704 south to Route 15 and head south to Route 50 and travel west to **Middleburg**. Every fall, during fox hunting season, horses and hounds gather in the streets here. The scene looks like that portrayed in many an English painting.

From Middleburg take Route 626 to **The Plains** or Route 50 to **Upperville** for more great scenery. If you continue south on Route 626 to Route 71 you'll arrive in **Warrenton**, site of the **Flying Circus Airshow**, in Bealeton, 703/439-8661, a precision aerobatic airshow. Exploring the region will take approximately two driving hours.

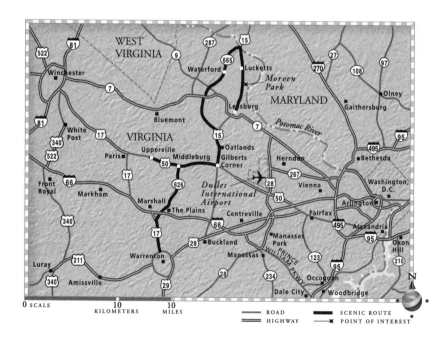

4
RICHMOND

The capital of Virginia is both a big city and a small town. City leaders have fiercely protected Richmond's historic districts, buildings, and monuments. The result is a city with block after block of stunning architecture, juxtaposed against tastefully modern high-rises and commercial buildings. The Richmond area is often overlooked by travelers who tend to focus only on Colonial Williamsburg, the beach, and the mountains when they visit the state. What a shame! The area arguably has the most significant collection of historic sites in the state. In addition, it offers a superior selection of affordable hotels and restaurants than many other regions in Virginia.

A PERFECT DAY IN RICHMOND

Start at the Richmond Visitor Center to board a Historic Richmond Tour. Drive to the Virginia Historical Society and Virginia Museum of Fine Arts just minutes away on Boulevard. Then head downtown and park near the Museum and White House of the Confederacy. Tour the Civil War museum and White House and the nearby Valentine Museum or take the State Capitol tour. End your day having dinner in Shockoe Bottom or Shockoe Slip at one of the great restaurants there. To catch a glimpse of the future of the city, stroll down along the riverfront to see all of the new development taking place.

SIGHTSEEING HIGHLIGHTS

★★★★ AGECROFT HALL
4305 Sulgrave Rd., 804/353-4241

Agecroft Hall is an impressive English manor house that was rescued from destruction in Lancashire, England, when it traveled across the Atlantic to its current home. The house is reminiscent of Tudor and early-Stuart England (1485–1660), with exposed timbers, moss-accented roof, lead-glass windows, a courtyard and English knot, boxwood and flower gardens.

Details: *Tue–Sat 10–4, Sun 12:30–5, $5 adults, $4.50 seniors, $3.50 students, free for children under age 6. (45 minutes)*

★★★★ CHURCH HILL/ST. JOHN'S CHURCH
2401 E. Broad St., 804/648-5015

Church Hill, named for its most famous landmark St. John's Church, has lovely eighteenth- and nineteenth-century homes and

HISTORIC RICHMOND

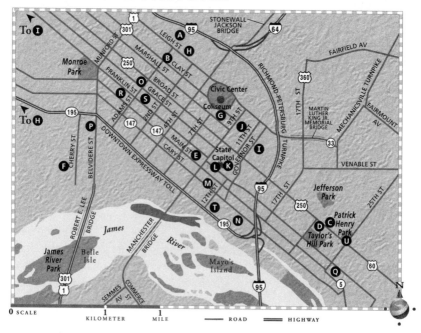

atmospheric gas lanterns lining the streets. St. John's Church is Richmond's oldest church (1739). It was here that the Second Virginia Convention was held in 1775 and Patrick Henry delivered his famous "Give me liberty, or give me death" speech. Reenactments of his fiery speech are presented on Sundays between Memorial Day and Labor Day.

In the church graveyard are buried John Marshall, Henry Clay, and Edgar Allan Poe's mother, among others. Other significant sites in Church Hill include the house where Edgar Allan Poe's childhood sweetheart once lived (2407 E. Grace Street) and Libbie Hill Park with its Soldiers and Sailors monument.

Details: Daily Mon–Sat 10–4, Sun 1–4, last tour begins at 3:30 p.m., re-enactments on summer Sun at 2 p.m. $3 adults, $2 seniors, $1 students. (45 minutes)

★★★★ HISTORIC RICHMOND TOURS
707 E. Franklin St., 804/780-0107

Historic Richmond Tours offers the only regular van tours of the city and battlefields. It picks up at some area hotels and at the main visitor center. The guides on these tours are well informed and entertaining.

SIGHTS

- **A** Bill "Bojangles" Robinson Monument
- **B** Black History Museum and Cultural History Center of Virginia
- **C** Church Hill/ St. John's Church
- **D** Edgar Allen Poe Museum/Old Stone House
- **E** Historic Richmond Tours
- **F** Hollywood Cemetery
- **G** John Marshall House

SIGHTS (continued)

- **H** Maggie Walker National Historic Site
- **I** Museum and White House of the Confederacy
- **J** Valentine Museum/ Wickham-Valentine House
- **K** Virginia's Executive Mansion
- **L** Virginia's State Capitol
- **C** Richmond National Battlefield Park

FOOD

- **M** Dining Room at the Berkeley Hotel
- **N** Frog and the Redneck
- **O** Lemaire
- **P** Mamma 'Zu
- **Q** Millie's Diner

LODGING

- **M** Berkeley Hotel
- **R** Jefferson Hotel
- **S** Linden Row Historic Inn
- **T** Omni Richmond
- **U** William Catlin House

Note: Items with the same letter are located in the same place.

Details: $16 Old Richmond Today historical tour, $13 Highlights Tour, $22 Battlefield Tour. (time varies depending on tour)

★★★★ MAGGIE WALKER NATIONAL HISTORIC SITE
110½ E. Leigh St., 804/780-1380

Walker, an African American, was an integral part of the Jackson Ward community. She was the first black woman in the United States to become a bank president, and she lived here for 30 years.

Her historic home, operated by the National Park Service, contains a wonderful slice of life from the nineteenth and early twentieth centuries. Her bank, today Consolidated Bank and Trust, is the oldest surviving black-operated bank in the U.S. The furnishings and the audio-visual presentation are very personal and revealing, making this historic house a breath of fresh air among the long list of Richmond's more stately homes.

Details: Wed–Sun 9–5. Free. (1 hour)

★★★★ MAYMONT
1700 Hampton St., 804/358-7166

Major James H. Dooley and his wife, Sally May, gave this former turn-of-the-century estate to the city. The stunning gardens on the park's 100 acres include English and herb gardens and an extravagant Italian garden with a classical columned–walkway and romantic fountains. There's also a peaceful Japanese garden complete with waterfall and pagodas. A nature center and wildlife habitat feature native Virginia animals such as bobcats, red foxes, bison, and black bears. Tours are also available of the Dooleys' furnished Victorian home (1890), with its swan-shaped bed and Tiffany pieces and an outstanding carriage collection.

Details: Generally Tue–Sat noon–5 p.m., grounds 10–5, call for additional hours. Free. Carriage and tram rides $2 adults, $1 children. (2–4 hours)

★★★★ MONUMENT AVENUE/THE FAN

Row after row of restored turn-of-the-century townhouses are only part of the appeal of Richmond's Fan District, named for how its streets fan out from Monroe Park. The country's largest intact Victorian neighborhood is home to numerous unique bistros and shops, and on its outskirts is Monument Avenue. This dazzling boulevard features one-of-a-kind statues of (in order from east to west)—General J.E.B. Stuart, General Robert E. Lee, Confederate president Jefferson Davis, General Thomas Jonathan "Stonewall" Jackson, scientist/oceanographer Matthew Fontaine Maury, and tennis ace Arthur Ashe Jr.

Details: (2–3 hours)

★★★★ MUSEUM AND WHITE HOUSE OF THE CONFEDERACY
1201 E. Clay St., 804/649-1861

This acclaimed museum contains the largest collection of Confederate artifacts. The museum creatively presents changing exhibits on various subjects (women during the war, African American soldiers, etc.). Mainstays of the museum include Lee's headquarters flag, sword, and personal effects; and J.E.B. Stuart's famous plumed hat. Also displayed are some emotionally stirring artifacts from the war: letters, photos,

A Downtown Block Ticket may be purchased from Historic Richmond Tours, Metro Richmond Visitor Centers, None Such Place Restaurant, or Borders Books and Music for $15 (valid for 30 days). It includes admission to many of the most popular attractions.

and items reflecting the people involved in the heart of the conflict. The adjacent White House (1818) was the home of Confederate president Jefferson Davis and his family during the war. The home has been completely restored to its wartime appearance. The museum's gift shop sells a variety of hard-to-find Civil War books, posters, and memorabilia.

Details: Mon–Sat 10–5, Sun noon–5. $8 adults, $7 seniors/AAA members/military, $5 students. (1–2 hours)

★★★★ VALENTINE MUSEUM/WICKHAM-VALENTINE HOUSE
1015 E. Clay St., 804/649-0711

One of the grandest homes in Court End is the Wickham-Valentine House (1812). Today it has been meticulously restored and furnished with extraordinary period furnishings. In the basement of the house is a state-of-the-art exhibit detailing servant life at the mansion. Next to the house is Richmond's city history museum, the Valentine Museum. Special exhibitions focus on urban and social history, decorative arts, costumes, and architecture—presented in an intriguing fashion that is never dull or ordinary. The Valentine's gift shop is loaded with special items like Victorian notecards and great nostalgic toys.

Details: *Mon–Sat 10–5, Sun noon–5. $5 adults, $4 seniors/students, $3 children ages 7–12, free for children under age 7. (1½ hours)*

★★★★ VIRGINIA HISTORICAL SOCIETY
48 N. Blvd., 804/358-4901

This museum houses the state's most priceless historical treasures—J.E.B. Stuart's blood-stained uniform, Patrick Henry's walking cane, and the most extensive collection of Confederate weapons anywhere. The Virginia Historical Society is a must for anyone wishing to explore Virginia's history. The museum is housed in historic Battle Abbey, which was built in 1913 as a monument to those who lost their lives fighting for the Confederacy. A new expansion recently doubled the museum's size.

Details: *Mon–Sat 10–5, Sun 1–5. $4 adults, $3 seniors, $2 students and children ages 6 and over. (1½ hours)*

★★★★ VIRGINIA HOUSE
4301 Sulgrave Rd., 804/353-4251

Next to Agecroft Hall, the stately stone mansion, à la *Wuthering Heights,* is known as Virginia House. Operated by the Virginia Historical Society, its original structure dates back to the twelfth century, when it was an English priory. Virginia House was moved to its current site in the 1920s. The gardens behind the mansion are gorgeous when they are blooming.

Details: *Tue–Sat 10–4, Sun 12:30–5. $4 adults, $2 students and children ages 6 and over. Entry to the gardens is $2. (45 minutes)*

★★★★ VIRGINIA MUSEUM OF FINE ARTS
2800 Grove Ave., 804/367-0844

The Virginia Museum is the largest art museum in the Southeast and contains works by Monet, Renoir, Degas, Picasso, Warhol, and others. The museum features an impressive assortment of art nouveau, art deco, contemporary, impressionist, and British sporting art. An equally significant variety of artifacts from ancient Egypt, Greece, Rome, and the Americas goes as far back in time as the third millennium before Christ. International masterpieces have been collected from Africa,

China, Japan, India, and the Himalayas. Tours are offered to help guide you through the enormous collection.

Details: Sun 11–5 p.m., Thu 11–8. Donation suggested. (2 hours)

★★★ BLACK HISTORY MUSEUM AND CULTURAL CENTER OF VIRGINIA
00 Clay St., 804/780-9093

This museum provides an overview of Richmond's African American history. Exceptional photography and artifacts tell the story of Virginia's first black residents, the growth of Jackson Ward into a vital entrepreneurial center, and leadership in today's community.

Details: Tue–Sat 11–4. $2 adults, $1 seniors, children, students. (45 minutes)

★★★ HOLLYWOOD CEMETERY
Albemarle and Cherry Sts., 804/648-8501

Hollywood is one of the nation's most historic and picturesque burial grounds. Overlooking the James River are the graves of presidents James Monroe and John Tyler, Confederate president Jefferson Davis, more than 18,000 Confederate soldiers, J.E.B. Stuart, Matthew Fontaine Maury, Fitzhugh Lee, and authors Ellen Glasgow, James Branch Cabell, and Douglas Southall Freeman. One of the more unusual monuments in the city, a 90-foot-tall granite pyramid, is dedicated to Confederate soldiers who died during the Civil War.

Details: Daily 8–5, office open mainly for maps and research Mon–Fri 8–5. Free. (1 hour)

★★★ JOHN MARSHALL HOUSE
818 E. Marshall St., 804/648-7998

Chief Justice, John Marshall, and his family, lived in this Court End home for more than 40 years. Today it has been restored and contains many personal artifacts and furnishings.

Details: Tue–Sat 10–5, Oct–Dec closes at 4:30, Jan–Mar open by appt. only. $3 adults, $2.50 seniors 55+, $1.25 children ages 7–12. (30 minutes)

★★★ LEWIS GINTER BOTANICAL GARDEN
1800 Lakeside Ave., 804/262-9887

This botanical garden features varied floral displays year-round with perennials, daylilies, daffodils, Children's Garden, and picturesque waterways. Bloemendaal House is the site for many weddings, receptions, and special events, and contains a great gift shop filled with horticultural goodies.

Details: *Mon–Sat 9–4:30. $4 adults, $3 seniors, $2 children ages 2–12. (2 hours)*

★★★ RICHMOND NATIONAL BATTLEFIELD PARK
3215 E. Broad St., 804/226-1981

The park headquarters is housed on Church Hill, in what was one of the largest Confederate hospitals. If you plan on visiting several battlefields, a stop here is warranted. The center has a film, many Civil War artifacts, park rangers on site, and a great gift shop with hard-to-find Civil War books. Some of the sites located around the Richmond area include Cold Harbor, Chickahominy Bluffs, Drewry's Bluff, Beaver Dam Creek, Gaines Mill, Garthright House, White Oak Swamp, Savage Station, Glendale, and Malvern Hill.

Details: *Daily 9–5, parks dawn until dusk. Free. (Headquarters 45 minutes)*

★★ BILL "BOJANGLES" ROBINSON MONUMENT
Leigh and Adams Sts.

A statue of vaudeville legend Bill "Bojangles" Robinson stands near an intersection where Robinson paid to have a stoplight installed for the safety of neighborhood children.

Details: *(10 minutes)*

★★ EDGAR ALLAN POE MUSEUM/OLD STONE HOUSE
1914 E. Main St., 804/648-5523

Richmond's oldest house is a museum in Shockoe Bottom dedicated to the memory of former Richmond resident Edgar Allan Poe. The museum contains artifacts, personal effects, and an intriguing model of Richmond during Poe's time. Spend some time here strolling in the garden and studying the model of Richmond. Other historic sites near the museum include the 17th Street Farmer's Market, Main Street Station, and the nation's oldest continuously used Masonic lodge.

Details: *Sun–Mon noon–4, Tue–Sat 10–4, call for winter hours. $6 adults, $5 seniors/students. (45 minutes)*

★★ WILTON HOUSE MUSEUM
215 S. Wilton Rd., 804/282-5936

Located just a few blocks away from Agecroft and Virginia House, this historic home was constructed by William Randolph III in 1753 in the traditional Georgian style. The house is meritorious as a fine example of a colonial plantation home equal to the Shirley and Berkeley plantation houses along the James River.

Details: Tue–Sat 10–4:30, Sun 1:30–4:30, $3.50 adults, $3 seniors, $2 students, free children ages 6 and under. (45 minutes)

★ VIRGINIA'S EXECUTIVE MANSION
Capitol Square, 804/371-TOUR

This historic neoclassical home is located on the grounds of the capitol. It has been the residence of Virginia governors since 1813 and is the oldest continuously occupied governor's mansion existing in the country.

Details: Sep–May Mon 2–4, Tue–Fri 10–noon, Jun–Aug Mon 2–4, Tue–Fri 10–noon and 2–4. Free. (30 minutes)

★ VIRGINIA'S STATE CAPITOL
Ninth & E. Grace Sts., 804/786-4344

Designed by Thomas Jefferson, this capitol is home to the oldest legislative body in the Western Hemisphere. A treasured statue of George Washington, created by famed artist Jean Antoine Houdon, stands in the rotunda. Guided tours are available on the second floor and are highly recommended.

Details: Mon–Sun 9–5, call for winter hours. Free. (1 hour).

FITNESS AND RECREATION

Richmond offers urban white-water rafting. Rapids along the James River running through the heart of the city are Class IV. Outfitters include **Richmond Raft Company**, 4400 W. Main Street, 804/222-7238, and **Adventure Challenge**, 8225 Oxer Road, 804/276-5936. Cast your line on the James River or one of the region's lakes (especially **Lake Chesdin** and **Pocahontas State Park**), and experience some great fishing. Call **Game and Inland Fisheries**, 804/367-1000, for regulations and boat launch information.

Richmond has a AAA baseball team, the Richmond Braves, which is the farm team for the Atlanta Braves. It plays home games at **The Diamond**. For more information, call 804/359-4444. Tickets are a bargain at $7 for box seating, $6 for press box seating, and $5 for adult general admission/$3 youth and seniors. An ECHL ice hockey team, the Richmond Renegades, draws record crowds and

GREATER RICHMOND

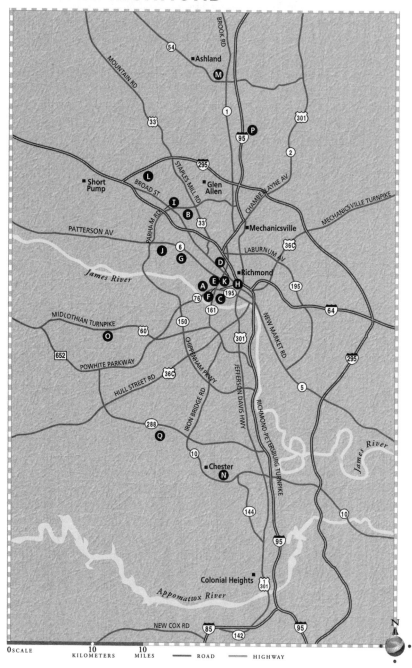

even won the Riley Cup in 1994–1995. Call 804/643-PUCK for more information. The area also has an abundance of college basketball and a minor league soccer team. **Richmond International Raceway**, 804/345-RACE, is one of the finest NASCAR racetracks in the country.

FOOD

Try fancy grits with haute Southern cuisine at the **Frog and the Redneck**, 1423 E. Cary Street, 804/648-3764. Celebrity chef Jimmy Snead uses the freshest local ingredients to prepare a variety of unusual dishes. Try the red pepper soup with crab meat, or the grilled fresh cobia with parmesan butter.

For more formal consumption, **Lemaire**, at the Jefferson Hotel, Franklin and Adams Streets, 804/788-8000, serves well-bred Virginia cuisine including its famous spoonbread, venison, and traditional peanut soup. Another in the formal category is the **Dining Room at the Berkeley Hotel**, 1200 E. Cary Street, 804/780-1300. This quiet and reserved restaurant is one of Richmond's finest dining experiences with entrées such as lamb chops and venison.

For a totally different dining experience, **Millie's Diner** at 2603 E. Main Street, 804/643-5512, offers inventive dishes served up in an atmospheric diner. The cuisine includes items like *platanos fritos* and Thai spicy shrimp.

At **Mamma 'Zu**, 501 S. Pine Street, 804/788-4205, get a true taste of Italy in an unlikely place. The small, uninspiring environment in a no-frills Oregon Hill neighborhood definitely does not reflect the food. The chef uses fresh ingredients to prepare authentic Italian dishes such as oxtails Roman-style, rabbit

SIGHTS

Ⓐ Agecroft Hall
Ⓑ Lewis Ginter Botanical Garden
Ⓒ Maymont
Ⓓ Monument Avenue/The Fan
Ⓔ Virginia Historical Society
Ⓐ Virginia House
Ⓕ Virginia Museum of Fine Arts
Ⓖ Wilton House Museum

FOOD

Ⓗ Amici
Ⓘ Azzurro
Ⓙ Fox Head Inn
Ⓚ Granite on Grove

LODGING

Ⓛ Hampton Inn West
Ⓜ Henry Clay Inn
Ⓝ Holiday Inn Express Chester
Ⓞ Sheraton Park South

CAMPING

Ⓟ Americamps, Richmond North Best Holiday Trav-L-Park
Ⓠ Pocahontas State Park

Note: Items with the same letter are located in the same place.

cacciatore, *zuppa di pesce*, and ricotta cheesecake. Mamma 'Zu serves dinner only. Two other great Italian restaurants are **Azzurro**, 6221 River Road, 804/282-1509, and **Amici**, 3343 W. Cary Street, 804/353-4700.

Looking for a sleek, sophisticated restaurant that is a definite departure from lamb chops and white linen? **Granite on Grove**, 5702 Grove Avenue, 804/288-3600, is a modern new bistro offering contemporary cooking like mile-high shredded chicken salad, fresh fish, and pasta.

West of Richmond near Tuckahoe Plantation, the **Fox Head Inn**, 1840 Manakin Road, 804/784-5126, offers traditional fare in individual rooms of a renovated nineteenth-century farmhouse. Antiques and fireplaces complement the meal (set price $45).

LODGING

The region has a multitude of accommodations on a variety of price levels and styles. In Richmond, the **Jefferson Hotel**, Franklin and Adams Streets, 804/788-8000 or 800/424-8014, is one of the most spectacular hotels in the country. From the elegant Palm Court with its noble statue of Thomas Jefferson and stained-glass ceiling to the breathtaking Rotunda with its grand staircase and marbleized columns, this is truly a hotel that reflects the splendour of another era. Each room features a hair dryer, terry cloth robes, and many other little comforts that make staying here special. Other amenities offered include two full-service restaurants, lounge/bar, and room service. Rates are $185 to $225.

In Shockoe Slip, the **Berkeley Hotel**, 1200 E. Cary Street, 804/780-1300, is an alternative to a giant hotel. The smaller, European-style hotel features comfortable, tastefully decorated rooms, a full-service restaurant, room service, a bar/lounge, and valet parking. The average room rate is $135.

Another interesting hotel option is **Linden Row Historic Inn**, 100 E. Franklin Street, 804/783-7000 or 800/348-7424. Listed on the National Register of Historic Places, Linden Row is a series of 1847 Greek Revival townhouses with rooms furnished with antiques. Amenities also include a full-service restaurant, bar/lounge, and room service. Rates are $89 to $169.

For more traditional upscale accommodations, there is the **Omni Richmond**, 100 S. 12th Street, 804/344-7000 or 800/THE OMNI. The hotel overlooks the Shockoe Slip historic area and features nicely appointed rooms, two full-service restaurants, bar/lounge, indoor swimming pool, health club, and room service. Rates are $99 to 169.

The **William Catlin House**, 2304 E. Broad Street, 804/780-3746, is located in Church Hill and features five rooms—several with four-poster beds (some canopied) and antiques. Rates are $75 to $95. The **Henry Clay Inn**,

PARAMOUNT'S KINGS DOMINION AND SCOTCHTOWN

North of Richmond off I-95 in Doswell, **Paramount's Kings Dominion**, 804/876-500, offers more than 100 rides, live shows, and a complete water park. There are six roller coasters including the new 70-MPH. Volcano, and the park features several movie/television-themed rides and attractions. For the younger set there is a KidZville play area, a Nickelodeon themed area, and many traditional kid-oriented rides. The full-scale water park features a Lazy River, daring slides, and wave pool. Changing areas are located in the area and lockers are available to place valuables and store clothes. Entertaining shows include a laser music show, kid circus, and Nickelodeon show for kids.

Head a little further north to Hanover County located on Route 2 to visit **Scotchtown**, 804/227-3500. Scotchtown was the eighteenth-century home of Patrick Henry during most of his active political years. Costumed guides give tours of the farmhouse with stories of Henry's life during the time. Scotchtown is open April through October.

114 N. Railroad Avenue, Ashland, 804/798-3100, offers 15 guest rooms with a variety of bed styles including canopied, pencil post, acorn, turned post, cannonball, and sleigh beds. The average room rate is $80 to $145.

For more basic accommodations, the **Hampton Inn West**, 10800 W. Broad Street, Glen Allen, 804/747-7777 or 800/HAMPTON, is a new budget hotel with a long list of amenities. Rates are $86 to $105. The **Sheraton Park South**, 9901 Midlothian Turnpike, 804/323-1144 or 800/525-9538, in Richmond's south side recently underwent a massive renovation and now features an elegant marble lobby and comfortable rooms. Rates are $85 to $100.

For more economical accommodations in Richmond's south side, the new **Holiday Inn Express Chester**, 1911 W. Hundred Road, 800/HOLIDAY, offers basic accommodations at low rates. Rooms are $45 to $75.

CAMPING

Camping is allowed at several parks in the area including **Pocahontas State Park**, 800/933-7275, south of Richmond. Only one full-service campground is available, however. **Americamps, Richmond North Best Holiday Trav-L-Park**, 396 Air Park Road, Ashland, 804/798-5298, is located near Paramount's Kings Dominion with 146 campsites (116 with water and electric hookups and 33 full hookup pull-thrus). Tiled restrooms have hot showers, and amenities include propane, a dumping station, after-hour security, RV supplies and storage, Laundromat, groceries, car rental, and on-site telephone hookups. Americamps also has a variety of recreational facilities.

NIGHTLIFE

Richmond's two leading entertainment districts are located in former warehouse neighborhoods with most of the buildings dating back to the 1800s and early 1900s.

Shockoe Slip underwent a dramatic transformation in the 1970s, and today its cobblestone streets continue to provide shopping, dining, and nightlife. One of the city's landmark restaurants, the **Tobacco Company**, 12th and Cary Street, 804/782-9555, is located here, as is the acclaimed **Frog and the Redneck** restaurant, 1423 East Cary Street, 804/648-3764.

Just a few blocks away, Shockoe Bottom has only recently sprung to life following the construction of a flood wall. The Cuban-themed Havana '59 restaurant, 16 N. 17th Street, 804/649-2822, is an interesting spot where patrons can light up a cigar and dance the night away on a rooftop dance floor.

PERFORMING ARTS

The acclaimed **Richmond Symphony**, 300 W. Franklin Street, 804/788-1212 or 804/225-9000, presents concerts year-round. The **Virginia Opera**, 300 W. Franklin Street, 804/643-6004, appears in Richmond at the Carpenter Center several times a year. The **Richmond Ballet**, 614 N. Lombardy Street, 804/262-8100 or 804/353-6161, is a very well-respected East Coast dance company. Highly lauded theatrical performances can be enjoyed at **TheatreVirginia**, the Virginia Museum, 2800 Grove Avenue, 804/353-6161; **Barksdale Theatre**, The Shops at Willow Lawn, 804/282-2620; and dinner theater at the **Swift Creek Mill Playhouse**, Route 1, Colonial Heights, 804/748-5203.

5
VIRGINIA'S COAST

Virginia's coastline offers up a diverse mélange of sights and impressions. While small skiffs calmly sail in and out of the Northern Neck, enormous ships carrying tons of weaponry and cargo cut a deep path from the shores of Norfolk out into the Atlantic. And while to the south there are scores of modern high-rise hotels with turquoise swimming pools, Virginia's northern coastline contains only beach homes and sand dunes. And then there is the bay—Chesapeake Bay remains one of the country's great treasures teaming with wildlife and beautiful waters.

The town of Portsmouth has a terrific historic district. Newport News is lush and green with some impressive museums and parks. Hampton has a lovely waterfront with a first-rate Air and Space Museum. Norfolk is gaining momentum as a tourism destination with a growing waterfront and Virginia Beach has given itself a snazzy facelift to appeal to more families.

A PERFECT DAY ON VIRGINIA'S COAST
Begin your journey along Virginia's coast in the Northern Neck region. Rummage through the many antique shops in Tappahannock via Route 3 south to Route 360 west. Retrace Route 360 eastward to Route 3 south to Irvington and have lunch while watching sailboats and yachts glide by at the lovely Tides Inn. Then take Route 3/33 south to Route 17 south to I-64 east and arrive in

87

VIRGINIA'S COAST

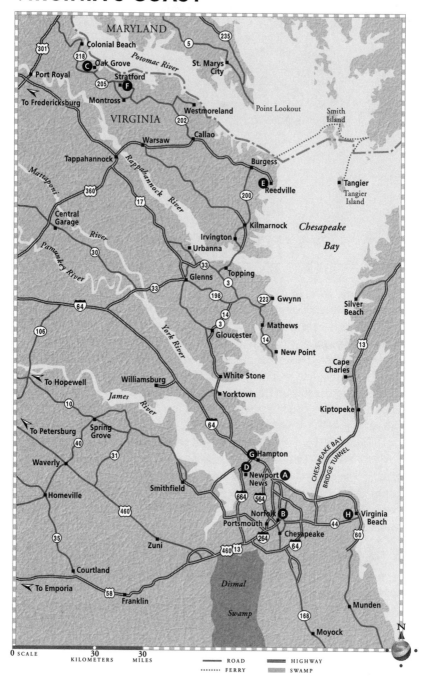

MARYLAND

301
Colonial Beach
218
235
5
Oak Grove
C 205 Stratford
Port Royal **F**
To Fredericksburg Montross

Potomac River

St. Marys City

VIRGINIA
Westmoreland
202
Point Lookout
Smith Island

Warsaw
Callao

Tappahannock
Burgess
360 17
200 **E** Reedville
Tangier
Tangier Island

Mattaponi

Rappahannock River

Central Garage
30
River
Kilmarnock
Chesapeake Bay

Pamunkey River

Irvington
Urbanna
33
33
198
Glenns
Topping
3
223 Gwynn
Silver Beach

14
3 Mathews
14
Gloucester
New Point
Cape Charles
13

64
106

York River

White Stone
Yorktown
Kiptopeke

To Hopewell
Williamsburg

James River

10
64

To Petersburg
Spring Grove
40
31

CHESAPEAKE BAY BRIDGE TUNNEL

G Hampton
D Newport News **A**
664 564

Waverly

Smithfield

Homeville

460
Norfolk **B**
Portsmouth
H Virginia Beach
44
60

35

Zuni
264
Chesapeake
64

Courtland

To Emporia
58
Franklin
460 13

Dismal Swamp

168
Munden

Moyock

N

0 SCALE
30 KILOMETERS
30 MILES

—— ROAD
····· FERRY
HIGHWAY
SWAMP

Newport News to visit the dramatic Mariners' Museum. Continue on I-64 east to I-44 toward Virginia Beach. Keep heading towards the beachfront for a sunset walk along the water. Have dinner at one of Virginia Beach's great seafood restaurants.

THE TIDEWATER PENINSULA

The Tidewater Peninsula includes the towns of Newport News, Norfolk, Hampton, and Virginia Beach.

The nautical town of **Newport News** has a wealth of history, plenty of grassy, tree-filled spaces (unusual in this part of the state) and a number of notable museums. There are also a number of historic homes and Civil War attractions in Newport News. If you are planning to be in the Tidewater area, plan to spend several hours here. You won't be disappointed. For more details contact the Newport News Visitor Information Center located at 13560 Jefferson Avenue, 757/886-7777, or 888/4WE-R-FUN.

The city of **Norfolk** is part military town, part seafaring town, part shipbuilding town, and part tourist attraction. In the past decade, the city has built up its waterfront area to contain nice hotels, shopping venues, museums, and attractions. Now, this area has become a hub for visitors to the area. For more information contact the Norfolk Convention and Visitors Bureau, 232 Virginia Beach Boulevard, 757/664-6620 or 800/368-3097; or the Norfolk Visitor Center, Fourth View Street, 757/441-1852 or 800/368-3097.

Virginia Beach has evolved from one of the premier beach destinations in the country to a resort area struggling with the challenges of erosion and upkeep. Now it is again gaining momentum as a family resort destination with new boardwalk area and improved shopping/entertainment areas. It certainly

SIGHTS

- **A** Casemate Museum/ Fort Monroe
- **B** Chrysler Museum
- **B** Douglas MacArthur Memorial
- **C** George Washington's Birthplace National Monument
- **C** Ingleside Winery
- **D** Mariners' Museum
- **B** Nauticus
- **B** Norfolk Naval Base
- **E** Reedville Fisherman's Museum
- **F** Stratford Hall Plantation
- **G** Virginia Air and Space Center and NASA Langley Research Center
- **D** Virginia Living Museum
- **H** Virginia Marine Science Museum
- **B** Virginia Zoo

Note: Items with the same letter are located in the same place.

would be accurate to say that this resort city is making valiant strides to keep up with its competition to the north and south. The resort area contains a clean, well-monitored beachfront with more than 10,000 hotel rooms ranging from economical to luxurious. There are biking/jogging trails, a small amusement park, bungee jumping ride and the usual bevy of kitschy beach shops and wax museums. Parking is plentiful throughout the resort with clearly marked municipal lots for visitors. Umbrellas can be rented on the beach and floats, boards and other water sport equipment can be rented all along the beach. Trolley and boat tours of the area are available. For more information contact the Virginia Beach Convention and Visitors Bureau, 2101 Parks Avenue, Suite 500, 800/VA BEACH.

The city of **Hampton** is the birthplace of America's space program where the first Mercury astronauts trained in 1959. The city also contains the world's largest naval base. For an overview of the city, trolley tours are available.

The city boasts two historic churches that are well worth a visit. **St. John's Church**, 100 W. Queens Way, 757/722-2567, was established in 1610 and has been restored and features a recorded history of the church for visitors. St. John's has a beautiful stained-glass window depicting the baptism of Pocahontas in the country's oldest continuous English-speaking parish. The **Little England Chapel**, located at 4100 Kecoughtan Road, 757/723-6803, was built in 1879 and is Virginia's only-known African American missionary chapel. For more information about Hampton's many attractions contact the **Hampton Visitor Center**, 710 Settlers Landing Road, 757/727-1102 or 800/800-2202.

TIDEWATER PENINSULA SIGHTSEEING HIGHLIGHTS

★★★★ MARINERS' MUSEUM
100 Museum Dr., Newport News, 800/581-SAIL

The city's, and perhaps the state's, crowning jewel of museums is the extraordinary Mariners' Museum. Truly one of the finest maritime museums in the world, this dazzling collection of more than 35,000 nautical artifacts will mesmerize even the most rock-solid landlubbers. Each gallery is more remarkable than the last—room after room of ornate figureheads, detailed ship models, gorgeous paintings, and exotic vessels. Historic artifacts include the anchor from the Civil War–era USS *Monitor,* Captain John Smith's map of the Chesapeake Bay, and the polar bear figurehead from Admiral Richard Byrd's Antarctic expedition vessel. Visitors can inspect the amazing detail with magnifying viewers.

Details: Daily 10–5. $5 adults, $3 students, free children ages 5 and under, $13 family combination ticket for four people any ages. (2–4 hours)

★★★★ NORFOLK NAVAL BASE
9079 Hampton Blvd., Norfolk, 757/640-6300 or 757/444-7955

From any point in downtown Norfolk it is hard to miss the more than 100 ships docked at the Norfolk Naval Base—the world's largest. You can take a guided bus tour of the base where you will pass enormous aircraft carriers, destroyers, and the latest in assault vessels and submarines.

Details: Tours operate year-round, but times and departure locations vary. $5 adults, $2.50 children/seniors. (2–3 hours)

★★★★ VIRGINIA AIR AND SPACE CENTER AND NASA LANGLEY RESEARCH CENTER
600 Settlers Landing Rd., Hampton, 800/296-0800 or 757/727-0900

The city's crowning gem, the Virginia Air and Space Center, is located on the harbor in downtown Hampton. This sleek, modern museum is the official visitors center for the nearby NASA Langley Research Center. Tours depart from here daily for the research facility where visitors can see NASA technicians and engineers at work. Back at the museum, you'll find more than 100 air and space exhibits including the *Apollo 12* Command Module. There is also an IMAX theater.

Details: Daily 10–5. Museum/planetarium $9 adults, $8 military/seniors, $7 children ages 3–11; Museum only $6 adults, $5 military/seniors, $4 children ages 3–11. NASA Langley Tour 757/727-0900. Sat 11 p.m., 2 p.m., Sun 2 p.m. (2–3 hours)

★★★★ VIRGINIA MARINE SCIENCE MUSEUM
717 General Booth Blvd., Virginia Beach, 757/437-4949

This state-of-the-art aquarium and marine center is one of the top marine science museums in the country and one of the top 10 aquariums and marine science centers in the country. Inside the center, you wander through a rocky tunnel to come face-to-face with giant sharks in a 300,000-gallon aquarium. You can watch sea turtles glide by in one aquarium and see speedy otters glide through the water in another. The museum has numerous touch tanks where you can get cozy with stingrays and crabs. Staff members are available at each exhibit to answer questions and explain more about each animal. There's also an aviary, IMAX theater, outdoor theater, classroom, gift shop, and restaurant. The center also offers dolphin and whale-watching boat trips.

Details: Daily 9–5. Museum/IMAX $11.95 adults, $9.95 children. Museum $7.95 adults, $5.95 children. (2–4 hours)

★★★ CHRYSLER MUSEUM
245 W. Olney Rd., Norfolk, 757/664-6200
One of the finest art museums on the East Coast, the Chrysler Museum is well-known for its glass collection which includes works from the fifth to the second centuries B.C., as well as carved and blown glass by Tiffany, Galle, and Lalique. The museum also contains a strong collection of European paintings, sculptures, and drawings by such artists as Renoir, Matisse, and Picasso. Another highlight of this museum is the fantastic collection of American art with works by Sargent, Cassatt, Hopper, and Warhol. A group of nineteenth-century American neoclassic sculptures is considered one of the most important of its kind. The Chrysler Museum also administers three historic homes—the **Adam Thoroughgood House**, the **Moses Myers House**, and the **Willoughby-Baylor House**.

Details: Tue–Sat 10–4, Sun 1–5. Donation requested. (1–3 hours)

★★★ NAUTICUS
1 Waterside Dr., Norfolk, 800/664-1080 or 757/664-1000
The creators of Nauticus have concocted a one-of-a-kind, hands-on maritime experience. However, it takes focus and a definite interest in the subject matter to truly get the most out of this museum. Particularly well done are the Aquaria section with its touch pools and working sea labs and the Virtual Adventures offering visitors a virtual reality experience in search of the Loch Ness Monster's eggs.

Also notable are the Aegis Command Center, which allows visitors to be a part of an interactive battle aboard a destroyer ship, and the Nauticus Theater which shows award-winning IMAX films.

The Hampton Roads Naval Museum on the second floor of Nauticus displays a nice collection of naval artwork, ship models, and underwater artifacts.

Details: Memorial Day–Labor Day daily 10–5, Oct–Apr Tue–Sat 10–5 and Sun noon–5. $7.50 adults, $5 students ages 6–17, $6.50 *seniors/AAA members/military personnel with I.D., free children under age 5. (1–4 hours)*

★★★ VIRGINIA LIVING MUSEUM
524 J. Clyde Morris Blvd., Newport News, 757/595-1900

Just minutes away from the Maritime Museum, the Virginia Living Museum offers an up-close look at regional wildlife. In addition to the zoo-like natural habitats for deer, raccoon, bald eagles, beavers, otters, foxes, bobcat, birds, and other critters, there are many indoor exhibits.

Details: *Summer Mon–Sat 9–6, Sun 10–6, Thu 9–9; Winter Mon–Sat 9–5, Sun noon–5, Thu 7–9 p.m.; Museum/Observatory $6 adults, $4 ages 3–12. (2 hours)*

★ CASEMATE MUSEUM/FORT MONROE
P.O. Box 341, Fort Monroe, 757/727-3391

This fort houses the prison cell of Confederate president Jefferson Davis and many Civil War weapons. You can take a walking tour of Fort Monroe, the largest stone fort ever built in America and the country's only active-duty, moat-encircled fort.

Details: *Daily 10:30–4:30. Free. (1 hour)*

★ DOUGLAS MACARTHUR MEMORIAL
MacArthur Sq., Bank St., and Hall Ave., Norfolk 757/441-2965

MacArthur is buried at this memorial, which also contains a museum, theater, and special exhibit galleries profiling the life of the American hero. A 25-minute film on the general's remarkable life is shown in the museum's theater.

Details: *Daily Mon–Sat 10–5, Sun 11–5. Free. (1 hour)*

★ VIRGINIA ZOO
3500 Granby St., Norfolk, 757/441-5227

The Virginia Zoo has been around since 1899 but has never gained enough attention to be considered a world-class zoo. Now the folks at this zoo are making plans to expand and improve the quality of animal exhibits and habitats. A 10-acre "African Okavango River Delta" exhibit is planned for the near future. The current 53-acre zoo still offers a wide variety of animals that include elephants, monkeys, reptiles, Siberian tigers, and rhinos.

Details: Daily 10–5. $2 adults, $1 seniors/children ages 2–11. (1–2 hours)

NORTHERN NECK SIGHTSEEING HIGHLIGHTS

★★★ STRATFORD HALL PLANTATION
Stratford, 804/493-8038

In nearby Stratford, you will enjoy touring the childhood home of another famous name, Robert E. Lee. The house is an impressive brick H-shaped manor house built in the 1730s and is especially enjoyable because you are able to tour the entire house—not just a few rooms. The house is situated in a spectacular setting with a glorious view of the river just minutes away.

Details: Daily 9–5. $7 adults, $3 children. (2 hours)

★★ GEORGE WASHINGTON'S BIRTHPLACE NATIONAL MONUMENT
Hwy. 3, Oak Grove, 804/224-1732

North of Tappahannock, in Westmoreland County, this monument is a living historical farm recreating our first president's childhood world.

Details: Daily 9–5. $2 adults. (1–2 hours)

★★ INGLESIDE WINERY
P.O. Box 1038, Oak Grove, 804/224-8687

Cruises to this nearby winery are available in Tappahannock through Rappahannock River Cruises, Route 1, in Reedville, 804/453-3638 or 800/598-2628. It makes for a lovely day if you take this cruise along the river, passing an abundance of wildlife and scenery along the way, to arrive at the winery for a tour and wine tasting. To drive to Ingleside Winery, just take Route 360 east to Route 3 north to Oak Grove.

Details: Mon–Sat 10–5, Sun noon–5. Free. (1 hour)

★ REEDVILLE FISHERMAN'S MUSEUM
504 Main St., Reedville, 804/453-6529

At this museum you will find exhibits about the area's watermen and fishermen, as well as artifacts such as boats and an 1875 waterman's home.

Details: Wed–Mon 10:30–4:30. $2 general admission. (30 minutes)

ESSEX COUNTY MUSEUM

Tappahannock's history can be explored at the Essex County Museum, 227 Prince Street, 804/443-4690.

CRUISES

Miss Hampton II Harbor Cruise, 710 Settler's Landing Road, (downtown waterfront at the pier), 757/722-9102, offers dining aboard a luxury tour boat Memorial Day through Labor Day. Fishing charters are also available from the harbor.

The **American Rover**, 757/627-SAIL, is a three-masted tall ship that offers two- and three-hour narrated harbor cruises under full sail along the Elizabeth River. **Carrie B**, 757/393-4735, is a paddle-wheel riverboat that tours Norfolk's naval shipyards and naval operating base. **Elizabeth River Ferry**, 757/640-6300, offers leisure cruises every half-hour on the quarter-hour. **Spirit of Norfolk**, 757/627-7771, offers tours aboard its sleek luxury yacht. It features lunch and dinner cruises with dancing, live shows, and sight-seeing.

Although Reedville does have a few antique shops and restaurants of interest to visitors, what this town is mostly known for are its cruises to Tangier and Smith Islands on the Chesapeake Bay.

Cruises depart for Tangier Island via **Tangier and Chesapeake Cruises**, 804/453-2628, aboard the **Capt. Thomas** at 10 a.m. every day, May through October. On Tangier there are no cable, no cellular towers, no cars, and few commercial businesses. The people still speak with faint traces of an Old English accent.

Also from Reedville, cruises are available to Smith Island via **Smith Island & Chesapeake Bay Cruises**, 382 Campground Road, 804/453-3430, aboard the **Capt. Evans**. Cruises depart at 10 a.m. daily, May through October 15. This remote island is filled with wildlife and natural scenery.

FITNESS AND RECREATION

On the Northern Neck, there is fantastic deep-sea fishing on the Chesapeake Bay. There's also outstanding fishing on the Rappahannock, Potomac, Mattaponi, and Pamunkey Rivers. In Tidewater, deep-sea fishing charters are numerous for half-day or full-day excursions.

VIRGINIA'S COAST

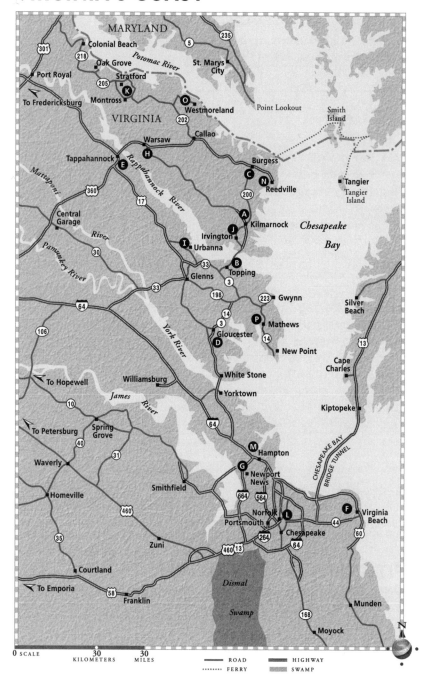

MARYLAND

Colonial Beach
Oak Grove
Port Royal
218
205
301
Stratford
Montross
To Fredericksburg
K
VIRGINIA
Potomac River
St. Marys City
5
235
O
Westmoreland
202
Point Lookout
Smith Island
Warsaw
Callao

Tappahannock
H
E
360
17
Rappahannock River
Burgess
C
N
Reedville
200
Tangier
Tangier Island

Central Garage
River
30
Pamunkey River
Mattaponi
A
Kilmarnock
J
I
Irvington
Urbanna
33
Glenns
B
Topping
3
Chesapeake Bay

64
106
York River
198
14
3
D
Gloucester
P
Mathews
14
223
Gwynn
Silver Beach
13
New Point

To Hopewell
Williamsburg
James River
White Stone
Yorktown
64
Cape Charles

To Petersburg
Spring Grove
10
40
31
Waverly
Kiptopeke

Homeville
Smithfield
460
35
Zuni
M
Hampton
G
Newport News
664
564
Norfolk
L
Portsmouth
460 13
264
Chesapeake
64
F
Virginia Beach
44
60
CHESAPEAKE BAY BRIDGE TUNNEL

Courtland
To Emporia
58
Franklin
Dismal Swamp
168
Munden
Moyock
N

0 SCALE   30 KILOMETERS   30 MILES

ROAD   HIGHWAY
FERRY   SWAMP

In Virginia Beach private charters and party boats are available from **Bubba's Marina**, 757/481-3513; **Fisherman's Wharf Charters**, 757/428-2111; **Lynnhaven Seafood Marina**, 757/481-4545; **Rudee Inlet Station Marina**, 757/422-2999; and **Virginia Beach Fishing Center**, 757/422-5700. Some fishing charters in Northern Neck include **Capt. Billy's Charters**, 804/580-7292, out of Wicomico Church, and bay fishing aboard the *Jeannie C*, 804/453-4021, out of Reedville.

Sight-filled trails in the Northern Neck include **Bushmill Stream Natural Area**, 804/462-5030, to spot herons; marshlands at the **Caledon Natural Area**, 540/663-3861; and **Westmoreland State Park**, 804/493-8821, through woods, meadows, and riverfront. In Virginia Beach are opportunities for whale-watching, surfing, boogie-boarding, windsurfing, Jet skiing, para-sailing, scuba diving, canoeing, sailing, miniature golf, volleyball, softball tournaments, bowling, roller-skating, and kayaking. Recreational equipment can be rented along the beach.

Of the more than 20 golf courses on Virginia's Coast, **Hell's Point**, 2700 Atwood Town Road, 757/721-3400, in Virginia Beach, has one of the highest ratings.

FOOD

You don't have to try hard to find great affordable seafood restaurants along Virginia's Coast.

FOOD

- **A** Crab Shack
- **A** de' Medici
- **B** Eckhard's
- **C** Horn Harbor House
- **D** Kelsick Gardens
- **E** Lowery's Seafood Restaurant
- **F** Rockafeller's
- **F** Rudee's On The Inlet
- **F** Three Ships Inn
- **F** Timbuktu

LODGING

- **G** Best Western King James Motor Inn

LODGING (continued)

- **H** Best Western Warsaw
- **I** Cavalier Hotel
- **I** Founders Inn & Conference Center
- **J** Hewitt Plantation
- **J** Hope and Glory Inn
- **K** Inn at Montross
- **L** Marriott Waterside Norfolk
- **M** Radisson Hotel Hampton
- **I** Ramada Virginia Beach
- **J** Tides Inn
- **J** Tides Lodge
- **J** Windmill Point

CAMPING

- **I** BethPage Camp Resort
- **N** Chesapeake Bay/Smith Island KOA Kampground
- **O** Cole's Point Plantation
- **P** Holiday Trav-L-Park
- **P** New Point Campground
- **Q** Seashore State Park
- **I** Virginia Beach KOA Campground

Note: Items with the same letter are located in the same place.

In the Northern Neck, the most popular are **Horn Harbor House**, 804/453-3351, near Burgess; **Lowery's Seafood Restaurant**, 528 Church Lane, 804/443-2800, in South Tappahannock; and the **Crab Shack**, 804/435-2700, in Kilmarnock. These places have fresh crab dishes (especially good crab cakes), oysters, shrimp, and fish.

Other notable eateries in the region include **Kelsick Gardens**, 804/693-6500, in Gloucester, with its gourmet sandwiches, salads, and wine tastings; **de' Medici**, 51 School Street, 804/435-4006, in Kilmarnock, serving fine Italian cuisine; and **Eckhard's**, Routes 3 & 621, 804/758-4060, in Topping, offering authentic German dishes.

Many of the tourist-laden seafood restaurants in Virginia Beach are genuinely good. Be a purist, however, and order the catches without lots of sauces and accoutrements. Most of these spots have early-bird specials and inexpensive Sunday brunches.

On Rudee's Inlet in Virginia Beach, **Rockafeller's**, 308 Mediterranean Avenue, 757/422-5654, and **Rudee's On The Inlet**, 227 Mediterranean Avenue, 757/425-1777, are both crowd pleasers with family-style atmospheres. At Rockafeller's order the catch of the day, the BBQ shrimp wrapped in bacon, or the crab cakes.

Virginia Beach locals flock to **Timbuktu**, 32nd Street & Atlantic Avenue, located in the Days Inn hotel, 757/491-1800. And for years tourists have been coming to the **Three Ships Inn**, 4110 East Ocean View, 757/362-4659. With its roaring fireplace and candlelight, this local landmark consistently serves great seafood.

LODGING

The best known resort in the Northern Neck region is the **Tides Inn**, 480 King Carter Drive, Irvington, 804/438-5000 or 800/843-3746, known for its lovely setting amidst docked yachts and sailboats. Although this resort property is in need of a good sprucing up, the food and amenities still draw loyal guests. Rates are $320 Sunday through Thursday and $350 Friday and Saturday.

Across the water from the Tides Inn are the **Tides Lodge**, 1 St. Andrews Lane, Irvington, 804/438-6000, and **Windmill Point**, Route 695, White Stone, 804/435-1166; both offer less expensive, yet comfortable accommodations. The Tides Lodge has cheerful, yet simple rooms. Rates range from $145 to $165. Windmill Point's beachfront hotel has clean, adequate rooms with an average room rate of $110.

The **Hope and Glory Inn**, 634 King Carter Drive, Irvington, 804/

438-6053, has been getting raves for its Victorian-style decor and ambiance. The former 1890 elementary school has seven rooms and four cottages with private baths. Rates range from $95 to $175. The **Inn at Montross**, 21 Polk Street, Montross, 804/493-0573, has comfortable rooms (many with four-poster beds), private baths, and above par dining. This is a homey kind of place with the family pets wandering about. Rates are $85 including a full breakfast. **Hewitt Plantation**, Virginia State Highway 602/615, Urbanna, 804/758-4214, is a bed-and-breakfast inn located on a 1678 plantation site. The property is owned and operated by 10th-generation descendants of the original owner.

For basic, inexpensive accommodations in Northern Neck, try the **Best Western**, Route 360, Warsaw, 804/333-1700. The rooms are clean and basic Best Western fare with cable TV, swimming pool, and continental breakfast. Rates run from $64 to $70 June through September.

In Hampton, the **Radisson Hotel**, 700 Settlers Landing Road, 757/727-9700, is located on the waterfront; some rooms offer lovely views of docked boats. Rooms are large and comfortable and full-service restaurants and room service are available. The average room rate is $139.

In nearby Newport News, the **Best Western King James Motor Inn**, 6045 Jefferson Avenue, 757/245-2801, offers basic accommodations at reasonable rates.

The **Marriott Waterside**, 235 E. Main Street, 757/627-4200, in Norfolk, is one of the more luxurious hotels in the region and is located across the street from Waterside and Nauticus. Room rates average $139.

On Virginia Beach's oceanfront, the old landmark **Cavalier Hotel**, 42nd and Oceanfront Streets, 757/425-8555, has been recognized for excellence over the years. Further north up the beachfront, the **Ramada Virginia Beach**, 57th and Oceanfront Streets, 757/428-7025, has a large addition and includes an indoor/outdoor swimming pool with swim-up bar, gym, sauna, whirlpool, and other upgraded amenities. Rates range from $150 to $195.

Not on the beach, but well worth a minor inconvenience, the **Founders Inn & Conference Center**, 5641 Indian River Road, 757/424-5511, is owned by the Christian Broadcasting Network and is one of the most luxurious hotels in the state. The lobbies are decorated with fine antiques and antique reproductions, and the rooms are spacious and tastefully decorated. The average room rate here is $125.

CAMPING

All over the Northern Neck you'll find campgrounds with the dramatic backdrop of Chesapeake Bay. The largest campground in the area is **BethPage**

URBANNA/MIDDLESEX & MATHEWS COUNTIES

Most people in Virginia know Urbanna as the site of the annual **Urbanna Oyster Festival** *in November—a Virginia tradition for 20 years. This small bayside town is also home to some great antique shops, bed-and-breakfast inns, a historic waterfront port with marinas, and great local restaurants.*

In nearby Mathews County, **Gwyn's Island Museum***, Route 633, Gwynn, 804/725-2656, details the area's Native American history with artifacts and exhibits. Urbanna, Deltaville, and Regatta Point offer full-service yachting centers/marinas with restaurants, shops, and more.*

Camp Resort, 804/758-4349, in Urbanna with 600 sites. BethPage features full electric/water/sewer hookups, swimming pool, marina, boat ramp, showers, laundry facilities, picnic areas, and planned activities like crab feasts and pig roasts. The **New Point Campground**, 804/725-5120, in Mathews, contains 300 campsites with modern hookups and supplies, as well as a boat ramp, miniature golf, playground, swimming pool, camp store, laundry, and planned activities. **Cole's Point Plantation**, 804/472-3955, in Westmoreland, is a marina and campground on the Potomac River. The 100 wooded campsites surround a freshwater lake and the facility offers boat slips, marine supplies, laundry facilities, hookups, private beach, and watercraft rentals. **Chesapeake Bay/Smith Island KOA Kampground**, 804/453-3430, in Reedville, has 82 sites, most with electric and water. The facility contains a marina, boat ramps, fishing pier, showers, laundry, camping cabins, and boat and bike rentals.

One of the the most popular camping areas in Virginia Beach is at **Seashore State Park**, 800/933-7375. Reservations are required at the 2,700-acre park and it is suggested that you call far in advance during busy seasons. The **Holiday Trav-L-Park**, 800/548-0223, is the closest campground to the Virginia Beach resort. The oceanfront campground contains 1,000 wooded sites (210 with full hookups). The recreation room at the campground contains a big-screen television, and hayrides are offered every night. Other amenities/activities include miniature golf, volleyball, bike rentals, playgrounds, four swimming pools, three camp stores, lounge, restaurant, and laundry facilities. **Virginia Beach KOA Campground**, 800/562-4150, contains 400 campsites (125 with full hookups) and features a camp store, recreation room, snack bar, showers, laundry facilities, camping cabins, swimming pool, playground, transportation to the beach, and miniature golf.

NIGHTLIFE

The usual line-up of beach bars and clubs can be found in Virginia Beach. The long-running **Abbey Road**, 203 22nd Street, 757/425-6330, is known for excellent live acoustic and folk music. The **Jewish Mother**, 31st Street and Pacific Avenue, 757/422-5430, offers the best in live rock 'n' roll, with a popular dance club playing all the latest tunes.

A sparkling new amphitheater has been built in Virginia Beach for nationally known concert performances. Other venues for concerts include **The Boathouse**, 757/622-6395, and the **Pavilion Convention Center**, 1000 19th Street, 757/428-8000, in Virginia Beach; **Chrysler Hall** and **Scope** (part of one facility), Brambleton and St. Paul's Streets, 757/664-6464, in Norfolk; and the **Coliseum**, 1000 Coliseum Drive, 757/838-5650, in Hampton.

PERFORMING ARTS

Every year, Virginia Beach presents one of the largest music festivals in the country with the **American Music Festival** on Labor Day weekend. The line-up of performers is always impressive and well worth fighting the crowds.

The **Virginia Opera**, 757/623-1223, is based in Norfolk, and the **Virginia Symphony**, 757/623-2310, is found in Virginia Beach.

SHOPPING

In the Northern Neck area, there is a large number of antique stores that invite exploration for hidden treasures. One of the best antique shops in the region is **Nadji's Nook**, 303 Queen Street, 804/443-3298, in Tappahannock. You could spend hours in here wandering around hunting for treasures.

In Tidewater, Norfolk's **Waterside** has nautical atmosphere to go along with its few distinct shops mostly catering to tourists. New stores like Nordstrom and Restoration Hardware are scheduled to arrive soon.

6
EASTERN SHORE
VIRGINIA

Far from the maddening crowds and smell of suntan oil, the Eastern Shore of Virginia is a peaceful refuge made up of quiet fishing villages and undisturbed shoreline. The area is generally split into two separate counties—Accomack and North Hampton. This wonderful region is a world unto itself and a perfect place to unwind from everyday tensions.

Stay at a seaside bed-and-breakfast to get a real sense of this community. You'll meet folks here whose families have been residents for generations. Homes and businesses here are are like a slice of life from a simpler time. Here, everyone is proud that this slender portion of land has remained quiet and picturesque.

A PERFECT DAY ON THE EASTERN SHORE

After crossing the world-famous Chesapeake Bay Bridge-Tunnel, one of the first sights you'll see on the Shore is the Cape Charles Lighthouse. Drive up U.S. 13 to Cape Charles then onto Melfa and visit the Turner Foundry and Gallery. Visit Onancock and the Hopkins and Bros. Store. Keep going on U.S. 13 to Oak Hall and visit The Decoy Factory. Finally, watch the sunset in Chincoteague National Wildlife Refuge and do a little wildlife-spotting for egrets, loons, swans, and a few wild ponies. Make sure to sample some of the freshest seafood available as you make your way through the region.

EASTERN SHORE VIRGINIA

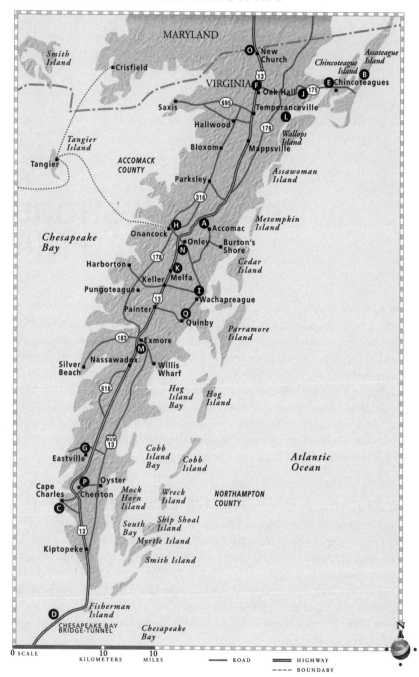

MARYLAND

Smith
Island

Crisfield

New Church **O**

Chincoteague
Island

Assateague
Island

Chincoteagues **E** **B**

VIRGINIA

Oak Hall **F** 13

Saxis 695

Temperanceville

J 175

Hallwood

176 **L**

Tangier
Island

Bloxom

Mappsville

Wallops
Island

Tangier

ACCOMACK
COUNTY

Parksley

Assawoman
Island

316

Metompkin
Island

Chesapeake
Bay

Onancock **H** **A** Accomac

Onley

Burton's
Shore

N

178

Harborton

Keller **K** Melfa

Cedar
Island

Pungoteague

13

I Wachapreague

Painter

Q Quinby

Parramore
Island

183 Exmore

M

Silver
Beach

Nassawadox

Willis
Wharf

618

Hog
Island
Bay

Hog
Island

BUS
13

Cobb
Island
Bay

Cobb
Island

Atlantic
Ocean

G

Eastville

P Oyster

Cape
Charles

Cheriton

Mock
Horn
Island

Wreck
Island

NORTHAMPTON
COUNTY

C

13

South
Bay

Ship Shoal
Island

Myrtle Island

Kiptopeke

Smith Island

D

Fisherman
Island
CHESAPEAKE BAY
BRIDGE-TUNNEL

Chesapeake
Bay

N

0 SCALE   10   10
KILOMETERS   MILES

ROAD
HIGHWAY
BOUNDARY

ACCOMACK COUNTY SIGHTSEEING HIGHLIGHTS

★★★★ ASSATEAGUE

Chincoteague Chamber of Commerce Visitor Center
6733 Maddox Blvd., 757/336-6161

Originally Native American tribes inhabited the island of Assateaugue for thousands of years. In the 1670s the island was settled by English explorers. Today the island is a federally owned wildlife preserve.

The **Chincoteague National Wildlife Refuge**, located in Assateague, was created in 1943 to protect the diminishing migrating waterfowl population. Bird-watching for herons, egrets, terns, sandpipers, warblers, and other species is a popular activity. The visitors centers offer a bird checklist and special rules regarding threatened animals.

The **Assateague National Seashore**, a protected shoreline, is home to crashing waves, undisturbed beachfront, and the occasional wild pony. Legend says that the famous wild horses on Assateague island are descendants of mustangs who survived a shipwreck in the sixteenth century. The National Park Service reports that these horses are descended from domesticated stock brought

---

SIGHTS

- Ⓐ Accomac
- Ⓑ Assateague
- Ⓒ Cape Charles
- Ⓓ Chesapeake Bay Bridge and Tunnel
- Ⓔ Chincoteague
- Ⓕ The Decoy Factory
- Ⓖ Eastville
- Ⓗ Onancock
- Ⓘ Wachapreague
- Ⓙ Wallops Island/NASA Visitor Center
- Ⓚ Willis Wharf

FOOD

- Ⓔ Island Creamery's
- Ⓘ Island House Restaurant
- Ⓔ Landmark Crab House
- Ⓔ Pony Tails
- Ⓔ Steamers
- Ⓛ Wright's Seafood Restaurant and Crab Galley

LODGING

- Ⓒ Bay Avenue's Sunset
- Ⓜ Best Western Exmore
- Ⓔ Channel Bass Inn
- Ⓝ Comfort Inn Onley

LODGING (continued)

- Ⓒ Days Inn Cape Charles
- Ⓞ Garden and the Sea Inn
- Ⓔ Island Manor House Inn

CAMPING

- Ⓟ Cherrystone Family Camping and RV Resort
- Ⓔ Maddox Family Campground
- Ⓠ Thousand Trails' Virginia Landing

Note: Items with the same letter are located in the same place.

---

here by seventeenth-century planters. Here horses could graze freely on the island and their owners could avoid tax restrictions.

The mystique of the ponies grew even more in 1947 after the popularity of Marguerite Henry's novel, *Misty of Chincoteague*, which became a motion picture in the 1960s. The horses are a little smaller than many other breeds and have adapted to the harsh environment with shaggy coats. Although they started out domesticated, they are wild today. The famous annual Pony Swim and Pony Penning are held every July (last Wednesday and Thursday).

Assateague Island Boat Tours, offers *Misty* boat tours, 757/336-6155. Prices are $10 for adults and $5 for children.

Details: *Visitor Center is open Mon–Sat 9–4:30. (full day)*

★★★★ CHINCOTEAGUE

Chincoteague Chamber of Commerce Visitor Center
6733 Maddox Blvd., 757/336-6161

Just like Assateague, the island of Chincoteague was inhabited by Native American tribes until it was settled by English explorers in the 1670s. Today the island is mostly residential, with a number of small shops, inns, and cafés that cater to tourists.

Fishing charters, nature cruises, and custom cruises are offered by **Chincoteague View Cruises**, 757/336-6861, $30 per person for fishing charter, $10 per person for one-hour nature cruises, $15 per person for two-hour nature cruises. Cruises aboard *The Osprey*, 757/336-5511, are offered daily during the summer and on select days during the off-season. Admission prices are $10 adult for a 1 1/2-hour trip.

In Chincoteague, the **Oyster and Maritime Museum**, 757/336-6117, features live marine exhibits including a small aquarium, as well as shells and maritime/seafood industry artifacts. The **Refuge Waterfowl Museum**, 7059 Maddox Boulevard, 757/336-5800, features carved waterfowl exhibits, antique decoys, artwork, boats, weapons, and traps. There are a number of small motels and charming bed-and-breakfast inns throughout the area, and shops sell folk art, hand-carved decoys, saltwater taffy, and more. The town of Chincoteague springs to life every July during the annual running of the wild ponies. Many of the horses are driven across the channel for sale at the annual auction.

Details: *Visitor Center is open Mon–Sat 9–4:30. (full day)*

★★★★ ONANCOCK
Eastern Shore Visitors Center, P.O. Drawer R, Melfa
757/787-2460

This is perhaps the most scenic and charming village on the Eastern Shore. Founded in 1680, Onancock has recently renovated its deep-water harbor with improved docking facilities and a boat launching ramp. Wander around the Hopkins and Bros. Store, 2 Market Street, 757/787-3100, one of the oldest general stores in the country, and peruse merchandise from dry goods to arts and crafts. The **Blue Crab Bay Co.**, 108 Market Street, 757/787-3602, sells seafood seasonings and specialty food items. In addition to the many 1700s homes and public buildings, **Kerr Place** (1799), 69 Market Place, 757/787-8012, is a fine restored home opened for tours and headquarters of the Eastern Shore Historical Society.

Visitors can also cruise to historic Tangier Island (see Chapter 5: Virginia's Coast) from Onancock. Cruises are available aboard the *Capt. Eulice*, P.O. Box 27, Tangier Island, 757/891-2240.

Details: *Visitors Center is open weekdays 8:30–4, weekends 9–4. (2–4 hours)*

WATERFRONT IN ONANCOCK

Virginia Tourism Corporation

★★★ WALLOPS ISLAND/NASA VISITOR CENTER
Wallops Island, 757/824-1344 or 757/824-2298

The Goddard Space Flight Center on Wallops Island is a special complex for suborbital, aeronautical, and space research operated by NASA. Here, more than 1,000 NASA scientists conduct research on rockets, balloons, and aircraft to gain an understanding of all kinds of phenomena related to Earth and its space environment. The center also operates a NASA satellite-tracking station and studies the interaction of the oceans, atmosphere, and land. At the visitors center, exhibits chronicle the history of flight. One of the most compelling points of interest is a display area of current and future NASA projects. Model rocket demonstrations are conducted the first Saturday of every month March through November at 1 p.m. and the third Saturdays of summer months. NASA souvenirs are available at the gift shop.

Details: Mar–Nov Thu–Mon 10–4, July 4–Labor Day daily. Free for taxpayers. (2 hours)

★★ ACCOMAC
Eastern Shore Visitors Center, P.O. Drawer R, Melfa
757/787-2460

The town of Accomac has a definite colonial feel and contains a large concentration of restored 1700s buildings making for a great walking tour. Located in the town is a 1784 jailer's residence that was turned into a debtor's prison in 1824. Today it is an example of a jailer's home.

Details: Visitors Center is open weekdays 8:30–4, weekends 9–4. (2–4 hours)

★★ THE DECOY FACTORY
6301 Lankford Hwy., Oak Hall, 757/824-5621

South of Chincoteague you'll find the world's largest decoy factory, where you can watch carvers create wonderful wooden ducks, geese, and other native waterfowl. There is also a gift shop where you can buy decoys, folk art, gifts, and crafts.

Details: Daily 9–5. Free. (1–2 hours)

★ WACHAPREAGUE
Eastern Shore Visitors Center, P. O. Drawer R, Melfa
757/787-2460

Wachapreague is home to only 200 residents who undoubtedly appreciate the unspoiled wetlands and barrier islands that make the area ideal for fishing, boating, and bird-watching. Fishing takes priority in this town known for flounder, tuna, and marlin tournaments. It has four marinas and several charter companies—whose boats have names like *Trashman* and *Nomad*—to take you out for a fishing expedition. After all, this is the "Flounder Fishing Capital of the World."
Details: Weekdays 8:30–4, weekends 9–4. (2 hours)

NORTHAMPTON COUNTY SIGHTSEEING HIGHLIGHTS

★★★★ CHESAPEAKE BAY BRIDGE AND TUNNEL
P.O. Box 111, Cape Charles, 757/331-2960

It took just four years, beginning in 1960, to construct the Chesapeake Bay Bridge and Tunnel, in an effort to improve transportation between Virginia and its Eastern Shore. The project would become the world's largest bridge-tunnel complex and in a worldwide competition with more than 100 other major projects, the Chesapeake Bay Bridge and Tunnel was named "One of the Seven Engineering Wonders of the Modern World" in 1965. The amazing link stretches for 17.6 miles and contains 12 miles of trestled roadway, two milelong tunnels, two bridges, almost two miles of causeway, four manmade islands, and five and a half miles of approach roads. Even more amazing, the bridge/tunnel is set to expand from two lanes to four lanes by 1999. The first island features a 625-foot fishing pier with bait and tackle available. It also has a full-service restaurant, souvenir and gift shop, and scenic-view area.

Details: Open daily. Two-axle, four-tire vehicles $10/Class 1, vehicles towing a one-axle trailer $13/Class 1, vehicles towing two-axle vehicle/trailer $16/Class 1, vehicle towing three-axle trailer $19. (1 hour)

★★ CAPE CHARLES
Eastern Shore Visitors Center, P.O. Drawer R, Melfa 757/787-2460

Located at the southern top of the Eastern Shore peninsula, Cape Charles is the first town you approach after departing the Chesapeake Bay-Bridge Tunnel. It has a high concentration of late-Victorian and turn-of-the-century buildings lining its small-town streets. Established in 1884, Cape Charles was born when the New York/Philadelphia/

Norfolk Railroad extended its line southward through the peninsula. The town's railroad history continues as it is the headquarters for the Eastern Shore Railroad, one of the largest shortline roads in the country. There's a scenic boardwalk overlooking the Chesapeake Bay here and a slew of seafood restaurants, specialty/antique shops, pottery, public beach area, marina, and bed-and-breakfast inns.

Martha Custis, wife of George Washington, was born and raised on Arlington Plantation here and her family's tombs are located on the site. Kiptopeke State Park, 757/331-2267, contains 375 areas with swimming beach, camping, and boating opportunities, as well as fishing and bird-watching.

Details: Weekdays 8:30–4, weekends 9–4. (2–4 hours)

★ EASTVILLE
Eastern Shore Visitors Center, P.O. Drawer R, Melfa
757/787-2460
The Clerk's Office in Eastville houses the oldest continuous court records in the country (1632). The historic little village voted the Stamp Act unconstitutional 10 years before the signing of the Declaration of Independence. The town's courthouse and its historic gardens, located at an 1866 manor, and the 1735 Eyre Hall mansion also make for interesting stops.

Details: Weekdays 8:30–4, weekends 9–4. (1 hour)

★ WILLIS WHARF
Eastern Shore Visitors Center, P.O. Drawer R, Melfa
757/787-2460
Located northeast of Cape Charles, the wharf attracts visitors from around the country who enjoy stopping at the oyster house to see the fall and spring oyster shucking. The Eastern Shore National Wildlife Refuge is yet another great place to bird-watch; it also includes a museum and a waterfowl carving collection.

Details: Weekdays 8:30–4, weekends 9–4. (2–4 hours)

FITNESS AND RECREATION
One of the great pleasures about outdoor adventuring in Virginia's Eastern Shore is its peacefulness and gentility. The waters, shoreline, and wildlife have been faithfully protected. The results are long bike tours with all-natural backdrops, nature walks where you can spot abundant wildlife, and boating on

TURNER FOUNDRY AND GALLERY

In Melfa, just south of Onancock, the Turner Foundry and Gallery, 27314 Lankford Highway, (Route 13), 757/787-2818, features bronze sculptures created by William and David Turner. Their amazing wildlife creations grace national museums, zoos, corporations, private homes, and even the White House. The 3,350-square-foot gallery displays most of their current editions as well as works from other local and national wildlife artists.

waters that have changed little over the centuries. Bikers and kayakers of all levels can enjoy the special trips connecting lovely scenery with bed-and-breakfast lodging. Some tours include garden visits, yoga and fitness classes, and education on wildlife and history. For more information on special itineraries and packages for bikers and kayakers provided by **Eastern Shore Escapes**, call 888/VASHORE. Eastern Shore Escapes also offers bird-watching trips during peak migration seasons. Visitor centers offer bird checklists for those with tours or out spotting waterfowl alone.

FOOD

Naturally there is no shortage of fresh seafood along the peninsula. One local and tourist favorite is **Wright's Seafood Restaurant and Crab Galley**, Watts Bay, Atlantic, 757/824-4012, near Wallop's Island. There are three dining rooms and a new all-you-can-eat Crab Galley area overlooking Watts Bay. Offerings include the usual bevy of seafood including flounder, crab of all types, lobster, shrimp, and clams. The **Island House Restaurant**, 17 Atlantic Avenue, Wachapreague, 757/787-2105, has an attractive setting modeled after an old 1880s life-saving station. Its specialty is, of course, seafood—especially its signature crab cakes. At **Landmark Crab House**, N. Main Street, Chincoteague, 757/336-5552, diners can enjoy water views and live entertainment with their seafood and quality steaks.

Also in Chincoteague, but with a decidedly more casual atmosphere, **Steamers**, 6251 Maddox Boulevard, 757/336-6238, offers all-you-can-eat crab and shrimp by the bucket loads.

Aside from seafood, **Island Creamery's**, 6251 Maddox Boulevard,

Chincoteague, 757/336-6236, sells homemade ice cream, and **Pony Tails**, 7011 Maddox Boulevard, 757/336-6688, sells saltwater taffy.

LODGING

The majority of hotels and motels on Virginia's Eastern Shore are outside-entry motor inns, most of which are clean and perfectly suitable. However, if you need that national chain name on the marquis, there are a **Best Western**, 2543 Lankford Highway, Exmore, 757/442-7378; a **Comfort Inn**, Four Corner Plaza, Onley, 757/787-7787; and a **Days Inn**, 29106 Lankford Highway, Cape Charles, 757/331-1000.

In New Church, the **Garden and the Sea Inn**, P.O. Box 275, 800/824-0672, is one of the prettiest bed-and-breakfast inns around with special touches like antiques, oriental rugs, fresh flowers, and stained glass windows. Built circa 1802, the Victorian house contains six nicely decorated guest rooms with private baths—many with whirlpool tubs. The inn serves up dinner as well as breakfast in a fine dining restaurant using fresh local seafood and produce. Rates range from $65 to $165 based on the season.

The **Island Manor House Inn** (1848), 4160 Main Street, Chincoteague, 800/852-1505, is a historic T-shaped federal-style house that has been restored and contains antiques, gardens, and water views. There are eight guest rooms in all and the inn serves a fantastic breakfast and afternoon tea with homemade desserts. Rates range from $70 to $115 depending on the season.

The **Channel Bass Inn**, 6228 Church Street, Chincoteague, 757/336-6686, has six spacious guest rooms with attractive furnishings. Breakfasts are hearty and an afternoon English tea with homemade scones is served daily. Rates range from $125 to $175.

Bay Avenue's Sunset, 108 Bay Avenue, Cape Charles, 757/331-2424, aims to make you feel at home with rockers on the front porch, four homey guest rooms, full breakfasts, televisions/VCRs in the rooms, fireplaces, and classic movies on tape. Room rates are $85 to $105.

CAMPING

There are three major campgrounds throughout Virginia's Eastern Shore offering hookups, places to pitch a tent, and more. **Cherrystone Family Camping and RV Resort**, 757/331-3063, in Cheriton, is not only the largest campground on the Eastern Shore, but is one of the largest in the mid-Atlantic area. Three hundred acres of waterfront contain more than 700 campsites shaded by tall trees. There are camping cabins, on-site trailer rentals, swimming pools, fishing piers, a bait and tackle shop, and a well-stocked general merchandise store. Each day during the summer there are activities like clamming (Cherrystone harvests its own) and fiddler crab races. Daily rates for campsites are approximately $19 during the high season, with an additional charge for water, electric, and sewer. Rates for cabins sleeping four are approximately $38 per day or $235 per week. Tent rentals are $33 per day during high season.

Thousand Trails' Virginia Landing, Route 605, 800/723-6226, in Quinby, offers an inviting setting with RV hookups, a pool, miniature golf, paddle boats, clamming, cabins, a private marina, and a boat launch with 21 slips. The **Maddox Family Campground**, 757/336-3111 or 757/336-6648, in Chin-coteague, offers grassy sites, pool, playground, grocery store, gift shop, laundry, bath houses, crabbing, and more.

7
THE HISTORIC
TRIANGLE

The Historic Triangle consists of Jamestown, Williamsburg, and Yorktown. Each of these towns is a destination in itself. There is simply no denying that Colonial Williamsburg is America's premier living historical park and one of the most visited destinations in the country. Hoping to mix a little education with their summer fun, families have been coming here for decades to show their children what it was like during colonial times. In the reproduction British town, authentically garbed townsfolk speak of their unrest on the eve of the American Revolution. Visitors are encouraged to become a part of history and play along.

Not only is the colonial capital a worthwhile attraction in itself, but America's first English settlement is also located minutes away at Jamestown. Here, visitors can see reproductions of seventeenth-century English and American Indian villages, as well as reproductions of the vessels that brought European settlers across the sea. Here, visitors learn about true courage and marvel at the settlers' ingenuity.

And finishing off the historic region is the dramatic site of Yorktown, where the British surrendered and America became free. One visit here is guaranteed to give your patriotic fervor a boost.

The region has also taken great care to balance heavy-handed history lessons with loads of entertainment. Minutes away from colonial streets and horse-drawn carriages are two world-class theme parks, one of the East

THE HISTORIC TRIANGLE

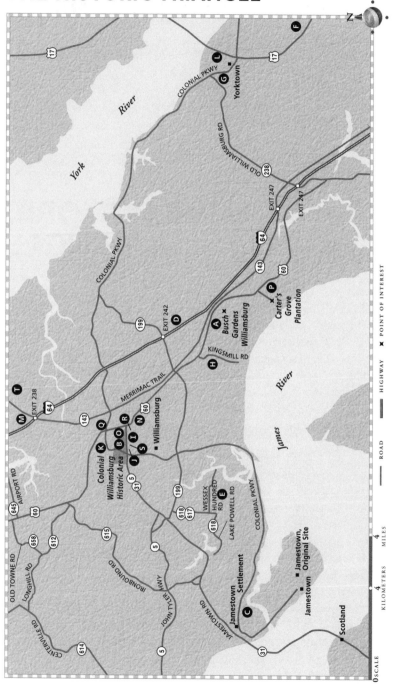

N

F

177

L

Yorktown

G

COLONIAL PKWY

River

York

EXIT 247

EXIT 247

238

64

OLD WILLIAMSBURG RD

COLONIAL PKWY

143

60

P

Carter's
Grove
Plantation

199

EXIT 242

D

A

Busch
Gardens
Williamsburg

KINGSMILL RD

H

River

James

MERRIMAC TRAIL

T

EXIT 238

64

M

143

Q R

O N

B I

K S

J

Colonial
Williamsburg
Historic Area

Williamsburg

5

31

199

WESSEX
HUNDRED
RD E

618
617

LAKE POWELL RD

COLONIAL PKWY

AIRPORT RD

645

60

615

5

IRONBOUND RD

618

Jamestown,
Jamestown Original Site

OLD TOWNE RD

658

612

LONGHILL RD

JOHN TYLER HWY

5

JAMESTOWN RD

Jamestown
Settlement

C

Scotland

31

CENTERVILLE RD

614

POINT OF INTEREST

HIGHWAY

ROAD

SCALE   KILOMETERS   MILES
0   4   4

Coast's largest outlet shopping areas, top-rated golf courses, and an unbelievable assortment of restaurants and hotels.

A PERFECT DAY IN THE HISTORIC TRIANGLE

This is one place where frequenting the tourist hangouts truly does pay off. Start out your day by having breakfast at Shields Tavern to get into a historic frame of mind. Stop at the Colonial Williamsburg Visitor Center, then visit the Governor's Palace and spend a couple of hours wandering the streets for atmosphere absorption. Have a sandwich and a tankard of beverage at a tavern, then drive along the Colonial Parkway to Jamestown Settlement. You can also visit the original site nearby where archaeologists are making exciting discoveries every day.

Then, get back on the Colonial Parkway and head to the Yorktown Victory Center for exhibits on the American Revolution. Before heading back to Williamsburg, stop at Yorktown Battlefield Park to see firsthand the ground where independence was fought for and won. Dine back in Colonial Williamsburg at The Trellis and end with a little Death by Chocolate.

SIGHTS

- **A** Busch Gardens Williamsburg
- **B** Colonial Williamsburg
- **C** Jamestown Settlement
- **D** Water Country USA
- **E** The Williamsburg Winery
- **F** Yorktown Battlefield
- **G** Yorktown Victory Center

FOOD

- **H** Bray Dining Room
- **I** Cascades Restaurant
- **J** Christiana Campbell's Tavern

FOOD (continued)

- **K** Dynasty Chinese Restaurant
- **L** Nick's Seafood Pavilion
- **M** Pierce's Barbecue
- **J** Shields Tavern
- **J** The Trellis
- **N** Williamsburg Inn Regency Dining Room

LODGING

- **O** Days Inn Historic Area
- **P** Fort Magruder Inn
- **Q** Governor's Trace
- **K** Hampton Inn and Suites Historic Area

LODGING (continued)

- **H** Kingsmill Inn & Conference Center
- **Q** Legacy of Williamsburg
- **Q** Liberty Rose
- **R** Williamsburg Inn
- **S** Williamsburg Lodge
- **G** York River Inn Bed and Breakfast

CAMPING

- **C** Jamestown Beach Campsites
- **T** Williamsburg KOA Resort

Note: Items with the same letter are located in the same place.

HISTORIC TRIANGLE SIGHTSEEING HIGHLIGHTS

★★★★ COLONIAL WILLIAMSBURG
P.O. Box 1776, I-64 (Exit 238), 800/HISTORY

It was in the 1920s that the Rockefeller Foundation created this reproduction of America's colonial capital and opened it as a history theme park. The park is located on Williamsburg's 173-acre historic area. The town's buildings line dusty streets and grassy lawns where the clippety-clop of hooves announce the arrival of horse-drawn carriages. Wander through the streets and you'll find townsfolk tending their gardens, forging metal in the blacksmith shop, selling wares in merchant areas, and transforming wood into everyday items. You'll also get a glimpse of the tide of political change that ocurred during America's early days as she struggled to be free of English oppression. All this makes for high entertainment once you lift yourself out of the twentieth century and place yourself among the townspeople and their world 200 years ago.

If you've never visited Colonial Williamsburg before, you'll want to take a guided tour to get the lay of the land and a feel for what was

COLONIAL WILLIAMSBURG

Virginia Tourism Corporation

going on at the time the town was the colonial capital. Then you can visit the significant buildings on site, especially the grand **Governor's Palace**. Other notable buildings to visit include the **Peyton Randolph** urban plantation, the **Capitol**, the **James Geddy site**, and **Anderson Blacksmith Shop**.

Just outside the historic area, **Carter's Grove** is one of the most significant homes in the country. The 400-year-old plantation contains slave quarters and an archaeological museum detailing the discovery of Wolstenholme Towne, (an early English settlement rediscovered less than 30 years ago). **Bassett Hall** is an eighteenth-century home that was once the home of Abby Aldrich and John D. Rockefeller Jr. At the **DeWitt Wallace Gallery** you will find an enormous collection of colonial furnishings and decorative arts. The **Abby Aldrich Folk Art Center** features the largest and oldest collection of folk art in the country.

A ticket is necessary for guided tours and entrance into the major buildings and exhibits in the park. Some tours and taverns are extremely popular so it's important to make reservations ahead of time.

Details: Dawn–dusk. Patriot's Pass (1-year pass to everything and discounts off special tours, concerts, shopping, and more) $34 adults, $19 children ages 6–12; Colonist's Pass (2-day pass) $30 adults, $17 children ages 6–12; Basic Pass (1-day) $26 adults, $15 children ages 6–12. (full day or more)

★★★★ JAMESTOWN SETTLEMENT
off Rte. 31, Jamestown (east of Williamsburg on the Colonial Pkwy. between the York and James Rivers) 757/229-1607

Just a short distance from the original settlement site, Jamestown Settlement was built in 1957 as a living museum with costumed interpreters, working farms, and outbuildings. The Virginia Company of London sponsored the expedition which sent 104 colonists aboard the *Susan Constant, Godspeed,* and *Discovery* to the New World. On May 14, 1607, the brave explorers stepped ashore on a marshy peninsula of Virginia. Jamestown was the capital of the Virginia colony from 1607 to 1699.

The reconstructed site includes a reproduction of a church and the excavated foundations of several seventeenth-century buildings. Three living history areas consist of an English fort, reproductions of the *Susan Constant, Godspeed,* and *Discovery,* and an Indian village. Make certain that you board these reproduction ships to gain an understanding of the challenges the first settlers' had to endure throughout their voyage.

A visitor center and museum focuses on the reasons behind the colonization, what Jamestown was like during its early years, and the story of the Powhatan Indians. The original settlement site is adjacent to the reconstructed park.

Details: *Daily 9–5 p.m. $9 adults, $4.25 children ages 6–12. A combination ticket is available with the Yorktown Victory Center $12.50 adults, $6 children ages 6–12. (There is an additional $8 admission fee for visiting the original site.) (3 hours)*

★★★★ YORKTOWN BATTLEFIELD
National Park Service, 757/989-3400

At Yorktown Battlefield, the National Park Service presents exhibits and film and tour information of the siege and battle area. It is a good idea to rent the audio tape tour of the battlefield area to get a full explanation of the significance of the site; maps are also available for you to tour on your own, however. The 16-minute film *Siege of Yorktown* is a great way to understand the strategies behind the important events of October 1781. Exhibits of wartime artifacts include field tents used by General Washington's troops. Spend some time just walking Yorktown's streets and get a feeling for the times.

Details: *Daily 8:30–5. $4 adults, free children ages 16 and under. Jamestown-Yorktown Pass $7 for adults. (2 hours)*

★★★★ YORKTOWN VICTORY CENTER
Old Rte. 238 and the Colonial Pkwy., I-64, (Exit 247)
888/593-4682 or 757/253-4838

At the Yorktown Victory Center visitors can explore the final days of English rule through living-history demonstrations, exhibits, and audio-visual presentations. Exhibits detail the days leading up to the definitive battle in 1781 and the Yorktown campaign (these include a film set in a military encampment at night and an exhibition about the sea scuttles in the York River). Living-history presentations include soldiers, craftspeople, and farmers.

Details: *Daily 9–5. $7.25 adults, $3.50 children ages 6–12; combination tickets with Jamestown Settlement $13.50 adults, $6.50 children ages 6–12. (2 hours)*

★★★ BUSCH GARDENS WILLIAMSBURG
I Busch Gardens Blvd. (3 miles east of Colonial Williamsburg on Rte. 60 or off I-64 exit 242A) 757/253-3350

More than 500 acres of hilly, forested land have been transformed into seventeenth-century France, Italy, England, and Germany at Busch Gardens Williamsburg. Here you can walk from country to country and past some extraordinary landscaping and authentic-looking architecture. Even the roller coasters are especially designed for the landscape, instead of being constructed down in any convenient spot.

The park's many rides include the fierce **Loch Ness Monster** and **Alpengeist** roller coasters, **Da Vinci's Garden of Inventions**, and a **Roman Rapids** white-water raft ride. Busch has also recently built an area in the park for the younger set with a dragon theme.

Entertainment includes a Broadway-style magic show and an animatronics spectacle for kids, (complete with fire-breathing dragon). Shops sell everything from magic supplies to Hummel figurines.

The famous **Anheuser-Busch Clydesdale** horses are also on view. You can take a monorail to the park's adjacent Anheuser-Busch brewery for a complimentary tour and sample. (It is not necessary to visit the theme park for the brewery tour. Brewery tours are free.)

Details: Daily 10–7 early May–Labor Day (extended hours during the summer), Fri–Tue 10–7 Sep–Oct 31. Call for additional hours. Admission (includes park entrance, shows, rides, and exhibits) $33 adults, $26 children ages 3–6. Parking $4. (6+ hours)

★★ WATER COUNTRY USA
P.O. Box 3088, I-64 (Exit 242A), 757/253-3350

Water Country, also owned by Anheuser-Busch, is one of the country's largest water parks with tons of nerve-shattering slides, raft rides, a wave pool, and attractions for small children. One of the park's latest attractions is the **Nitro Racer**, a super-speed slide that drops 382 feet. The **Aquazoid** is billed as the world's largest special-effects, family raft ride and takes four-person rafts through white-water streams and tunnels complete with laser light images, eerie sound effects, and an underground finale. There's also a 4,500-square-foot heated pool and a special children's playland for the younger set.

Details: Season runs May–Oct, opens at 10 a.m. and closes at various hours based on the time of year. Call for details. $33 adults, $26 children ages 3–6. (2–4 hours)

★ THE WILLIAMSBURG WINERY
5800 Wessex Hundred, 757/229-0999

One of a long list of fine wineries in Virginia, the Williamsburg Winery offers award-winning vintages using age-old wine-making traditions reminiscent of the early settlers. Guided tours are offered of the winery, and there are a seventeenth-century wine tasting room, a casual restaurant, and a museum of wine-making artifacts.

Details: *Mon–Sat 10–5:30, Sun noon–5:30; tours and tastings $5 (includes etched wine glass as souvenir). (1 hour)*

FITNESS AND RECREATION

Along with the theme park adventures, visitors to the Historic Triangle can enjoy jogging and biking trails in a historic setting. Trails along the York River at York River Park take bikers/hikers past pretty waterways and wildlife. In Walter Mill Park, Williamsburg, mountain-biking trails are hilly, steep, and difficult.

A number of premier golf destinations are in the area including the nationally renowned **Kingsmill Resort**, 1010 Kingsmill Road, 757/253-3906; **Legends at Stonehouse**, 9446 Overpass Road, Toano, 888/VA LEGENDS; **Williamsburg National Golf Club**, 3700 Centerville Road, 800/826-5732; **Ford's Colony Country Club**, 240 Ford's Colony Drive, 757/258-4100; and the new **Kiskiack Golf Club**, off James Country Parkway, 800/989-4728.

Two especially interesting tour options include the **Historic Air Tours**, Williamsburg Airport, 757/253-8185, and boat tours near **Jamestown Island National Park**, Jamestown Yacht Basin, 757/259-0400.

FOOD

The Trellis, 403 Duke of Gloucester Street, 757/229-8610, near Colonial Williamsburg, is one of those celebrity-status restaurants well worth its fanfare. Chef Marcel Desaulniers is considered an unparalleled culinary talent who has written cookbooks, received prestigious awards, and is known for desserts of pure fantasy. *Death by Chocolate* is his invention—a flourless chocolate concoction to die for. The seasonally changing menu features fresh regional foods with artistic flair.

The **Williamsburg Inn Regency Dining Room**, 136 E. Francis Street, 757/229-1000, is heavy on the elegant atmosphere with a little less emphasis on the food, but still worth a visit. Try this for afternoon tea with homemade scones and pastries. Kingsmill Resort's **Bray Dining Room** at 1010 Kingsmill

Road, 757/253-1703, is an elegant setting with above-par dining. The Sunday brunch here is especially popular.

Any of the colonial taverns in the historic district serve up loads of historic milieu with enjoyable food. **Shields Tavern**, Duke of Gloucester Street, serves 200-year-old recipes, and **Christiana Campbell's Tavern**, Duke of Gloucester Street, is heavy on seafood. Breakfast is a grand tradition at the **Cascades Restaurant**, 103 Visitor Center Drive, in the Colonial Williamsburg Visitor Center. Call 800/HISTORY to make reservations at any of these Colonial Williamsburg taverns.

In Yorktown, **Nick's Seafood Pavilion**, Water Street, 757/887-5269, has been around since the 1940s serving fresh seafood. This place has a loyal following and big crowds year-round.

Two mainstays worth mentioning in the area include the **Dynasty Chinese Restaurant** at 1621 Richmond Road, Williamsburg, 757/220-8888, located in a distinct pagoda-influenced restaurant, and **Pierce's Barbecue**, I-64 (from west Exit 234, from east Exit 238), 757/565-2955, known for legendary saucy barbecue and fixings.

LODGING

If you plan on staying at a Colonial Williamsburg property, you may want to consider special packages. Colonial Williamsburg properties include the Williamsburg Inn, Colonial Houses, Williamburg Lodge, Williamsburg Woodlands, and the Governor's Inn.

Williamsburg's five-star, AAA four-diamond **Williamsburg Inn**, 136 E. Francis Street, 800/HISTORY, is one of the most prestigious hotels in the country. The white-columned classical hotel offers luxurious accommodations just minutes from the historic area. Oriental rugs, antiques, and museum-quality oil paintings adorn the public areas, which is decorated in elegant, understated Williamsburg fashion. The hotel features a sauna, whirlpool, fitness center, indoor/outdoor pool, massage services, and more. The average room rate is $290.

Kingsmill Inn & Conference Center, 1010 Kingsmill Road, Williamsburg, 757/253-1703, with its top-rated golf course, is not just for golfers. The resort features deluxe villa accommodations a few miles from the droves of tourists near the historic area. In addition, the resort offers a great full-service spa, tennis, sports club, three restaurants, and an indoor/outdoor pool. The golf course here is home to the PGA Michelob Championship. There is a complimentary shuttle to the historic area and Busch Gardens. Rates are $179 to $259.

American folk art is the theme at the comfortable **Williamsburg Lodge**, 310 S. England Street, Williamsburg, 800/HISTORY, also within a short distance of the historic area. The hotel features a full-service spa, an indoor/outdoor pool, golf, and tennis. Rooms are tasteful and very comfortable. The average room rate is $185.

Economical accommodations worth mentioning in the Historic Triangle include the **Days Inn Historic Area**, 331 Bypass Road, Williamsburg, 757/253-1166, $49 to $79, located near the historic area. It features an adjacent full-service restaurant, a swimming pool, in-room safes, a Jacuzzi spa, hair dryers in rooms, and complimentary tea and cookies. **Fort Magruder Inn**, Route 60 East, Williamsburg, 757/220-2250, is located in a wooded area around an original Civil War redoubt and contains both indoor and outdoor pools and a fitness center. Rates average $129. The new **Hampton Inn and Suites Historic Area**, 1880 Richmond Road, 757/229-4900, has comfortable cheerfully decorated rooms, a fitness center, and a swimming pool. Rates average $60. Three of the loveliest bed-and-breakfast inns in Williamsburg are the Governor's Trace Bed and Breakfast, Liberty Rose Bed and Breakfast Inn, and the Legacy of Williamsburg Bed and Breakfast. **Governor's Trace**, 303 Capitol Landing Road, 757/229-7552, offers three antique-filled guest rooms— one with a wood-burning fireplace. Rates are $105 to $125. **Liberty Rose**, 1022 Jamestown Road, 757/253-1260, features four sumptuous bedrooms with luxuries such as private baths, ornate beds, and televisions. Rates are $135 to $195. **Legacy of Williamsburg**, 930 Jamestown Road, 757/220-0524, contains four guest rooms with canopy beds, fireplaces, and private baths. Rates are $95 to $140.

In Yorktown, the **York River Inn Bed and Breakfast**, 209 Ambler Street, 757/887-8800, offers waterfront accommodations with Virginia antiques and all the comforts of home. Breakfasts here are hearty and unforgettable. Rates range from $110 to $130.

CAMPING

The most amenities at area campsites are offered at the **Williamsburg KOA Resort**, 5210 Newman Road, Williamsburg, 757/565-2907, with 150 campsites, swimming pool, grocery store, game room, lounge, laundry facilities, and free shuttle to area attractions. The largest campground is **Jamestown Beach Campsites**, across from Jamestown Settlement, 757/229-7609 or 757/229-3300, on the James River, 10 minutes from Colonial Williamsburg. The campground offers 600 sites, grocery store, game room, lounge, swimming pool, fishing, and boating.

PERFORMING ARTS

The **Music Theatre of Williamsburg** at 7575 Richmond Road, (I-64, Exit 231A), 888/687-4220 or 757/564-0200, offers nightly performances featuring a mix of big band, blues, jazz, gospel, show tunes, country, and rock 'n' roll. The **Liberty Theatre** at 5351 Richmond Road, Williamsburg, 757/565-443, presents live performances such as *1776*, which ran in 1998.

SHOPPING

It is hard to believe that the colossal **Williamsburg Pottery Factory**, Route 60 West, Lightfoot, 757/564-3326, started out as a roadside stand by a potter named Jimmy Maloney. Today, the pottery has more than 200 acres of shops and outlets including lamps, gardenware, wooden items, custom framing, silk/dried floral arrangements, baskets, brass, candles, china, giftware, housewares, food items, and even plants grown in the pottery's nurseries.

Just down the street are three major outlet centers and a host of other specialty shops in between. **Berkeley Commons Outlet Center**, Route 60 West, Williamsburg, 757/565-0702, features more than 80 stores including outlets for OshKosh, Anne Klein, Liz Claiborne, Nike, Nautica, Cole Haan, Coach, Tommy Hilfiger, Eddie Bauer, Waterford, Wedgwood, and Brooks Brothers. The **Williamsburg Outlet Mall**, Route 60 West, Lightfoot, 757/565-3378, is fully enclosed and features Levi's, London Fog, Jockey, L'Eggs, Hanes, Bali, Playtex, Dexter Shoes, and more. Upscale **Patriot Plaza**, Route 60 West, Williamsburg, 757/564-7570, features outlets for Polo Ralph Lauren, Villeroy & Boch, WestPoint Pepperell, Dansk, Lenox, and Fila.

Specialty shops offering everything from books and chocolates to toys and fine clothing are available in wonderful surroundings at **Merchants Square**, Duke of Gloucester Street, 757/220-7751, near Colonial Williamsburg. Here you'll find 41 locally owned shops lining brick walkways.

8
CENTRAL/
SOUTHSIDE VIRGINIA

Central Virginia, surrounding Richmond, is mostly residential and rural. The region includes some of Virginia's most recognizable and worthwhile attractions, such as Appomattox, where Lee and Grant signed the close of the Civil War, stately James River Plantations, and the historic city of Petersburg—home to the longest siege in American history.

The rural countryside of Southside Virginia is a pastoral place dotted with farms and small towns. The region is famous for growing peanuts and tobacco, not to mention curing country hams. The land here is settled, but not bustling or commercial. The communities here like their towns quiet and simple—Fourth of July cook-outs, Main Street parades, and county fairs. Here, you'll find lots of home-cookin' restaurants, a few Civil War sites, and a lot of warm hospitality.

A PERFECT DAY IN CENTRAL/SOUTHSIDE VIRGINIA

Start the day off by heading east on I-460 to Petersburg. Browse a few antique shops, visit the Siege Museum, and then have lunch at Old Town. From Petersburg take I-295 north to Route 5 and travel to Virginia's plantations. Pick one to tour and then have dinner at either the Coach House Tavern or Indian Fields Tavern. Berkeley is perhaps the most historically significant, and the Coach House Tavern is located on its grounds.

CENTRAL/SOUTHSIDE VIRGINIA

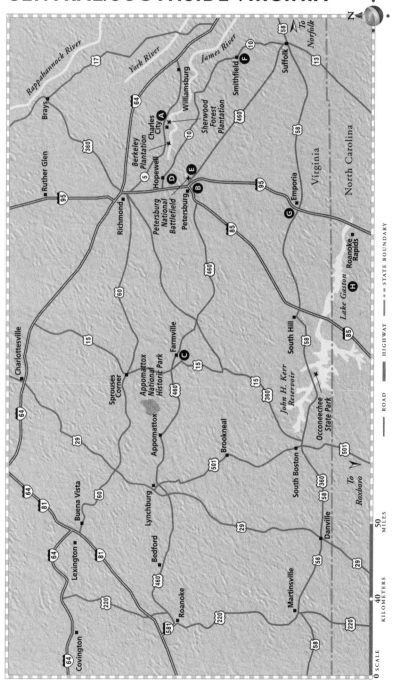

SIGHTSEEING HIGHLIGHTS

★★★★ BERKELEY PLANTATION
12602 Harrison Landing Rd., Charles City, 804/829-6018
This plantation is believed to be the site of the first Thanksgiving in the New World in 1619 based on the writings of explorer John Smith who wrote in his journal that settlers participated in such a celebration on this site. The estate is also the birthplace of Benjamin Harrison, who signed the Declaration of Independence, and William Henry Harrison (ninth U.S. president). *Taps* was composed here in 1682, and the first bourbon whiskey was distilled here (circa 1621–1622). It is also the ancestral home of the 23rd president, Benjamin Harrison.

In addition to its claims to fame, the house is a wonderful example of a typical colonial home with period antiques, terraced boxwood gardens, and a sweeping lawn to the James River.

Details: Daily 9–5. $8.50 adults, $6.50 children ages 13–16, $4 children ages 6–12, 10% off adult ticket price for seniors and AAA members. (1 hour)

★★★★ SHERWOOD FOREST
14501 John Tyler Hwy., Charles City, 804/829-5377
Since being built circa 1730, this plantation has had two U.S. presidents as owners. William Henry Harrison inherited the estate in the late

---

SIGHTS
- Ⓐ Berkeley Plantation
- Ⓑ Blandford Church
- Ⓑ Centre Hill Mansion
- Ⓐ Evelynton
- Ⓒ Farmville
- Ⓓ Hopewell
- Ⓑ Pamplin Park Civil War Site
- Ⓔ Petersburg National Battlefield Park
- Ⓓ Plantations South of the James

SIGHTS (continued)
- Ⓐ Sherwood Forest
- Ⓐ Shirley Plantation
- Ⓑ Siege Museum
- Ⓕ Smithfield/Wakefield

FOOD
- Ⓐ Coach House Tavern
- Ⓓ Kan Pai
- Ⓑ King's Barbecue
- Ⓖ Marie's Restaurant
- Ⓕ Smithfield Station
- Ⓕ Virginia Diner

LODGING
- Ⓖ Best Western Emporia
- Ⓖ Hampton Inn Emporia
- Ⓐ Piney Grove at Southall Plantation
- Ⓕ Smithfield Station

CAMPING
- Ⓗ Americamps Lake Gaston
- Ⓗ Occoneechee State Park
- Ⓖ Yogi Bear's Jellystone Campground

Note: Items with the same letter are located in the same place.

JAMES RIVER PLANTATIONS

On the north side of the James River in Charles City County are Virginia's best-known plantation homes. Block tickets are available at any of the plantations for $25.50 and include admission to Berkeley, Evelynton, Sherwood Forest, and Shirley plantations. The ticket also includes discounts for dining at the Coach House Tavern and Indian Fields Tavern, and lodging at Edgewood Plantation Bed and Breakfast and North Bend Plantation Bed and Breakfast. For more information, write to James River Plantations, P.O. Box 218, Charles City, VA 23030, or call 800/704-5423.

eighteenth century. In 1842, many years and many owners later, John Tyler purchased Sherwood Forest. Tyler succeeded Harrison as president upon his death. He was the 10th U.S. president, serving the country from 1841 to 1845. The house has remained in the family since that time and was restored in the 1970s by John Tyler's grandson and wife–the current owners. The house is Virginia Tidewater in architectural design and is the longest frame dwelling in the country. The home is a wonderful museum to John Tyler with many of his personal possessions, furnishings, silver, and paintings. The grounds contain formal gardens, more-than-a-century-old trees, a seventeenth-century tobacco barn, a garden house, a milk house, a smokehouse, a law office, and a kitchen/laundry area.

Details: Daily 9–5. $7.50 adults, $7 seniors, $6 AAA members/ active military, $4.50 students. (45 minutes)

★★★★ SHIRLEY PLANTATION
501 Shirley Plantation Rd., Charles City, 804/829-5121

This plantation dates back to 1613, making it Virginia's oldest. The land was granted to Edward Hill I in 1660, and the present home was begun in 1723 for his great-granddaughter, Elizabeth, upon her marriage to John Carter. The house is nearly as it was then and remains home to 10th and 11th generations of the Hill-Carter family. The house's famous hanging staircase rises three stories without any visible means of support. The outbuildings form a Queen Anne forecourt and is believed to be the only remaining example of this architectural style in

America. (A forecourt is an arrangement of dependencies that lead to the main house. The dependencies decrease in size based on their perceived importance to the house.) The site was the supply center for the Continental Army and twice it was a listening post for both American and British sides during the Revolution. During the Civil War it survived the Peninsula Campaign and the fighting around Richmond.

In addition, it is the ancestral home of Robert E. Lee's mother, and Robert E. Lee and his cousins were educated here.

Details: Daily 9–5. $7.50 adults, $6.50 seniors/military, $6 AAA members, $5 children ages 13–21, $3.75 children 6–12, free for children ages 5 and under. (1 hour)

★★★ EVELYNTON
6701 John Tyler Hwy., Charles City, 800/473-5075 or 804/829-5075

This plantation was reconstructed in the 1930s long after the house and grounds were destroyed by Union soldiers during the Civil War. The original home was part of William Byrd's Westover Plantation and was named after Byrd's daughter, Evelyn. The plantation has been home to the Ruffin family for four generations. One of the Ruffin ancestors, Edmund Ruffin, is said to have fired the first shot of the Civil War. The Duncan Lee–designed house is beautifully decorated with family antiques and furnishings.

Details: Daily 9–5. $7.50 adults, $6.50 seniors/military, $6 AAA members, $3.50 children. (45 minutes)

★★★ HOPEWELL VISITORS CENTER
4100 Oaklawn Blvd., 800/863-TOUR or 804/541-2461

The little industrial town of Hopewell is the site of one of the Civil War's largest Union fortifications, some of Virginia's most important plantation homes, and a wildlife refuge. Stop at the visitors center for a walking tour brochure and a map of the Old Town of City Point. The town, named "Bermuda Cittie" by Sir Thomas Dale in 1613, is a lovely historic district overlooking the Appomattox and James Rivers.

In addition, a driving-tour brochure directs you past some charming Sears, Roebuck and Company houses. During the 1920s and 1930s, the neighborhood was literally ordered from Sears. Today it contains 44 original mail-ordered homes. Another must-see site in Hopewell is the **City Point National Historic Site**, located at

Petersburg National Battlefield Park, 804/458-9504. It served as the supply base and headquarters for General Ulysses S. Grant from 1864 to 1865. During its time, City Point was the world's busiest port supplying 100,000 troops during the Siege of Petersburg. Free guided tours are available.
Details: *The visitors center is open daily 9–5. (2 hours)*

★★★ PLANTATIONS SOUTH OF THE JAMES
Visitors center at 4100 Oaklawn Blvd.
Hopewell, 800/863-TOUR or 804/541-2461
Several historic plantation homes and sites along the southern side of the James River near Hopewell are well worth a visit. **Flowerdew Hundred**, 1617 Flowerdew Hundred Road, 804/541-8897, is a significant archaeological site with museum, windmill, and replicated colonial kitchen.

In Hopewell, **Weston Manor**, Weston Lane and 21st Avenue, 804/458-4682, is a beautifully-restored eighteenth-century Tidewater Plantation mansion that offers tours. **Bacon's Castle**, in Surry, 757/357-6159, is one of Virginia's oldest plantations with a seventeenth-century manor house and gardens. **Smith's Fort**, also located in Surry, 757/294-3872, was Pocahontas's dower land. Today there are tours of the eighteenth-century manor house, gardens, and fort.
Details: *Open daily 9–5. (2 hours)*

★★ FARMVILLE VISITORS CENTER
116 N. Main St., 804/392-3939
Farmville is a quiet college town that is home to Hampden-Sydney University and Longwood University. The downtown area offers a riverfront park, lots of gift and furniture shops, and restaurants. If you're interested in Civil War history, spend a half hour at **Sailor's Creek Battlefield Historical Park**. This park marks the site of the last major battle of the Civil War. History enthusiasts will also enjoy the **1786 Debtor's Prison**, one of the only remaining structures of its kind in the country.
Details: *(4 hours)*

★ SMITHFIELD/WAKEFIELD
Isle of Wight Tourism, 130 Main St., Smithfield
800/365-9339
South of the James River are several small farm communities known as

purveyors of fine country hams and peanuts. The nearby town of Waverly has a museum dedicated to a favorite American snack food—the peanut. There's also a favorite Virginia restaurant locatd in Wakefield—the Virginia Diner—known to serve many peanut specials. Smithfield has recently renovated its downtown historic area and offers guided walking tours from the Old Courthouse, 130 Main Street.

Details: *Daily 9–5. (3 hours)*

PETERSBURG SIGHTSEEING HIGHLIGHTS

The city of Petersburg has had its share of anguishes. Once held for the longest siege in American history, Petersburg reveals a story of a city steeped in wartime dramas. The city began as a wilderness outpost in 1645 and thrived as a center of commerce, warehousing, and transportation. During the Revolution, the city was occupied by British troops in 1781. It would again be occupied during the longest siege of any American city during the Civil War in 1865.

Today Petersburg contains a charming restored historic district with restaurants, shops, and museums. Several years ago the district was devastated by a tornado, but it has been rebuilt and is slowly coming back. Other sites not listed in the highlights below, but noteworthy, include the First Baptist Church and Trapezium House. For more information write to The Petersburg Visitors Center, P.O. Box 2107, Petersburg, 23804, or call Petersburg, 800/368-3595 or 804/733-2400.

★★★★ PAMPLIN PARK CIVIL WAR SITE
6523 Duncan Rd., 804/861-2408

This technologically modern battlefield park has preserved the ground where Union soldiers broke through General Robert E. Lee's defenses on April 2, 1865. The park ends the conception that battlefield parks are all about reading signs and looking at an empty field. The unique Interpretive Center is designed to have the shape of the Confederate defensive line.

Inside, the 7,000-square-foot exhibit space features Civil War artifacts and an impressive fiber-optics battle map. Interactive video programs present the dramatic story of the Union breakthrough. There are trails to well-preserved fortifications, and park interpreters are available throughout the year to give interpretation and details of those dramatic days ending the longest siege in American history.

Details: *Daily 9–5 p.m. $4 adults, $1.50 children ages 6–11. (1 hour)*

★★★ PETERSBURG NATIONAL BATTLEFIELD PARK
Off E. Washington St., 804/732-3531
The Petersburg National Battlefield Park (site of the Battle of the Crater) is a 1,500-acre park that contains landmarks associated with the nearly 10 months of fighting for Petersburg. Other sites in the park include Fort Stedman and Poplar Grove National Cemetery.
Details: *Daily 8–5. $3 adults. (1–2 hour)*

★★ BLANDFORD CHURCH
Crater Rd. at Rochelle Ln., 804/733-2400
This historic 1735 church was the target of a Union attack during the Battle of the Crater. The church contains some lovely Tiffany windows, and a cemetery with a Confederate burial section is located on the grounds.
Details: *Mar–Oct Mon–Sat 9–5, Sun 12:30–5; Nov–Feb Mon–Sat 10–4, Sun 12:30–4. $2 adults. (30 minutes)*

★★ SIEGE MUSEUM
15 W. Bank St., 804/733-2400
You can gain an understanding of the events surrounding the siege and the role that Petersburg played during the war at the Siege Museum.
Details: *Mon–Sat 9–5, Sun 12:30–5 p.m. $2 adults. (45 minutes)*

★ CENTRE HILL MANSION
1 Centre Hill Circle, 804/733-2400
This restored 1823 plantation is said to be haunted annually by Confederate soldiers.
Details: *Mar–Oct Mon–Sat 9–5, Sun 12:30–5; Nov–Feb Mon–Sat 10–4, Sun 12:30–4. $2 adults. (30 minutes)*

FITNESS AND RECREATION

Throughout Central Virginia are numerous jogging and bicycling trails, especially along Route 5 between Richmond and Williamsburg and along the James River. Cast your line on the James River or one of the region's lakes (especially **Lake Anna** and **Lake Chesdin**), and experience some great fishing.

Free ferry rides into the **Presquile National Wildlife Refuge**, in Hopewell, reveal bald eagles and abundant wildlife. Call 804/458-4797 to schedule an appointment for a ferry ride.

Southside Virginia contains one of the state's most popular fishing areas. The communities surrounding Lake Gaston are primarily residential and retreat home areas. Both bodies of water offer an abundance of fishing and water sport opportunities. There are public boat landings all along the shoreline and public beach areas at Occoneechee and North End Park. Fishing lakes in this area include **Gaston Lake**, **Buggs Island Lake**, **Nottoway Lake**, **Briery Creek Lake**, and **Brunswick Lake**.

Call Game and Inland Fisheries, 804/367-1000, for regulations and boat launch information, as well as information on hunting in the area.

FOOD

While visiting the plantations on Route 5, make plans to dine at the **Coach House Tavern** at Berkeley Plantation in Charles City, 804/829-6003 or 800/291-6003. Regional fare such as rack of lamb and Chesapeake-style crab cakes are on hand in a historic setting. In Hopewell, **Kan Pai**, 5303 Oaklawn Boulevard, 804/541-8853, offers Japanese cuisine that's far better than the usual fare at national chains.

In Petersburg, **King's Barbecue**, 2910 Crater Road, 804/732-0975, is a favorite among BBQ connoisseurs with North Carolina–style fare. Try the minced BBQ plates with some melt-in-your-mouth hush puppies.

In Wakefield, the **Virginia Diner**, 120 Fleetwood Street, 757/899-3106, is a tourist landmark with famous peanut pie and country ham. Although lacking in ambiance, this is a favorite among both locals and tourists. The gift shop is a Virginia food marketplace with virtually anything peanut available.

Smithfield Station, 415 S. Church Street, Smithfield, 757/357-7700, offers home-cooked meals using fresh ingredients, Smithfield ham, and a lot of creativity.

In Emporia, **Marie's Restaurant**, 825 S. Main Street, 804/634-2213, serves up barbecue, fish, chicken, and other home-cooked specialties so well you wonder why the folks in town bother ever to cook.

LODGING

Among the James River Plantations, **Piney Grove at Southall Plantation**, 16920 Southall Plantation Lane, Charles City, 804/829-2480, is a historic inn with five rooms appointed with antiques, fireplaces, and private baths. Rates are $130 to $175, including a complete breakfast and mint julep arrival drinks.

There are a few quality hotels/motels in Southside Virginia; most are of the chain persuasion. A few fairly new ones are in Emporia near the North Carolina border along I-95. The **Best Western Emporia**, 1100 W. Atlantic Street,

APPOMATTOX COURTHOUSE NATIONAL HISTORIC PARK

The Civil War ultimately ended in the village of Appomattox. In 1935 the National Park Service suggested that the entire village be restored as a park. In 1954, the park opened appearing much as it did at the time of the surrender on April 9, 1865. It was here that General Robert E. Lee and General Ulysses S. Grant sat down to agree upon surrender terms ending the Civil War. Three days later the Confederates marched before the Union Army and layed down their weapons. For more information contact the visitor center at 804/352-8987.

804/634-3200, is less than five years old, and the **Hampton Inn Emporia**, 1207 W. Atlantic Street, 804/634-9200, is less than 10 years old. Get a list of new hotels in South Hill and Danville. In Smithfield, there are 17 nicely appointed waterfront guest rooms at **Smithfield Station**, 415 S. Church Street, 757/357-7700, including two suites.

CAMPING

Campgrounds in the region include **Americamps Lake Gaston**, 409 Americamps Drive, Bracey, 804/636-2668, which features 275 sites with water and electric hookups, snack bar, boat ramp, camp store, marina, showers, playground, and planned activities; **Yogi Bear's Jellystone Campground**, U.S. 301, 804/634-3115, near Emporia, also offers campsites with hookups and basic amenities like dump station, showers, and laundry; **Occoneechee State Park**, 804/374-2210, in the Lake Gaston area, offers camping, boat launching, and picnicking among other amenities.

9

SOUTHWEST VIRGINIA

The region of Virginia that makes up the state's western tip is mountainous and pastoral. Here, people still know how to cane a chair and clog to bluegrass music. The few major cities sprung up as coal and railroad towns. The landscape probably appears much like it did when Daniel Boone pursued new territory and cut the Wilderness Trail. Besides boasting Virginia's highest peak, Mount Rogers, the region is also home to gorgeous streams, rapids, cliffs, and terrain that are just waiting for some adventurous spirit to conquer them.

Throughout Virginia's Wild West, you'll find small towns with general stores selling ice cold pop and local crafts. The residents want you to learn about the pioneer spirit that built the region and set the pace for further exploration of the country. Many area parks have pioneer exhibits, and throughout the year special events in the region are filled with century-old music and traditions.

A PERFECT DAY IN SOUTHWEST VIRGINIA

Start your day at the Historic Crab Orchard Museum & Pioneer Park in Tazewell County. Then take Route 460 to Route 61 to Burke's Garden for dramatic mountain views and shopping for wonderful Amish baked goods and local produce. Continue up Route 61 north to U.S. 77 South. Stop at Big Walker Lookout for more spectacular scenery. Continue on U.S. 77 South to I-81 North to Newbern to visit the Wilderness Road Regional Museum and learn

SOUTHWEST VIRGINIA

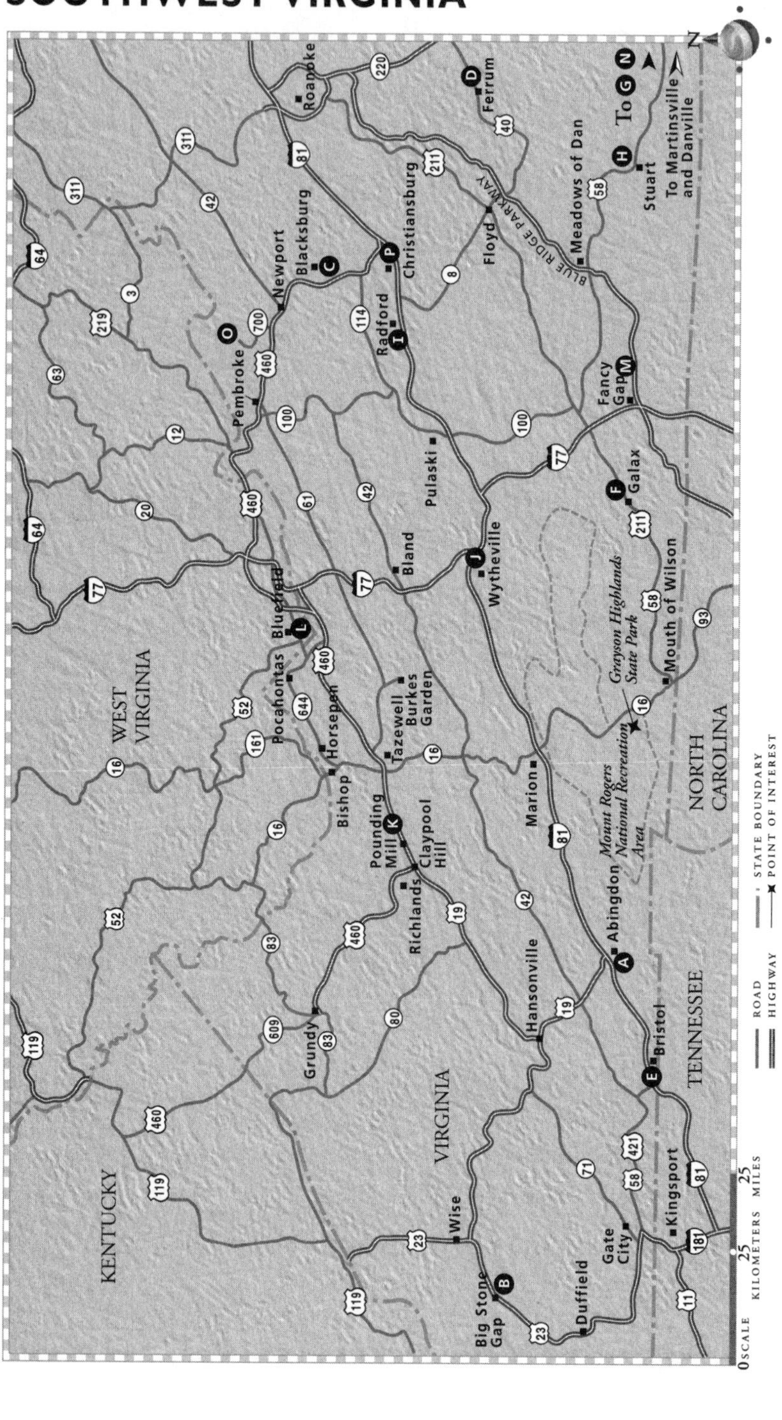

about America's early explorers and their quest to discover a new frontier west of the rugged mountains. Continue north on I-81 to Radford for an unforgettable evening of inspiration at *The Long Way Home* outdoor historical drama.

SIGHTSEEING HIGHLIGHTS
★★★★ ABINGDON VISITORS CENTER
335 Cummings St., Abingdon, 800/435-3440
The town of Abingdon (incorporated in 1778) is an arts hub for the region with the renowned Barter Theatre and a series of galleries and arts centers. The **Virginia Highlands Festival** draws more than 200,000 people every August to see the region's best arts and crafts, music and food. The more-than-65-year-old **Barter Theatre**, P.O. Box 867, 540/628-3991, (recently restored) began as a showplace, and during Depression days it bartered food to actors for their salaries. Over the years legendary actors such as Gregory Peck and Patricia Neal have graced the stage as up-and-coming performers. Today, productions here range from Broadway-style musicals to cutting-edge dramas to classic tried-and-true plays. Across the street from the Barter is one of Virginia's grand dame hotels, the **Martha Washington Inn** (see Lodging).

Downtown you can watch artisans at work at the **Arts Depot**,

SIGHTS
- Ⓐ Abingdon
- Ⓑ Big Stone Gap/Wise County
- Ⓒ Blacksburg
- Ⓓ Blue Ridge Institute and Farm Museum
- Ⓔ Bristol Area
- Ⓕ Galax/Old Time Fiddlers' Convention
- Ⓖ Martinsville
- Ⓗ Patrick County
- Ⓘ Radford
- Ⓐ Tazewell County
- Ⓙ Wytheville

FOOD
- Ⓔ Chops
- Ⓚ Cuz's Uptown Barbecue
- Ⓐ Hardware Company
- Ⓛ Mayflower Seafood
- Ⓖ Mutual Cafeteria
- Ⓐ Starving Artist Café
- Ⓑ Stringer's
- Ⓐ The Tavern
- Ⓔ Troutdale Dining Room
- Ⓔ The Vineyard

LODGING
- Ⓘ Allegheny Inn
- Ⓘ Best Western in Radford
- Ⓜ Doe Run Lodge
- Ⓝ House of Laird
- Ⓐ Martha Washington Inn
- Ⓞ Mountain Lake Resort
- Ⓟ Oaks Victorian Inn

CAMPING
- Ⓟ Interstate Overnight Park
- Ⓙ Wytheville KOA

Note: Items with the same letter are located in the same place.

314 Depot Square, 540/628-9091, or view exhibitions from local artists at the **William King Regional Arts Center**, 203 Academy Drive, 540/628-5005. There are also num-erous arts and crafts shops along Main Street, including the **Cave House Craft Shop**, 279 E. Main Street, 540/628-7721. You can shop till you drop at **Dixie Pottery**, 17507 Lee Highway, on U.S. 11, a 100,000-square-foot store with pottery and home accessories. (Dixie Pottery does not have a phone number.) **White's Mill**, 540/676-0285, in Abingdon, is a water-powered operational flour gristmill. Open for tours. A walking-tour brochure of the downtown historic district is available.

Southwest Highlands Gateway Visitor Center is located at Factory Merchants Mall in Fort Chiswell, Drawer B-12, Max Meadows, 800/446-9670. Appalachian Mountain Region Visitors Center, 17507 Lee Highway, Suite 2, Abingdon, 888/VAS-MTNS.

Details: *(2–4 hours)*

★★★ **BIG STONE GAP/WISE COUNTY TOURIST INFORMATION CENTER**
Gilley Ave. E., Big Stone Gap, 540/523-2060
Local resident John Fox Jr. created a dramatic story of pioneer struggles and victories. That story is played out in July and August at the *Trail of the Lonesome Pine* **Outdoor Drama**, 540/523-1235, here in Big Stone Gap. Outdoors, underneath the big wilderness sky, the outdoor play takes on more meaning, creating an uncommon experience in theater. Playwright **John Fox's home**, 17 Shoney Avenue E., 540/523-2747, is also a museum that is open for tours. **Southwest Virginia Museum**, located at West First Street, 540/523-1322, is a small museum chronicling the history of the region.
Details: *(2–4 hours)*

★★★ **DANVILLE AREA CHAMBER OF COMMERCE**
635 Main St., Danville, 804/793-5422
Perhaps the most significant reason to visit Danville is to take in the many Victorian and Edwardian mansions that make up the city's **Millionaires Row**. The prosperous tobacco planters and entrepreneurs who created today's Dan River, Inc., textile company built scores of homes along the Main Street area. A walking-tour brochure is available from the Chamber.

In the late 1850s Danville became a pioneer in the **tobacco auction** arena. Buyers using the Danville System could carefully weigh and examine the whole lot, not just see samples as before. Today visitors can watch tobacco auctions in progress mid-August through early-November, Monday through Thursday. Make every effort to do this if you are in the area during this time.

The **Danville Museum of Fine Arts**, 975 Main Street, 804/793-5644, features a nice collection of turn-of-the-century furnishings, decorative arts, and artifacts. The museum is housed in the Sutherlin Mansion. The mansion was once the home of Major William T. Sutherlin and his wife, who hosted Confederate president, Jefferson Davis, and the Confederate government during the last week of the Civil War after they had fled Richmond. Just a few blocks away is the **birthplace of Nancy Langhorne** and her sister, **Irene Langhorne Gibson** (who became known as "The Gibson Girl"). Nancy Langhorne became the first woman to sit in the British House of Commons. The house is currently undergoing restoration.

The town of Danville has recently renovated and upgraded many of its downtown historic sites (such as its 1899 train station), created a new amphitheater, renovated an 1885 Pepsi bottling building for meeting space, and created a festival area. The area undergoing significant change is called **The Crossing at the Dan** and also contains the Danville Science Center and the Danville Community Market.

Details: (2–3 hours)

★★★ THE HEART OF APPALACIA TOURISM AUTHORITY
311 Wood Ave., Big Stone Gap, 888/827-6867

Perhaps the best way to get an overview of the pioneer history of the region, is to visit the **Historic Crab Orchard Museum and Pioneer Park** off Route 19/460 in Tazewell, 540/988-6755. The museum is open Monday through Saturday 9 to 5, Sunday 1 to 5. Admission is $6 for adults and $5 for seniors. The museum chronicles the entire story of the region from prehistoric times to the present. **Burke's Garden** is a bowl-shaped indentation atop a mountain, dubbed "God's Thumbprint." It contains fertile soil attracting more than 280 residents who grow and sell their produce and baked goods here. On the Virginia/West Virginia border in Pocahontas, the **Pocahontas Exhibition Coal Mine and Museum**, 540/945-9522, allows you to view a 13-foot coal seam and take tours of a mine that operated for 73 years and produced 44 million tons of coal.

Details: (2–4 hours)

★★ BRISTOL CONVENTION AND VISITORS BUREAU
20 Volunteer Pkwy., Bristol, 423/989-4850

Bristol is partly situated in Virginia and partly in Tennessee. The town is home to a **NASCAR** speedway located off Volunteer Parkway. For the NASCAR speedway box office, call 423/764-1161.

Nearby Hiltons is the hometown of country music legends the Carter Family, and the **Carter Family Fold Music Concerts**, 540/386-9480, are presented here every Saturday night. A museum here profiles their rise to stardom on the Grand Ole Opry.

Also near Bristol, off U.S. 23, is **Natural Tunnel State Park**, 540/940-2674. The nature-carved tunnel is 850 feet long with an overlook 300 feet high. In Nickelsville, along Highway 71, Bush Mill is a restored and fully operational gristmill built in the late 1890s.

In nearby Gate City, the **Homeplace Mountain Farm Museum**, Route 4, 540/386-2465, is another recreated pioneer farm.

Details: (2–4 hours)

★★ MOUNT ROGERS NATIONAL RECREATION AREA
3714 Hwy. 16, Marion County, 540/783-5196

Hungry Mother State Park, 2854 Park Boulevard, Marion, 540/783-3422, is a more-than-2,000-acre park surrounding a 108-acre lake. Virginia's highest peak is **Mount Rogers** at 5,729 feet. The mountain is the site of a park offering unbelievable views, picnic facilities, fishing, hiking trails, and horseback riding. The **Mount Rogers High Country Outdoor Center**, P.O. Box 151, 540/677-3900, offers horse and wagon rides for a unique way to see the park.

Details: *(3 hours)*

★★ **PATRICK COUNTY CHAMBER OF COMMERCE**
138 S. Main St., Stuart, 540/694-6012
One of the most photographed gristmills in the country is located
along the Blue Ridge Parkway at **Mabry Mill**, 266 Mabry Mill Road,
SE, in Meadows of Dan, 540/952-2947. The working water-powered
mill is gorgeous regardless of the season, and especially picturesque
during peak fall foliage. Also in Meadows of Dan, there is a wonderful
winery offering tours, tastings, and great food—**Chateau Morris-
ette Winery and Restaurant**, 287 Winery Road, SW, 540/593-
2865. **Nancy's Homemade Fudge**, on Route 795, 540/952-2112,
is also located here—you may have seen the sweet stuff at shops
throughout the state or at craft sales. Confederate general J.E.B.
Stuart's home, called **Laurel Fork**, is located in Patrick County, and
there are a number of other historical buildings and landmark in Stuart.
Tobacco magnate, R.J. Reynold's restored nineteenth-century home,
Reynolds Homestead, 540/694-7181, is open for tours April
through October. And NASCAR fans may also be interested in the

GALAX OLD TIME FIDDLERS' CONVENTION

Wood Brothers Race Shop and Museum, 21 Peformance Drive, in Stewart, 540/694-2121. Two of Virginia's nine covered bridges in the county. **Jack's Creek Bridge** was built in 1914 (off Route 618) and the **Bob White Bridge** was built in 1922 (1½ miles south of Route 8 to Route 618 to Route 869). Just west of the Patrick County line off U.S. 58 is the town of Laurel Fork.

Details: (2–4 hours)

★★ RADFORD

This small college town, home to Radford University, is home to the region's other great outdoor drama, ***The Long Way Home***. The play depicts the capture and escape of pioneer Mary Draper Ingles and another woman by Indians in 1755. Ingles and her traveling companion escaped and made their way back from Kentucky by following the rivers home through some of the most rugged and then-unexplored terrain in North America.

Details: The Long Way Home *Outdoor Historical Drama, Radford, 540/639-0679. Mid-June–Aug. $10 adults, $9 seniors, $5 children ages 12 and under. (2–4 hours)*

★ BLACKSBURG REGIONAL CHAMBER OF COMMERCE
1995 S. Main St., Ste. 901, Blacksburg, 540/552-4061

Blacksburg is primarily a college town. It is home to **Virginia Polytechnic Institute** (Virginia Tech), 540/231-6000, whose student population supports many good restaurants and shops.

Also in Blacksburg, located on campus, is the **Virginia Museum of Natural History**, 540/231-3001, and an eighteenth-century pioneer home open for tours, **Smithfield Plantation**, 1000 Smithfield Plantation Road, 540/231-3947.

Details: (1–3 hours)

★ BLUE RIDGE INSTITUTE AND FARM MUSEUM
Ferrum College, Rte. 40, Ferrum, 540/365-4416

The institute and museum are located in **Ferrum**, on the small college campus of Ferrum College. The museum contains an 1800 pioneer farmstead and displays various folklife exhibits throughout the year.

Details: (1–2 hours)

★ MARTINSVILLE CHAMBER OF COMMERCE
115 Broad St., Martinsville, 540/632-6401

Situated near the North Carolina border, Martinsville is probably best known for its NASCAR speedway. The small furniture-milling town is also home to the **Virginia Museum of Natural History**, 1001 Douglas Avenue, 540/666-8600, a unique research museum with seven scientists on staff. Exhibits reflect the research that is going on at the facility. Especially interesting are the *Rock Hall of Fame*, an *Age of Reptiles* exhibit, and an *Age of Mammals* exhibit.

Details: *(1 hour)*

★ **WYTHEVILLE CONVENTION AND VISITORS BUREAU**
150 E. Monroe St., Wytheville, 540/223-3355
The town of Wytheville, south of Radford, features the mountaintop overlook at **Big Walker Lookout** (U.S. 52 North)—3,405 feet and quite spectacular. The observation tower also has a dining area and souvenir shop.

Details: *(3 hours)*

FITNESS AND RECREATION

As you'd expect the region's rugged terrain provides an excellent backdrop for camping, hiking, fishing, hunting, rafting/canoeing/kayaking, nature spotting, and more. White-water rafting is available through outfitters on the **Russell Fork River**, 540/835-9544. **Jefferson National Forest**, 110 Southpark Drive, Blacksburg, 540/552-4641, contains some of Virginia's most spectacular waterfalls, camping sites, hiking trails, fishing, hunting, wildlife, and more. The many fishing options include trout fishing at **Crooked Creek**, 540/236-6391; the **John Flannagan Dam and Reservoir**, 540/835-9544; **Fairy Stone State Park**, 540/930-2424; **Lake Keokee**, 540/328-2931; **Hungry Mother State Park**, 540/783-3422, in Saltville at the **Clinch Mountain Wildlife Management Area**; and at **Wallens Creek**, 540/346-4191, which also has catfish.

At **Claytor Lake**, near Radford, you can rent cabins, camp, fish, and rent boats to explore the 4,5000-acre lake, 4400 State Park Road, Dublin, Virginia 24084, 540/674-5492. There are some great bike trails at **Lebanon**, 504/889-8041; and challenging hiking and biking at **Mount Rogers National Recreation Area**, 540/783-5196; **Pinnacles of Dan** in the Dan River gorge; **Virginia Creeper Trail** near Abingdon, 540/676-2281; and **Flag Rock Recreation Area** in Norton, 540/679-0754.

Breaks Interstate Park, 540/865-4413, on the Virginia/Kentucky border, contains a 1,600-foot canyon called "the Grand Canyon of the South."

Overlooks include views of the gorge, rock formations, a cave, and springs.

Grayson Highlands State Park, 540/579-7092, offers camping, hiking, picnic facilities, and interpretive programs.

FOOD

Perhaps the most notable local joint is **Cuz's Uptown Barbecue**, 540/964-9014, in Pounding Mill (Tazewell County off U.S. 460 not far from the Crab Orchard Museum). What started as a little barbecue place with five tables in 1979 is now a legend with more than 100 seats in a barn and serving anywhere from 500 to 600 people on a Saturday night. There is great barbecue, enormously thick steaks, fresh seafood, and melt-in-your-mouth smoked prime rib— also Asian-influenced foods, quail and other game, and more than 20 kinds of beer. The decor is in-your-face-tacky and there's live bluegrass on weekends. The place has gotten so famous that folks travel here from several hours away, and certain coal executives have been known to helicopter in.

The Tavern, 222 E. Main Street, 540/628-1116, in Abingdon, is a fully restored 1779 stagecoach stop serving great American cuisine in atmospheric surroundings. Also in Abingdon, two other fine places to grab a bite are at the **Starving Artist Café**, 134 Wall Street, 540/628-8445, and the **Hardware Company**, 260 W. Main Street, 540/628-1111.

In Bristol, **Chops**, 3005 Linden Drive, 540/466-4900, serves hearty entrées including savory pork chops. The four-star **Troutdale Dining Room**, 412 Sixth Street, 423/968-9099, features consistently excellent continental cuisine. For great Italian food, **The Vineyard**, 603 Gate City Highway, 540/466-4244, is your best bet.

In Bluefield, **Mayflower Seafood** on Hockman Pike, 540/322-4578, is one of the few places to get good seafood in the region.

In Big Stone Gap, families and folks who like country cooking will like the buffet at **Stringer's**, 412 E. Fifth Street, 540/523-5388, and at **Mutual Cafeteria**, 314 Wood Avenue East, 540/523-1123, which is similar to an old Woolworth's cafeteria.

LODGING

The most distinguished hotel in the region is undoubtedly the **Martha Washington Inn**, 150 W. Main Street, 540/628-3161, in Abingdon. The small but stately hotel is an unmistakable landmark in an otherwise rustic and pioneer-influenced region. The original portion of the inn is the center building, which was built as a private residence, but was sold in 1858 to become Martha Washington College (a prestigious women's school). During the Civil War, it served as a military hospital, and in 1935 it opened as a hotel. The inn's public rooms are furnished with fine antiques, wallpaper, and oriental carpets. An $8-million renovation was undertaken in 1984 and the public and guest rooms have been modernized for comfort, but are not quite as spit-and-polished as other grand Virginia hotels.

Today the hotel features 51 guest rooms and 10 suites, each one different from the next. The hotel offers 24-hour room service, turn-down service, free newspaper, overnight shoe shine, valet parking, laundry service, dry cleaning, and babysitting service. The dining room, with its Sunday champagne brunch, is a mainstay of social gatherings for the town. Just some of the many ghost stories associated with "The Martha" include a riderless horse, strains of a violin, and reappearing bloodstains. Rates average $149.

Anyone who had the time of their life watching the movie *Dirty Dancing*, will recognize **Mountain Lake Resort**, State Route 700, 800/828-0490. The natural lake and hotel is surrounded by 2,600 acres of forest. The resort is very family-oriented with carriage and sleigh rides, boating, swimming, beach area, sauna, whirlpool, and tennis. Rooms are $130 to $250.

Doe Run Lodge, Milepost 189, Blue Ridge Parkway, Fancy Gap, 800/325-M189, offers chalet-style accommodations and activities for lovers of the great outdoors. The resort has a golf course, tennis court, fishing, bird hunting, hiking, restaurant, and live entertainment on the weekends. Rates are $95 to $130.

For chain-dependent folks, the **Best Western in Radford**, I-81, Exit 109, Radford, 800/628-1955, is 10 years old and contains an indoor pool, sauna, in-room coffee makers, and a full-service restaurant.

Several great bed-and-breakfast inns in the region include the **Oaks Victorian Inn**, 311 E. Main Street, in Christiansburg, 540/381-1500, with rates of $115 to $150; the super fancy **House of Laird**, in Chatham, 804/432-2523; and the **Allegheny Inn**, 1123 Grove Avenue, in Radford, 540/731-4466, known for its great food.

CAMPING

Two commercial campgrounds in the region include the **Interstate Overnight Park**, 2705 Roanoke Street, in Christiansburg, 540/382-1554, and the **Wytheville KOA**, Route 2, Box 122, 540/228-2601. Interstate offers spectacular campsites atop the Allegheny Mountains with a laundry center, showers, and water/sewer hookups. The Wytheville KOA has campsites, cabins, petting zoo, playground, and pool.

NIGHTLIFE

Nightlife options include college-oriented clubs or country and Western spots. The region is home to the famous Carter family, so bluegrass "is king" here. Your best luck for hearing some legendary bluegrass music include the **Virginia-Kentucky Opry**, 724 Park Avenue, Norton, 540/679-1901; the **Carter Family Fold**, A.P. Carter Highway, Hiltons, 540/386-6054; the **Friday Nite Jamboree**, 206 Main Street, Floyd, 540/745-4563; **Cuz's**, off U.S. 460, Tazewell County; and **Country Cabin**, Wise, 540/328-8108 or 540/679-2632.

PERFORMING ARTS

The region's premier theater stage is located in Abingdon at the **Barter Theatre**, 133 W. Main Street, 540/628-3991. The theater underwent a $1.7-million renovation in 1996, and today it seats 500 in its main space. The theater presents everything from drama to comedy to musicals year-round.

10
CHARLOTTESVILLE

So much of Charlottesville's identity is tied to Thomas Jefferson. Jefferson called the area home and built his pièce de résistance on a hillside overlooking the town. He founded the University of Virginia here in 1817. Signs of his influence can be seen everywhere here—from lots of neoclassical architecture to street and business names. Charlottesville is located in Albemarle County, which was founded in 1744. Charlottesville, named after Queen Charlotte, became the county seat in 1762, (but not incorporated as a city until 1888). Modern Charlottesville is a mixture of college town, preserved historic site, and residential base for the wealthy and the horsey set. The city is charming, yet sophisticated, with a variety of great restaurants, many bed-and-breakfast inns, two resort hotels in the area, and shopping at many antique and specialty shops.

The Historic Court Square downtown features an eighteenth-century courthouse which was used during its time as a jail, pillory, and whipping post. Surrounding the courthouse are public buildings that were erected around it during the early nineteenth century.

In addition to its historic sites, the Charlottesville area is home to a long list of wineries, the Virginia Discovery Museum (hands-on science museum for kids), and even the unlikely Beatles Museum (the only registered Beatles Museum and gift shop in America). Charlottesville is also considered "horse country." Drive along Route 22 near Keswick and you'll pass some of the most beautiful horse farms and estates in the nation. In September, extravagant tailgate parties are a highlight of Virginia's premier steeplechase horse racing event, the Foxfield Races.

A PERFECT DAY IN CHARLOTTESVILLE

Tour Thomas Jefferson's mountaintop creation, Monticello. Then tour Ash Lawn-Highland and have lunch at Michie Tavern. Tour the University of Virginia campus. Shop along Charlottesville's Downtown Mall for antiques and other special finds. End your day by having dinner in fine English style at Keswick or by the fire at Prospect Hill.

CHARLOTTESVILLE SIGHTSEEING HIGHLIGHTS
★★★★ MONTICELLO
State Rte. 53, (I-64 to Rte. 20 South for a ½-mile, then

CHARLOTTESVILLE

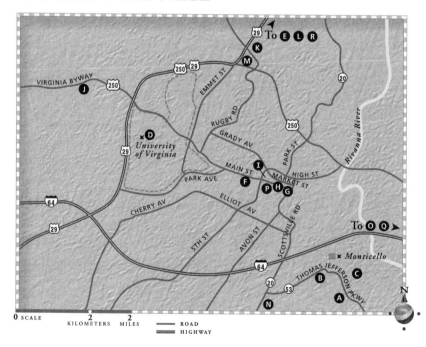

**east on Rte. 53 to the Monticello Visitor Center)
804/984-9822 or 804/984-9800**

Few historical homes in America rival the significance and sheer architectural splendor of Thomas Jefferson's magnum opus in the hills of the Blue Ridge Mountains. Jefferson was only 14 years old when he inherited from his father the 5,000 acres of land on which Monticello is located. He would spend the rest of his lifetime planning, designing, changing, and cultivating the center of his private world—his paradise outside of his role in politics and foreign affairs.

The exterior appearance of the house, with its domed roof and Roman columns, conveys his love of neoclassical architecture and his rejection of the traditional Georgian-style homes, which were so popular in Virginia at the time. He began construction of Monticello in 1770; it was not completed until 1809, after numerous renovations and additions by Jefferson, however. His finished masterpiece, as well as the estate's many outbuildings and grounds, has been pristinely restored.

Guided tours leave from a visitors center that contains the exhibition *Thomas Jefferson at Monticello*. Before or after the tours you can peruse the large collection of personal artifacts and architectural drawings/models and view a short film here. You then travel two miles aboard a tram to Monticello, where you can tour the house, grounds, and dependencies.

Although the main house contains 26 rooms, tours only take you through 10 rooms on the first floor due to fire and safety regulations. Rooms contain many of Jefferson's personal possessions. From the entry hall to Jefferson's bedroom, you can see an amazing collection of fine American and European antiques, as well as furnishings designed by Jefferson and made right on the premises. There is an

SIGHTS
- **Ⓐ** Ash Lawn-Highland
- **Ⓑ** Historic Michie Tavern
- **Ⓒ** Monticello
- **Ⓓ** University of Virginia (UVA)

FOOD
- **Ⓔ** Bavarian Chef
- **Ⓕ** Blue Ridge Brewing Company
- **Ⓖ** C&O Restaurant
- **Ⓗ** Hardware Store
- **Ⓘ** L'Avventura

LODGING
- **Ⓙ** Boar's Head Inn
- **Ⓚ** Courtyard by Marriott
- **Ⓛ** DoubleTree
- **Ⓜ** Hampton Inn
- **Ⓝ** Inn at Monticello
- **Ⓞ** Keswick Hall
- **Ⓟ** The Omni
- **Ⓠ** Prospect Hill Plantation Inn
- **Ⓡ** Silver Thatch Inn

enormous art collection and museum-quality artifacts, including many from the Western exploration of Lewis and Clark, which Jefferson sponsored as president.

The estate's dependencies include buildings associated with the operation of the house and farm (weaving, carpentry, etc.), stables, carriage bays, ice house, kitchen, and slave quarters. There were nearly 135 slaves working on the plantation. The graveyard, located at Monticello, was laid out in 1773 and continues to be a burial ground for Jefferson's descendants. Jefferson, who died at Monticello in 1826, is buried in the cemetery.

Jefferson's love of gardening and wine-making is evident when you tour the grounds of the estate. Intrigued by horticulture, Jefferson experimented at Monticello with numerous flowers, fruits, vegetables, and wines. The gardens and vineyards are cultivated today, and vegetables harvested here are given to Monticello employees. In the vegetable garden is a lovely pavilion where Jefferson often sat to relax and read. Jefferson was an American pioneer of wine making. The grapes harvested from the two vineyards here are used today to make wine under the Jefferson label. (The **Jefferson Winery** is located just two miles east of Monticello. Tours are available.)

Details: *Tours depart daily Mar–Oct 8–5, Nov–Feb 9–4:30; garden tours Apr–Oct daily 9:15–4:15 every hour. $9 adults, $5 children ages 6–11. A film,* Thomas Jefferson: The Pursuit of Liberty, *is shown daily on the hour June 15–Labor Day; 11 a.m. and 2 p.m. during the remainder of the year. (3–4 hours)*

★★★★ UNIVERSITY OF VIRGINIA (UVA)
804/924-3239

Thomas Jefferson designed and built the Academical Village at the University of Virginia. The area at UVA now known as "The Lawn" is much as it was during Jefferson's time, (except for the blue jean– and Nike-clad student body). Founded in 1817, Jefferson's university features a trademark neoclassical Rotunda, which connects by colonnade to pavilions and gardens on either side. The original university buildings were voted by the American Institute of Architects as the most significant architectural work in the nation. Tours of the historic buildings give visitors an understanding of Jeffersonian philosophies on education and higher learning. Tours are given by a student guide service that has a unique perspective on Mr. Jefferson and the ideals on which he based this institution.

PRESIDENT'S PASS

A President's Pass ticket is available offering discounted admission for touring Monticello, Ash Lawn-Highland, and Michie Tavern for $15.50 per person. Contact the visitors bureau ahead of time or stop by the Charlottesville Visitors Center, Route 20 South, Charlottesville, Virginia, 804/293-6789. It is open November through February daily 9 to 5, March through October 9 to 5:30.

Also on campus is the **Bayly Art Museum**, Rugby Road, 540/924-3592, which houses a permanent collection of European and American paintings, sculpture, prints, and photographs, as well as Asian, American Indian, African, and pre-Columbian artifacts.

> **Details:** *Tours Feb–Nov daily 10 a.m., 11 a.m., 2 p.m., 3 p.m., and 4 p.m. Free. (1–1½ hours)*

★★★ HISTORIC MICHIE TAVERN
683 Thomas Jefferson Pkwy., 804/977-1234

No visit to Monticello and Ash Lawn are complete without dining in colonial style at Michie Tavern. The 1784 tavern has been restored to its former glory and offers tours through the original building and its outbuildings. The inviting white-frame tavern and lovely adjacent **Meadow Run Grist Mill** greets diners who can play time traveler. Inside, costumed guides allow you to experience eighteenth-century social life by learning period dances and tasting age-old ale recipes in authentic tankards. Costumed hostesses serve a colonial-style buffet lunch in Michie's original tavern, called the Ordinary. A wine museum is located upstairs over the grist mill.

> **Details:** *Daily 9–5. Dining hours 11:30–3. Tours are $6 adults, $5.50 seniors/students/military, $2 children ages 6–11. Lunch $9.95 adults, $4.95 children. (1½ hours)*

★★ ASH LAWN-HIGHLAND
James Monroe Pkwy., I-64, Exit 121, 804/293-9539

Jefferson's neighbor was friend and fifth U.S. president James Monroe. Monroe picked the site because of its proximity to his friend and fellow statesman. Ash Lawn is a simpler white-frame farmhouse situated on

535 spectacular acres. It offers you a glimpse of plantation life in the nineteenth century with a working farm, craft demonstrations, children's games, farm animals, and tours of the home furnished with the Monroe family's personal possessions. Kids will enjoy watching the costumed interpreters and seeing the variety of animals on the grounds.

The plantation is the site of numerous special events and concerts during the year. The **Ash Lawn-Highland Summer Festival** presents classical music in the boxwood gardens from June to August. Fourth of July weekend, Ash Lawn comes to life with more than 50 costumed interpreters, soldiers, musicians, and craft demonstrators. Various winery tours are also offered to groups in conjunction with plantation tours.

Details: Mar–Oct daily 9–6, Nov–Feb daily 10–5. $7 adults, $6.50 seniors, $4 children ages 6–11. (45 minutes)

FITNESS AND RECREATION

Two great golf resorts in the area include **Wintergreen Resort**, 804/325-2200, which offers an outstanding golf school and great courses, and **Keswick**, 804/979-4440, which offers a peaceful setting with no waits, no crowds, and unbelievable scenery—it feels like your own private golf course.

FOOD

The **C&O Restaurant**, 515 Water Street, 804/971-7044, serves first-rate cuisine in either formal or informal settings depending on which dining room you choose. The menu offers exquisitely prepared French cuisine. Make your reservations far in advance.

Another delight with international flavor is **L'Avventura**, 220 W. Market Street, 804/977-1912, serving country Italian cuisine like penne pasta with walnut sauce and spaghetti with oregano and cherry tomatoes.

North of Charlottesville, the **Bavarian Chef**, on Route 29, Madison, 540/948-6505, is a truly outstanding German restaurant. Traditional dishes are served up here in huge portions. The sauerbraten and strudels are fantastic.

Families will enjoy the **Hardware Store**, 316 E. Main Street, 800/426-6001, in Charlottesville's Downtown Mall. The festival restaurant serves great sandwiches, burgers, and pasta. Another casual setting is the **Blue Ridge Brewing Company**, W. Main Street, 804/977-0017, with homemade American dishes and beer.

LODGING

Keswick Hall, 701 Club Drive, Keswick, 804/979-4440, 800/ASHLEY-I, is one of Virginia's most glorious hotels. When Lord Bernard Ashley (former husband of retail maven Laura Ashley) began Ashley House Hotels, he wanted his guests to feel as though were being hosted in private estates. His three properties include a castle in Wales, a waterfront inn in St. Michaels, Maryland, and this gem near Charlottesville. There is no front desk, no busy lobby, and absolutely no tipping. Instead, when you enter the sumptuous Keswick Hall you are greeted by someone who, by no accident, resembles the house staff of a glorious private mansion and calls you by name.

Throughout the house you'll find bowls of fresh fruit and fully stocked bars especially placed for you to help yourself. Each guest room has an individual theme carried out in its decor. The music room has antique prints of instruments on the wall, for example. Some rooms have private terraces and whirlpool tubs. One suite is stocked with antique books and contains a formal dining room (Margaret Thatcher stayed here). Other rooms are almost contemporary in feel—like the one Katie Couric stayed in with its pale gray walls and white furnishings. Amenities include an elegant restaurant serving breakfast and dinner, a café/grill near the spa area, and an uncrowded golf course. The spa contains an indoor/outdoor swimming pool, workout facilities, masseuse, saunas, and hot tubs. High tea is served every afternoon with a delectable assortment of scones, pastries, and hors d'oeuvres. Rates for such opulence don't come cheap, at $250 to $595.

The Charlottesville area's other highly rated resort is the **Boar's Head Inn**, Route 250 West, 800/476-1988. The old Virginia hunt club–influenced Boar's Head features well-appointed rooms with resort amenities such as a fitness center, spa, great golfing, and a restaurant serving traditional dishes. One of the most beautiful ways to see the Charlottesville countryside is by taking a hot-air balloon tour from the grounds. Rates are $165 to $315.

One standout in a long list of superior Virginia country inns is **Prospect Hill Plantation Inn**, 2887 Poindexter Road (take I-64 just east of Charlottesville to Trevilions), 800/277-0844. This historic plantation contains 13 cozy, yet elegantly decorated rooms—many in private cottages that were once outbuildings and slave quarters to the original farm. Rooms contain a variety of antiques and furnishings. Some contain canopy beds and silk wallcoverings, others are more rustic with hand-hewn beds and colonial antiques. All rooms contain fireplaces with snug seating areas. The owners trained extensively in culinary schools in France, so the meals have a decidedly French slant. Breakfast here is superb (pancakes stuffed with apples and cinnamon and omelets laced with sour cream and chives). At dinner, the innkeepers ring a bell to gather their guests together for the romantic candlelit five-course dinner. Rates include breakfast and a five-course dinner at $200 to $345.

The **Inn at Monticello**, Highway 20 South, 1188 Scotsville Road, 804/979-3593, is housed in an 1800s country manor house near Monticello, with five guest rooms furnished in period antiques and reproductions. All rooms have private baths and some have working fireplaces, a private porch, or romantic four-poster draped canopy bed. The breakfast served here usually includes freshly ground hazelnut coffee, home-baked breads, and crab quiche or orange-yogurt pancakes topped with in-season berries. Rates are $125 to $145.

Another notable inn in the Charlottesville area is the **Silver Thatch Inn**, 3001 Holly Mead Drive, 804/978-4686, with its cozy rooms and atmospheric dining rooms. Rates are $135 to $160.

Charlottesville also offers modern, upscale accommodations at **The Omni**, 235 W. Main Street, 804/971-5500, near the downtown mall area with rooms averaging $139 a night; and the **Doubletree**, 2350 Seminole Trail, 804/973-2121, off Route 29 west of the city, with rooms ranging from $89 to $144.

For economical lodging, the **Courtyard by Marriott**, 638 Hillsdale Drive, Route 29 N., 804/973-7100, features large, comfortable rooms and offers a full-service restaurant, indoor pool, fitness center, and room service. Rates are $69 to $89. The **Hampton Inn**, 2035 India Road, Route 29 N., 804/978-7888, also offers nicely appointed rooms for reasonable prices. The inn has a swimming pool and offers a complimentary continental breakfast each morning. Rates average $69 per night.

SKI RESORTS

Wintergreen, P.O. Box 706, Wintergreen, 804/325-2200, is the largest and most highly lauded ski resort in the state. It offers 17 ski slopes and trails, golf, tennis, hiking, horseback riding, swimming, spa facilities, and restaurants. The resort has a lighted snowboarding park and a variety of black diamond terrain with more than 1,000 feet of vertical drop, challenging runs, steep pitches, and cruising runouts. There are group lessons for skiing and snowboarding in specially designated areas ($12 midweek, $18 weekends/holidays) and private lessons are available. Such magazines as *Family Circle* and *Better Homes and Gardens* have rated the resort "One of the Best in the Country for Families"—a new Children's Terrain Garden and activities especially designed to entertain kids are reasons why. Lodging available includes family-style mountain villas and homes, studios, and lodge suites. Night skiing is available.

MONTPELIER/ORANGE COUNTY

Montpelier, located at 11407 Constitution Highway, Montpelier Station, 540/672-2728, was the home of the fourth U.S. president and author of the Constitution, James Madison. The white-columned home sits on 2,700 acres of rolling hills, formal gardens, and forests. The house is not your typical restored historic home with recreated rooms and decor, but a museum containing exhibits pertaining to topics such as family history, plantation life, political philosophy, and Dolley Madison. High-tech audio tours are available to truly get a feel for what it was like at the mansion during Madison's time. On the grounds are many outbuildings including a blacksmith shop, an African American cemetery, and a family cemetery. The house is open daily March through December from 10 to 4, weekends January through February 10 to 4. $7.50 adults, $6.50 seniors/AAA members, $2 children ages 6 to 12.

Other intriguing sites in Orange County include the **James Madison Museum**, 129 Caroline Street, 540/672-1776, featuring county history and exhibits on James Madison (furnishings, papers, etc.); the **Exchange Hotel Civil War Museum**, 400 S. Main Street, Gordonsville, 540/832-2944, a railroad hotel used during the Civil War as a hospital, that now offers living-history tours and medical re-enactments; and **St. Thomas Episcopal Church** (1833), 119 Caroline Street, 540/672-3761, where General Robert E. Lee worshipped for a time. For more information contact the Orange County Visitors Bureau, P.O. Box 133, Orange, 540/672-1653.

NIGHTLIFE

Nighttime attractions in the college town of Charlottesville include acoustic guitar at the **Biltmore Grill**, 16 Elliewood Avenue, 804/293-6700; rock 'n' roll at **Durty Nelly's**, 2000 Jefferson Park Avenue, 804/1278; jazz at **Miller's** downtown mall, 804/971-8511; and live country music at **Katie's Country Music Restaurant**, U.S. 29 N., 804/974-6969.

During the summer months, live performances are given at **Ash Lawn-Highland** in Charlottesville in the boxwood gardens.

VINEYARDS AND WINERIES

Perhaps the best-known and highly lauded of Virginia's wineries is **Oakencroft Vineyard and Winery**, 1486 Oakencroft Lane, 804/296-4188, in Charlottesville. The medal-winning winery offers tours and tastings daily from 11 to 5. (March weekends only).

SHOPPING

The **Downtown Mall** in Charlottesville has become the center of downtown activity in recent years. Main Street has been closed off to traffic and now features unique shops, antique dealers, and interesting restaurants and clubs. One especially good place to hunt for deals is the **Greene House Shops**, in Ruckersville (15 miles north of Charlottesville on Route 29), 804/985-6053.

11
SHENANDOAH VALLEY AREA

The Blue Ridge and Allegheny Mountain ranges are some of the oldest in the country. Their soft peaks snuggle up to the Virginia sky like old friends. As you travel through the region you discover it's the simple things that take your breath away. A white clapboard church sits like a beacon in the middle of a green valley. Vibrant red barns seem perfectly placed beneath a breathtaking mountain. A sparkling stream winds its way alongside a tree-lined roadway. Virginia's mountains are havens for scenery that melts away the stresses of everyday life. Less rugged and more populated than its West Virginia neighbor, the region is for lovers of the great outdoors who still need a touch of modern convenience. Here you'll find awe-inspiring scenery a stone's throw from hotels and bed-and-breakfast inns, family-oriented ski resorts, outlet shopping, historic sites, and museums.

A PERFECT DAY IN THE SHENANDOAH VALLEY AREA

Begin your journey near Staunton and take I-81 north to Shenandoah National Park. Take time to visit the New Market Battlefield. Spend the rest of the day enjoying scenery in the park and end the day on Hawksbill Mountain for dramatic views. Naturally, autumn offers the most colorful views, but the region is spectacular during any season.

SHENANDOAH VALLEY

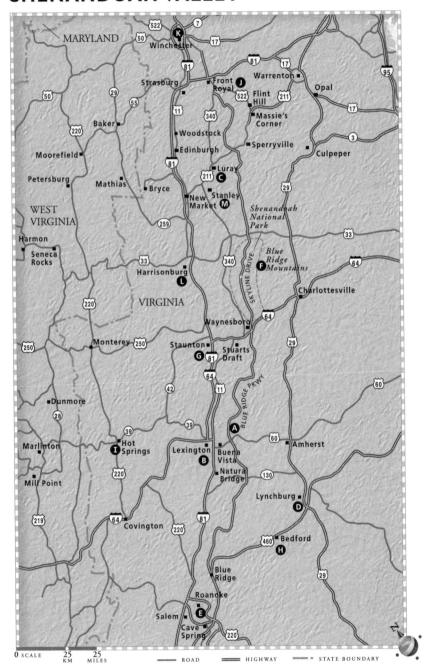

SIGHTSEEING HIGHLIGHTS

★★★★ BLUE RIDGE PARKWAY
2551 Mountain View Rd., Vinton, 540/857-2213
This famous scenic roadway extends 469 miles along the crests of the southern Appalachians, and links **Shenandoah National Park** and the **Great Smoky Mountains National Park**. Running north to south in Virginia, the parkway begins near Waynesboro and runs through Buena Vista, George Washington National Forest, east of Roanoke, past Mabry Mill, and exits Virginia's southern border east of Galax. Wildlife along the parkway include raccoon, opossum, chipmunk, skunk, fox, groundhog, whitetail deer, and black bear. The maximum speed on the parkway is 45 MPH.
Details: (half day)

★★★★ LURAY CAVERNS
P.O. Box 748, Luray, 540/743-6551
The largest and most popular caverns in Virginia are Luray Caverns with their enormous rock formations and famous organ. The ancient stone formations take on a variety of shapes, from majestic to whimsical. The U.S. Natural Landmark has an impressive scale—10-story-high rooms—as well as underground lakes and pools. Other

SIGHTS
- Ⓐ Blue Ridge Parkway
- Ⓑ Lexington/Rockbridge County
- Ⓒ Luray Caverns
- Ⓓ Lynchburg
- Ⓐ Natural Bridge/Natural Bridge Caverns
- Ⓔ Roanoke
- Ⓕ Shenandoah National Park/Skyline Park
- Ⓖ Staunton
- Ⓗ Thomas Jefferson's Poplar Forest/Bedford

FOOD
- Ⓝ The Homestead
- Ⓘ Inn at Little Washington
- Ⓘ Sam Snead's Tavern
- Ⓚ Violina

LODGING
- Ⓛ Days Inn
- Ⓘ The Homestead
- Ⓔ Hotel Roanoke
- Ⓙ Inn at Little Washington
- Ⓜ Jordon Hollow Farm Inn
- Ⓛ Shoney's Inn

CAMPING
- Ⓕ Dundo
- Ⓑ Lake A. Willis Robertson Recreation Area
- Ⓕ Shenandoah National Park

Note: Items with the same letter are located in the same place.

impressive caverns include **Dixie Caverns**, 5753 W. Main Street, 540/380-2085; **Endless Caverns** in New Market, 540/896-CAVE; **Shenandoah Caverns**, off of I-81, 540/477-3115; and **Skyline Caverns**, on U.S. 340, 800/296-4545.

Details: *Mar–May 9–6, Jun–Labor Day 9–7. $13 adults, $6 children 7–13. (2 hours)*

★★★★ NATURAL BRIDGE/NATURAL BRIDGE CAVERNS
P.O. Box 57, U.S. 11 and Rte. 130 (I-81 Exits 175 and 180) 800/533-1410 or 540/291-2121

Once a sacred native Indian site, Natural Bridge is today a retreat and vacation destination surrounding the famous rock formation. The bridge is believed to have been formed 100 million years ago when a waterfall flowing over the bridge washed away the limestone leaving sinks (a hole in the earth created by water flow) and resulting in one of the Seven Modern Wonders of the World. The Indian explanation for the bridge tells of the Monocan Indians in hot pursuit from the Shawnee and Powhatan tribes. The Monocans fled through the forest and came to 200-foot canyon with no way to cross. They called upon the Great Spirit to save them, and magically a stone bridge appeared. The bridge was deeded by George III to Thomas Jefferson in 1774. George Washington formally surveyed the bridge and his initials are in the southeast stone wall. The bridge is approximately 90 feet long, 150 feet wide at one end, and 50 feet wide at another.

Numerous hiking trails around the bridge past Saltpeter Cave, the Lost River, Natural Bridge Caverns, and Cathedral Wall offer breathtaking views. After dark, the bridge is illuminated to the strains of music and the Biblical story of creation. Look for the naturally sculpted figures of an alligator, lion, eagle, and Biblical characters. Also on site is an inn and conference center, a 170-item wax museum, and amenities such as tennis courts, swimming pools, miniature golf, and restaurants.

Details: *Natural Bridge daily 8–9, nighttime drama 9 p.m. $8 adults, $5 children ages 6–15. Natural caverns daily 10–5. $7 adults, $3.50 children; combination ticket for Natural Bridge and Caverns is $12 adults, $5.50 children. (2–4 hours)*

★★★★ SHENANDOAH NATIONAL PARK/SKYLINE DRIVE
Shenandoah National Park Headquarters, 3655 U.S. Hwy. 211 E., Luray, 540/999-3500

One of Virginia's most beautiful national parks is located north of Waynesboro along the Shenandoah River to Front Royal. Running through the length of the park is Skyline Drive. The area was designated as a park in 1926 by congress and was dedicated in 1936 to Franklin D. Roosevelt, who began the practice of allowing an overused area to return to a natural state.

Today more than 95 percent of the park is covered by forests with approximately 100 species of trees. Wildlife here includes bobcat, deer, bear, chipmunk, groundhog, turkey, ruffed grouse, woodpeckers, barred owl, timber rattlesnakes, and copperhead snakes. At any time of year there is something to see here, from wildflowers in spring to brilliant foliage in the fall (peak usually October 10 to 25). The ridges and valleys between Skyline Drive and the park boundaries offer up wonderful discoveries like sparkling mountain streams and cascading waterfalls. The headquarters for the park is located three miles west of Thornton Gap and four miles east of Luray on U.S. 211. You can pick up brochures, wildlife information, and backcountry passes at this location. Park visitors centers are open April through October and are located at Milepost 4.6 (Dickey Ridge) and Milepost 51 (Byrd). These visitors centers offer information and souvenirs.

Skyline Drive connects directly with the 469-mile Blue Ridge Parkway. Some of the highlights on Skyline Drive include the highest peak on the drive (Skyland, 3,680 feet), Mary's Rock Tunnel, Dark Hollow Falls, and Whiteoak Canyon's six waterfalls.

Details: Mon–Fri 9–5. Free. (4 hours)

★★★ LEXINGTON/ROCKBRIDGE COUNTY VISITORS CENTER
106 E. Washington St., 540/463-3777

Lexington is home to one of America's most prestigious military schools and the state's premier equestrian facility. **Virginia Military Institute**, founded in 1839, is the nation's oldest state-supported military college. There is also the **Washington and Lee University**, founded in 1749. The Lee Chapel on campus is the site of Robert E. Lee's grave. The school is a National Historic Landmark.

Other major historic sites in town include **General Thomas "Stonewall" Jackson's pre-Civil War home**, 8 E. Washington Street, and the **Stonewall Jackson Memorial Cemetery**, S.

Main Street, which contains the burial places of Jackson, his family, and more than 100 Confederate veterans.

Also in Lexington is the **Virginia Horse Center**, a year-round center for horse-related shows, auctions, educational clinics, and an annual horse festival.

Details: *The visitor center is open daily 9–5 (half day)*

★★★ ROANOKE VALLEY CONVENTION AND VISITORS BUREAU
Marketplace Center, 114 Market St., 540/342-6025

The Shenandoah region's largest city is a commercially successful business center featuring all the amenities of larger cities but with small town appeal. More than 270,000 residents live in and around the city that owes its early establishment to salt marshes. Originally named Big Lick, Roanoke was renamed in 1882 when the railroads brought new business and visitors to the region. Downtown is a growing modern area with a restored **Farmer's Market** (the oldest continuously operated in the state), museums, and an art center.

Center in the Square is an award-winning center for cultural arts housing the **Art Museum of Western Virginia**, 540/342-5760; the **History Museum of Western Virginia**, 540/342-5770; **Mill Mountain Theatre**, 540/342-5740; and the **Science Museum of Western Virginia/Hopkins Planetarium**, 540/342-5710.

Also downtown, **Virginia Museum of Transportation**, 303 Norfolk Avenue, SW, 540/961-1185, features steam locomotives, antique cars, carriages, buses, trolleys, and a model of a miniature traveling circus. Roanoke's innovative **Explore Park**, Blue Ridge Parkway, 540/427-1800, is an 1,100-acre attraction unlike any other. Here you can explore three areas depicting life in Virginia from A.D. 1,000 to 1850. Historic interpreters bring to life different aspects of Virginia's history—from Native American villages to pioneer farm life. The park is designed to be a sort of multi-dimensional Colonial Williamsburg. Kids will enjoy the **Mill Mountain Zoo**, Walnut Avenue to Parkway Spur Road, 540/343-3241, for close-up looks at 45 species of exotic and native animals. Animals at the zoo include a Siberian tiger, snow leopards, prairie dogs, lions, red pandas, reptiles, and more.

Details: *The visitor center is open daily 9–5. (3–4 hours)*

★★★ STAUNTON-AUGUSTA TRAVEL INFORMATION CENTER
1250 Richmond Rd., I-81 Exit 222, 800/332-5219 or 540/332-3972

Country music fans know that Staunton is home to the Statler Brothers, harmony legends. Don't miss the **Statler Complex**, 501 Thornrose Avenue, 540/885-7297, which features a mini-muse-um that displays Statler Brothers' memorabilia. Staunton is also home to another impressive Virginia attraction, the **Museum of American Frontier Culture**, 1250 Richmond Road, 540/332-7850. This living history museum brings to life pioneer farms of various cultures. The early eighteenth-century German and Irish, seventeenth-century English, and middle-nineteenth-century American farms feature authentic barns, homes, costumed interpreters displaying early trades, gardening techniques, agricultural methods, and traditions of their respective cultures.

Visitors to Roanoke will find it impossible to miss the 90-foot-tall illuminated star sitting atop Mill Mountain, giving the city its nickname, "The Star City of the South."

Staunton is also the birthplace of **Woodrow Wilson**, 18-24 N. Coalter Street, 703/885-0897. Wilson's birthplace home is open for tours as is a wonderful museum depicting his life through artifacts and photos.

Details: *The visitor center is open daily 9–5. (4 hours)*

★ LYNCHBURG VISITORS CENTER
12th and Church Sts., 800/732-5821

Lynchburg is a quiet, sleepy college town that is home to **Lynchburg College**, **Sweet Briar College**, and **Jerry Fallwell's Liberty University**. The town's beginnings are tied to a ferry house built by John Lynch in 1757. It was Lynch who built the nation's first tobacco warehouse in 1791. The city was used during the Civil War as a supply center for the Confederacy and was the site of the Battle of Lynchburg in 1864. Among the most notable attractions here is the **Maier Museum of Art**, showing nineteenth- and twentieth-century American paintings by artists like Mary Cassatt, Georgia O'Keefe, and Jamie Wyeth.

Details: *The visitor center is open daily 9–5. (half day)*

★ THOMAS JEFFERSON'S POPLAR FOREST/BEDFORD
804/525-1806

Located near the towns of Bedford and Lynchurg, Poplar Forest is an octagonal house designed by Thomas Jefferson. The extraordinary home was designed as a year-round retreat when Jefferson needed to get away from the activity at Monticello. Restoration of the house has recently been completed and there is archaeological work being undertaken on the grounds. Bedford is a slice of small town rural America with a historic downtown area, restored homes, and Smith Mountain Lake nearby.

   Details: *Poplar Forest is open Apr–Nov Wed–Sun 10–4. $6 adults, $5.50 for seniors, $3 for grounds only, $1 for youth. (half day)*

FITNESS AND RECREATION

Canoing, kayaking, and rafting are offered by various outfitters along the Shenandoah, Maury, and James Rivers. Two popular outfitters are **Shenandoah River Trips**, 800/RAPIDS 1, and the **Front Royal Canoe Company**, 800/270-8808. For a complete list of outfitters, call 888/42-FLOAT. Tubing is also available on the Shenandoah National River through **Shenandoah River Outfitters, Inc.**, 703/743-4159. Tube trips travel four miles and take four to five hours. Great fishing can be found at many lakes, streams, and rivers in the area. Some of the most popular fishing lakes are **Smith Mountain Lake, Claytor Lake**, and **Lake Moomaw**. All three lakes also feature public beach areas. Fishing for trout in mountain streams is allowed in **Shenandoah National Park**. Pick up a list of available streams from park visitors centers or the headquarters.

   Major parks in the region include **Douthat State Park**, 540/862-8100; **George Washington National Forest**, 540/265-5100; **Jefferson National Forest**, 540/265-5100; and **Shenandoah National Park**, 540/999-2266. **Shenandoah National Park** contains 280 square miles of outdoor paradise including hiking, camping, cabin rentals, educational programs, and horseback riding. There are more than 500 miles of trails in the park. Detailed hiking maps are available at park visitors centers and headquarters. An additional hiking and wildlife-spotting venue, more than 535 miles of the 2,144-mile **Appalachian Trail** runs through Virginia, 304/535-6331.

   You won't find flat, unimaginative golf courses here. **The Homestead**, U.S. 220 N., Hot Springs, 800/838-1766 or 540/839-7785, has one of the most challenging mountain courses in the country. Cited by *Golf Digest* as

"One of America's 100 Greatest Golf Courses," the Cascades course at The Homestead is the top-rated course in the state. **Bryce Resort**, 540/856-2121 or 800/821-1444, Exit 273 off Route 263 in Basye, also features great golf on its championship 18-hole, par 71 course. The resort is a four-season property with swimming, horseback riding, boating, tennis, grass skiing, miniature golf, biking, and snow skiing.

FOOD

While many of the choices in the Shenandoah region are home-cookin' spots (no complaints, really), the region also boasts some of the country's finest restaurants in lush settings. The **Inn at Little Washington**, Middle and Main Streets, Washington, 540/675-3800, just a few miles south of Front Royal and west of Warrenton, has been hailed as one of America's best restaurants and inns by virtually every major publication. Dining here is like a grand event—it's meant to be savored and reserved for special occasions. Each plate brought to the table is like an individual work of art prompting *oohs* and *aahs* from diners. Dishes change constantly, but some examples are veal sweetbreads sauted with crabmeat, gulf shrimp and shellfish sauce, braised local rabbit with chanterelle mushrooms and homemade angel hair pasta, and barbecued grilled boneless rack of lamb in a pecan crust with sweet potatoes two ways. For dessert, have a warm apple walnut tart with cinnamon ice cream or swans of white chocolate mousse swimming in a pool of passion fruit purée.

Many people have underlying culinary motives for choosing to stay at **The Homestead**, U.S. 220 N., Hot Springs, 540/839-1766. Its cuisine is legendary, along with the sumptuous surroundings. The main dining room has offered continental cuisine under the direction of the resort's executive chef, Albert Schnarwyler, for 35 years. For less formal dining, **Sam Snead's Tavern**, Hot Spings, 540/839-7666, (affiliated with The Homestead), offers the same quality menu with high quality beef, fresh trout, and more.

Violina, 181 N. Loudoun Street, Winchester, 540/667-8006, is a gem of an Italian restaurant in Old Town. Here, diners can enjoy elegant and romantic strains from violinists while enjoying authentic northern Italian cuisine.

LODGING

Virginia's grandest hotel is **The Homestead**, U.S. 220 N., 800/838-1766, in Hot Springs. The refined brick resort hotel is reminiscent of an age of civility and refinement. The property has recently undergone a much-needed massive restoration of the public rooms, as well as 200 guest rooms. Because of these efforts, the elegant lady is looking more beautiful than ever. The Men's Bathhouse, thought to have been used and designed by Thomas Jefferson, was built in 1761 and is the oldest spa structure in America. The first hotel here was built in 1766 by Lieutenant Thomas Bullitt and called The Homestead. In 1890 the hotel was bought by M.E. Ingalls to transform it into a complete resort. The current brick building was built in 1902 with additions added in 1903, 1914, and 1929.

The elegant Georgian-style resort is sumptuously decorated in calming muted colors and rich jewel tones. It has 517 guest rooms, including 89 suites—some with sun porches and fireplaces. Ten dining facilities, from casual to fine dining, are on site. A shopping area with upscale boutiques including new clothing and children's apparel retailers. Activities at the resort include world-class golf, tennis, skiing, ice skating, skeet and trap shooting, a movie theater, sporting clays, mountain biking, hiking/walking trails, indoor/outdoor swimming, water aerobics, horseback and carriage rides, bowling, and a fitness center. The spa offers full-service amenities including mineral baths, massages, loofah scrubs, herbal wraps, aromatherapy, and combination baths. Rates based on the Modified American Plan (includes breakfast and dinner) range from $137 per person on weekends (January through March) to $187 per person on weekends (May through October) for a standard room. Rates climb to $597 per person for super-deluxe suites.

North of Charlottesville, near Luray, the **Jordon Hollow Farm Inn**, 326 Hawksbill Park Road, Stanley, 540/778-2285, has snug rooms (many with gas fireplaces) and a complete menagerie of farm animals. Horseback riding is available for spectacular views, and the resident cats' sneaking in to your room are part of the package. Rates are $110 to $154.

Perhaps the most famous of all the inns in the state is the **Inn at Little Washington**, Middle and Main Streets, Washington, 540/675-3800. Each sumptuous room is furnished with fine antiques, oriental rugs, opulent beds, and exquisite architectural details. Some rooms have in-room Jacuzzi tubs and balconies overlooking a romantic garden. Also one of the most expensive inns around, double rooms are $240 to $450 a night, including dinner and breakfast.

For modern hotel conveniences, but with a historic, old hotel flair, the **Hotel Roanoke**, 110 Shenandoah Avenue, Roanoke, 540/985-5900, has been restored to sheer perfection. The Doubletree-owned property features elegant interiors inside an English Tudor–style, grand building with nicely decorated rooms and all the amenities of a modern hotel. The average room rate here is $99.

In Harrisonburg, economical options include the top-rated **Days Inn**, 1131 Forest Hill Road, 540/433-9353, located right across from James Madison University. It offers an indoor pool, continental breakfast, Jacuzzi, and privileges at a nearby Nautilus facility. **Shoney's Inn**, 45 Burgess Road, 540/433-6089, features a Jacuzzi, an indoor heated pool, and an exercise room.

CAMPING

Campsites are located at all major parks in the region. If you're interested in traditional campsites head to the **Lake A. Willis Robertson Recreation Area**, in Lexington, 540/463-4164.

In **Shenandoah National Park**, campgrounds are located at Milepost 51 (Big Meadows), Milepost 57.5 (Lewis Mountain), and Milepost 79.5 (Loft Mountain). These are more primitive sites, and hookups are not offered. Call ahead to make reservations, especially during peak visitation seasons in the summer and fall.

Also in the park, the **Dundo** group campground is available for organized groups by reservation and features running water and pit toilets. Backcountry camping is allowed at no charge throughout the park; campers must obtain a permit by mail or in person at entrance stations, visitor centers, and the park headquarters, however.

PERFORMING ARTS

The **Mill Mountain Theatre**, located in downtown Roanoke's Center on the Square, 540/342-5740, presents stage standards and new drama and musicals. Also in Roanoke, community theater productions are presented by **Showtimers**, Route 419, 540/774-2660.

In Lexington, the **Theater at Lime Kiln**, 14 S. Randolph Street, 540/463-7088, offers outdoor stage productions and concerts at stone ruins. Also in Lexington, the **Lenfest Center for Performing Arts**, Washington and Lee University, 540/463-8000, features two theaters for live concerts and plays at a modern arts center.

VINEYARDS AND WINERIES

Prince Michel Vineyards, U.S. 29, in Culpeper, 800/869-8242, is a great choice with some wonderful wines to taste and a lovely winery operation.

Other wineries worth trying in the region include **Barboursville Vineyard** and **Winery**, Orange County, 540/832-3824; **Jefferson Vineyards**, Charlottesville, 804/977-3042; **Stonewall Vineyards**, Concord, 804/993-2185; **Shenandoah Vineyards**, Edinburg, 540/984-8699; **Dominion Wine Cellar**, Culpeper, 540/825-8772; and **Naked Mountain Vineyard and Winery**, Markham, 540/364-1609.

SHOPPING

Outlet lovers will be thrilled to find the **Waynesboro Outlet Village**, 601 Shenandoah Village Drive, 540/949-5000, with famous brands at discount prices. Antique stores are plentiful throughout the area offering everything from rare, high-priced pieces to bargain-hunters' delights. The area is also a haven for buying goods from craftspeople practicing centuries-old techniques and skills. At the **Mountainman Woodshop and Caldwell Mountain Copper Kettles, Buckets and Other Vessels** shops, Eagle Rock (on U.S. 220 between Roanoke and Clifton Forge), the rare arts of woodworking and metal-working provide one-of-a-kind buys. For information on ordering products, or if you want to stop by to watch these nearly lost arts in the works, call 540/864-2197.

Shenandoah National Forest Area

Begin in **Winchester**, known as the apple capital of Virginia and the oldest town west of the Blue Ridge Mountains. Winchester has a nice restored eighteenth- and nineteenth-century district featuring a host of historic sites. They include a log cabin used by George Washington as a headquarters in 1755 and 1756, a 1754 restored former Quaker meeting house, and a Gothic-style house used by General Stonewall Jackson during the Civil War. Winchester is also the home town of music legend Patsy Cline. There are items relating to the singer at the Winchester Visitor Center. On a kooky note, **Dinosaur Land, Inc.**, may interest the younger set with its replicas of prehistoric creatures. Winchester is the site of the annual **Apple Blossom Festival**—one of Virginia's most festive special events.

From Winchester head to **Front Royal** and resist the impulse to dart onto the famous **Skyline Drive**. By taking a loop from this northern portion of the Shenandoah National Forest, you will get a flavor of the region's towns and culture, as well as be able to stop at a wide variety of attractions including vineyards, caverns, Civil War sites, and scenic vistas. Take Route 619 to

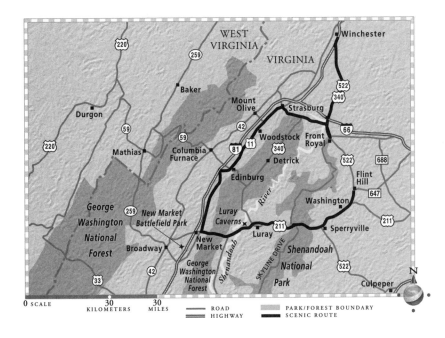

the mountain town of **Strasburg** for some great antique shops and galleries. The small, but respectable **Museum of American Presidents**, 130 N. Massanutten Street, 540/465-5999, contains many original historical documents, artifacts, portraits, and items relating to various U.S. presidents. The **Strasburg Emporium**, 150 N. Massanutten Street, 540/465-3711, features more than 100 antique dealers.

Then take Route 11 south to **Woodstock** where you can view the seven bends of the Shenandoah River from Massanutten Mountain on Woodstock Tower. Continue on through **Edinburgh** and then head to **New Market** to learn more about the Civil War. New Market is the site of the famous Civil War battle fought by Virginia Military Institute cadets against Union troops. The **Hall of Valor Museum**, New Market, 540/740-3101, open daily 9 to 5, is a comprehensive telling of the Civil War story. It has a nineteenth-century farm complex on site and offers walking tours of the battlefield park. Admission is $5 adults, $2 children ages six to 15. The **Bedrooms of America Museum and Pottery**, 9386 Congress Street, New Market, 540/740-3512, features 11 antique bedrooms from varying periods housed in a restored eighteenth-century building.

From New Market take Route 211 east to **Luray**, continue on to **Sperryville** for more great antiques and the popular **Faith Mountain Co.** retail store, located on Route 522/211, 540/987-8521. Continue on 211 to the pristine village of Washington and other great nearby mountain towns like **Massie's Corner** and **Flint Hill**. There are numerous vineyards in the region including the marvelous **Oasis Vineyards** in Hume. This route will take three to four hours driving time.

12
WEST VIRGINIA'S
EASTERN PANHANDLE

The rolling hills of West Virginia's Eastern Panhandle are often enjoyed as a retreat from the frenetic pace of Washington, D.C., and Baltimore only a short drive away. Nestled in the green landscape are some great bed-and-breakfasts, spas, Civil War attractions, and a horse racing center. Sandwiched between Maryland and Virginia, the region has a loyal following of visitors who consider it their special place to get away from it all.

It was here at Harpers Ferry that abolitionist John Brown raided a U.S. arsenal, which began a chain of events culminating in the Civil War. The town is still much as it was in the nineteenth century with cobblestone streets and original buildings. A few miles away, the atmosphere changes dramatically in Charles Town as the fast pace of horse racing pervades the scene. Even more exhilarating, Class II and III rapids are available for the close-to-D.C. rafting excursions. Further into the hills, warm springs famed for relaxation and healing waters feed the amenities at affordable spas and resorts. Combine it all and the Eastern Panhandle is truly therapy—for heart and soul.

A PERFECT DAY IN WEST VIRGINIA'S
EASTERN PANHANDLE

Begin your day in Harper's Ferry touring the National Historical Park. Drive to Martinsburg for shopping at great antique shops, outlets, and specialty stores.

End your day by checking into one of the many spas in Berkeley Springs. Schedule some pampering in the afternoon—a massage, golf round, facial or bath in the healing spring waters.

SIGHTSEEING HIGHLIGHTS

★★★★ HARPERS FERRY NATIONAL HISTORICAL PARK (HARPERS FERRY)
P.O. Box 65, Harpers Ferry, Virginia, 304/535-6298

Abolitionist John Brown brought the slavery issue to the forefront of American politics when he led a slave uprising in 1859. His raid on the U.S. arsenal here is credited with the beginning of a series of events leading up to the Civil War. Harpers Ferry is one of the most important African American sites in the country. During the war, Harpers Ferry was regarded by Union troops as a key for protecting the nation's capital. More than 12,000 Union soldiers were captured here

EASTERN PANHANDLE

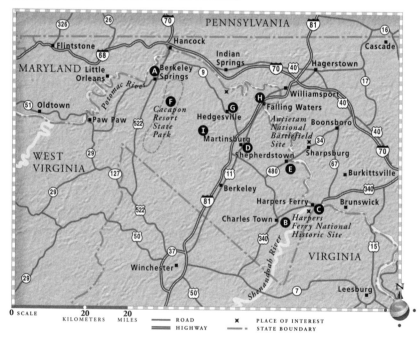

in 1861 by Stonewall Jackson in the days before Antietam. The streets of the historic town have been fully restored offering one of the most meaningful Civil War interpretation experiences you'll find. There are six paths of history to explore here—John Brown, Industry, Civil War, African American History, Environmental History, and Transportation. Nearby is an overlook offering panoramic views of three states.

Details: *Daily 9–5 . $5 per vehicle, $4 for adults. (2–4 hours)*

★★★★ MARTINSBURG

Martinsburg/Berkeley County Convention and Visitors Bureau, 198 Viking Way, 304/264-8801

The atmospheric town of Martinsburg is packed with historic buildings and sites, but is probably known today for being a shopping center for the region. The town, which was laid out in 1773, offers a walking-tour brochure of the downtown and other historic districts. Some important sites include the **Belle Boyd House**, 126 Race Street, 304/267-4713, which was once the home of a Confederate spy, and **Boydville** mansion, 10 Park Lake Acres, 304/263-1448, which was spared by President Lincoln during the Civil War. The **Adam Stephen House**, John Street, 304/267-4434, is a 1770 colonial stone mansion which has been restored to its original glory. Adam Stephen was a Scottish settler who accepted a pioneer military post which led him to Martinsburg. He provided leadership during the French and Indian War and was a major-general during the

---

SIGHTS

Ⓐ Berkeley Springs/Bath
Ⓑ Charles Town
Ⓒ Harpers Ferry National Historical Park (Harpers Ferry)
Ⓓ Martinsburg
Ⓔ Shepherdstown

FOOD

Ⓐ Appalachian Restaurant
Ⓔ Bavarian Inn and Lodge
Ⓓ Boomtown Restaurant

FOOD *(continued)*

Ⓓ Fannie's
Ⓐ Glens Country Inn Estate
Ⓓ Historic Market House Grill
Ⓓ Peppermill Restaurant
Ⓐ Tari's

LODGING

Ⓔ Bavarian Inn and Lodge
Ⓕ Cacapon Resort State Park

LODGING *(continued)*

Ⓐ Coolfont Spectrum Spa, Resort and Conference Center
Ⓖ The Woods

CAMPING

Ⓗ Falling Waters Campsite
Ⓖ Harpers Ferry KOA
Ⓖ Lazy A Campground
Ⓘ Nahkeeta Campsite

Note: Items with the same letter are located in the same place.

American Revolution. Stephen made a speech at the Virginia Constitutional Convention in 1788 that influenced delegates to ratify the U.S. Constitution. An adjacent museum, the Triple Brick Museum, houses memorabilia and artifacts from Martinsburg's history. The **Tuscarora Church**, 2335 Tuscarora Pike, 304/263-4579, established by Scots-Irish Presbyterians in 1740, still contains the pegs on which worshippers hung their guns. The **Apollo Civic Theater**, 128 E. Martin Street, 304/263-6766, has been in operation since 1913. Originally a vaudeville theater, it now houses a stage theater group, ballroom, and art studios. Two of the most popular tours in the area are the **Martinsburg Ghost Tours**, which feature graveyards on Fridays and buildings/historic areas on Saturdays.

Details: (2–4 hours)

★★★ BERKELEY SPRINGS/BATH COUNTY CONVENTION AND VISITORS BUREAU
304 Fairfax St., 304/264-8801

The soothing springs of Berkeley Springs were discovered by George Washington in 1748. Since then the town his family established, known as Bath (still the town's official name), and the surrounding area, is a haven for spas and resorts. Resorts/parks include the nationally acclaimed **Coolfont Spectrum Spa**, **Resort and Conference Center**, 1777 Cold Run Valley Road, 304/258-4500; **Cacapon Resort State Park**, 304/258-1022; **Berkeley Springs State Park**, 304/258-2711; and **The Woods**, Mountain Lake Road, in Hedgesville, 304/754-7977.

In addition, a very strong arts community is here. The new **Ice House Art Center**, 313 Independence Street, 304/258-2300, is home to top name concerts, galleries, community theater, and more.

Details: (2–4 hours)

★★ CHARLES TOWN
200 E. Washington St., 304/725-2055

This horse racing town was founded in 1786 and named for George Washington's brother, Charles.

In addition to its principal equestrian attraction, the town has some wonderful nineteenth-century historic buildings and sites. John Brown was tried here in 1859 at the Jefferson County courthouse, and a nearby museum houses artifacts from the area including Brown's gun and the wagon that carried him to his execution. At the

Charles Town Race Track, bettors and nonbettors enjoy both day and night racing.
Details: (2 hours)

★★ **SHEPHERDSTOWN VISITORS CENTER**
102 E. German St., 304/876-2786
Shepherdstown is one of the oldest towns in West Virginia. The town, founded in the 1730s, is utterly charming with wooden storefronts, bed-and-breakfast inns, and a popular art house cinema which is home to a **Contemporary American Theater Festival**. Shepherdstown was also the site of Civil War activity, due to its location along the Potomac and its proximity to Antietam in Maryland (one of the Civil War's bloodiest battles). The inventor of the steamboat, James Rumsey, was from this town, and a museum, 304/876-0910, features a replica of the first steamboat. A **Farmer's Market**, located on King Street, sells plants, herbs, perennials, vegetables, free-range eggs, baked goods, jams, and jellies.
Details: (2 hours)

FITNESS AND RECREATION

The region is home to milder white water than other areas in the state, so it may appeal to more families and less experienced thrill seekers. **Blue Ridge Outfitters**, 304/725-3444, and **River and Trail Outfitters**, 301/695-5177, offer Class II and III trips along the Potomac River out of Harpers Ferry. Hikers can traverse the **Appalachian Trail**, which runs through the region at Harpers Ferry. Other hiking opportunities are available at the **C&O Canal National Historical Park**. The former towpath trail runs 184.5 miles from Washington, D.C., to Cumberland, Maryland. Camping, fishing, and boating is also available at designated areas along the canal trail. The **Big Blue Trail** in Morgan County offers 66 miles of wildnerness trail. Bass fishing is plentiful near Charles Town on the **Shenandoah River**. The **Sleepy Creek Wildlife Management Area**, located on the Morgan and Berkeley County line, contains 22,000 acres of forest for hunting, 75 primitive campsites, and a 200-acre lake for boating and fishing.

Great golf can be had at **Cacapon State Park**, Route 1, Box 301, Berkeley Springs, 800/CALL WVA, with its Robert Trent Jones–designed course; the **Stonebridge Golf Club**, 304/263-GOLF, in Martinsburg; and the **Woods Resort**, Mountain Lake Road, 800/248-2222, in Hedgesville. Horseback riding is available at the **Homestead Farms Riding Stable** in Martinsburg, 304/267-6584. Cacapon State Park offers 6,000 acres of scenery, lodging, hiking and bridle trails, and a road climb that is 1,400 feet to the summit of Cacapon Mountain. The resort park also has swimming, fishing for bass and trout, boat rentals, tennis courts, volleyball, and cross-country skiing trails.

Unique to the area are spa facilities offered at one area park, **Berkeley Springs State Park**, 121 S. Washington Street, Berkeley Springs, 304/258-2711 or 800/CALL WVA. Here, you can enjoy the healing warm waters of Berkeley Springs without staying in a resort. The baths consist of two types, the Roman baths or conventional bathtub facilities. The tiled Roman baths are sunken pools containing 750 gallons of the 74.3-degree springwater. Five tubs and 13 Roman baths are in the park. The state park also offers various forms of physiotherapy including infrared heat, steam cabinets, and massage. Guests to the park must make reservations in advance. A deposit is required (Visa, MasterCard, and Diners Club are accepted.)

FOOD

One of the finest inns in the state is also one of the best dining spots around. The **Bavarian Inn and Lodge**, Route 480, Shepherdstown, 304/876-2551, offers hearty German and American cuisine. The Game Festival is a favorite occasion with roast pheasant, venison, rabbit, and wild boar on the menu. In Martinsburg, the **Peppermill Restaurant**, 200 W. Burke Street, 304/263-3986, is the fine dining establishment of choice with a varied wine list and a chef, trained at the Culinary Institute of America, who whips up fantastic prime rib, pork tenderloin in apple cider glaze, crab and corn crepes, and rock cornish hen.

For a romantic, candlelit seven-course dinner, the **Glens Country Inn Estate**, Route 2, Box 83, Berkeley Springs, 800/984-5367, serves up fancy dishes on fine china. The dinner is $35 per person.

In Berkeley Springs, reasonably priced country fare can be enjoyed at the **Appalachian Restaurant**, 209 North Washington Street, 304/258-3110. Home-cooked dishes include country ham, fresh local trout, and for the kids— a huge selection of pizzas. More innovative cuisine is available at **Tari's**, 123 N. Washington Street, Berkeley Springs, 304/258-1196. There's also a gourmet market with fresh breads, deli meats, seafood, and regional wines.

In Martinsburg, the **Boomtown Restaurant**, 522 W. King Street, 304/263-8840, the menu has definite international flair with great pasta and seafood, as well as a vegetarian menu. Some favorites include spinach-stuffed chicken breast, homemade crab cakes, and hand-cut Black Angus beef. Patrons range from dressy to casual, making families feel welcome. Housed in a historic 1852 building and decorated in fine Victorian style, the Boomtown also has outside dining in a garden with an antique goldfish pond.

Other worthwhile restaurants in Martinsburg include the **Historic Market House Grill**, 100 N. Queen Street, 304/263-7615, and **Fannie's**, 141 S. Queen Street, 304/263-1100.

LODGING

One of the most notable inns in the area is the the **Bavarian Inn and Lodge**, Route 480, Shepherdstown, 304/876-2551. The large four-star, four-diamond inn contains 72 rooms furnished with four-poster canopy beds, fireplaces, luxury baths, and balconies. The restaurant here is renowned.

The luxury of spa treatments at affordable prices can be found at the region's **Coolfont Spectrum Spa, Resort and Conference Center**, Cold Run Valley Road, 304/258-4500 or 800/296-8768, in Berkeley Springs. The famous spa features massage, facials, body wraps, mud baths, aromatherapy, reflexology, Reiki, Shiatsu, and meditation. There are fitness centers, whirlpool tubs, tennis, indoor swimming pool, hiking, fishing, boating, and special programs like smoking cessation and weight loss. Lodging includes the main lodge, chalets, cabins, and vacation homes with an average rate of $95 to $129 per person, per night, double occupancy including breakfast and dinner. Coolfont has recently added two-bedroom, two-bath chalets with two double-sized whirlpool tubs, wood-burning stove, wet bar, and spacious deck. The Tree Top Restaurant serves great healthy meals.

Cacapon Resort State Park, Route 1, Box 304, Berkeley Springs, 304/258-1022, offers accommodations in the Cacapon Lodge, in cabins, and the Old Inn. The handsome lodge is a reminder of times, not so long ago, when more families spent their summers in parks and not at big, beach resorts. The heavy, paneled lounge area has a crackling fireplace to welcome guests. The lodge has 50 simple, air-conditioned rooms with television, phone, and bath with showers. Within a short distance of the lodge is The Old Inn. Built in the 1930s by the Civilian Conservation Corps, the 11-room colonial-style inn has guest rooms with chestnut and knotty pine tongue-and-groove walls, low ceilings, stone chimneys, and wrought-iron fixtures. There are 13 standard, 11 modern, and six efficiency cabins. The modern cabins feature wood paneling, stone fireplaces, baths with showers, and kitchens. Standard cabins are log construction with no air-conditioning (open April through October). Efficiency cabins are one-room cabins with living and dining areas together in the room with beds. The efficiencies do, however, feature baths with showers and screened porches. There are full-service restaurants in both the inn and lodge. The Robert Trent Jones 18-hole golf course has rolling terrain, 72 sand traps, and some unique greens. Rates range from $60 to $115.

Another family resort is **The Woods**, P.O. Box 5, Mountain Lake Road, Hedgesville, 800/248-2222 or 304/754-7977, near Martinsburg. Golfers will especially enjoy the 27-hole course and special golf packages. The resort has two lodges and several cabins (as well as golf villas and vacation homes for rent), offering rooms ranging from $85 during the week to $135 on weekends. Cabins can be rented weekly for $850. Walden Lodge rooms have king-size beds, rustic pine furnishings, private whirlpool baths, and refrigerators. The Evergreen Lodge king or double rooms have large rooms with high ceilings, private whirlpool baths, wood-burning stoves, and refrigerators. Cabins are completely modern and feature heat/air-conditioning, wood-burning stoves, deck, two bedrooms, bath, kitchens, cable television, and phones. A Modified American Plan is available (includes complete breakfast and dinner in room rate).

CAMPING

Campsites, both primitive and modern, are abundant in the Eastern Panhandle. Near Harpers Ferry, the **Harpers Ferry KOA**, 304/535-6895 or 800/323-8899, has 257 sites (April through December) offering electricity, water, grocery store, dumping station, Olympic-size swimming pool, indoor swimming pool, game room, volleyball, horseshoes, basketball, and cabins.

In Berkeley County/Martinsburg, the largest campground is **Nahkeeta Campsite**, 304/754-3855, with 60 primitive sites, many within 100 feet of the 205-acre Sleepy Creek Lake. It has pit-type toilets and boat launching sites. **Lazy A Campground**, Hedgeville, 304/229-8185, contains 30 modern campsites with hookups and unlimited tent campsites. The amenities include hot showers, shaded picnic area, fishing and boating, and free dumping stations. **Falling Waters Campsite**, Route 2, Box 378, Falling Waters, 800/527-4902, contains 40 campsites, 10 for tents and 10 with full hookups, a bath house, and a store.

NIGHTLIFE

Locals in the region hang out at **Tari's Premier Café**, 123 N. Washington Street, 304/258-1196, a health food bistro and bar in Berkeley Springs. The restaurant has live music several nights a week.

PERFORMING ARTS

Theater and arts in the region includes live stage productions in Charles Town at the **Old Opera House Theatre**, 204 N. George Street, 304/725-4420. In

Martinsburg, the **Apollo Civic Center**, 128 E. Martin Street, 304/263-6766, presents plays, musicals, concerts, and more.

The **Contemporary American Theater Festival** is a wildly popular arts festival held in Shepherdstown every July presenting new American plays by a professional theater company. For tickets and information on plays, call 800/999-2283 or 304/876-3473.

SHOPPING

Martinsburg's shopping appeal includes two major outlet centers. The **Blue Ridge Outlet Center**, W. Stephen Street, located in restored woolen mills, contains more than 50 stores including outlets for Britches, Dooney and Bourke, Etienne Aigner, Lenox, Levi's, Polo/Ralph Lauren, and Tommy Hilfiger among others. The **Tanger Outlet Center**, W. King Street, contains factory-direct stores for Osh Kosh B'Gosh, Reebok, American Tourister, and Geoffrey Beene.

Also in Martinsburg, you'll find a variety of specialty stores selling antiques, home furnishings, arts and crafts, paintings, books, stained glass, and more. Delectable homemade ice cream is available from the **Rock Hill Creamery**, 313 South Queen Street, 304/264-2373.

In nearby Bunker Hill, at **Bunker Hill Antique Associates**, Runnymeade Road, 304/229-0709, antique hunters will find a buyers paradise at one of the top five antique centers in the country.

13
NORTHERN
WEST VIRGINIA

Northern West Virginia's location, near Ohio and Pennsylvania, make it more cosmopolitan than the state's rustic interior. The town of Wheeling has become an entertainment capital with live country music, river cruises, greyhound racing, gambling, and famous light displays during the holidays. Minutes away, there are wonderful family resorts and more outstanding West Virginia outdoor activities like white-water rafting, hiking, and skiing. Northern West Virginia is also home to many of the state's universities and schools including West Virginia University and Fairmont State.

A PERFECT DAY IN NORTHERN WEST VIRGINIA

Begin at Pricketts Fort State Park, located southwest of Morgantown. Then take I-79 north to Morrisville, Pennsylvania, and Route 21 to Moundsville to visit the largest ancient conical burial mound in the Americas. Then stop by an opulent palace that is beyond belief and tour the 1866 West Virginia Penitentiary. Take Route 2 north and spend your day in Wheeling. If it's a Saturday evening, take in a top-notch country music concert at the Capitol Music Hall. If not, take a stern-wheeler river cruise or have dinner at the lovely Oglebay Resort. Delight in the resort's magnificent gardens and buildings. If you're here during the holidays, you'l enjoy the citywide light displays.

NORTHERN WEST VIRGINIA

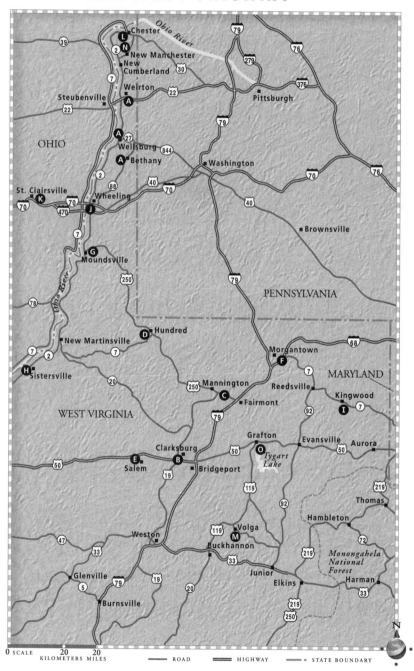

Ohio River

Chester

L
N
New Manchester
New Cumberland

39
2
7
30

Weirton
A
Steubenville
22

Pittsburgh

79
76
279
376
22

OHIO

A 27
Wellsburg
844
A Bethany

Washington

79

70
76

St. Clairsville
K
Wheeling
2
88
70
J
470

40
70
40

7

Brownsville

G
Moundsville
250

PENNSYLVANIA

79

78
Ohio River

D Hundred

New Martinsville
7
2
7

Morgantown
F
68
7

MARYLAND

H Sistersville
20

Mannington
250
C
Fairmont

Reedsville
92

Kingwood
I
7

WEST VIRGINIA
79

Grafton
O
Tygart Lake
Evansville
Aurora

Clarksburg
50
50
219

E
Salem
B
19
Bridgeport

119

92

Thomas

50

Hambleton

219

Weston
47
33

119
Volga
M
Buckhannon
33

Junior
Elkins

Monongahela National Forest
72
Harman
33

Glenville
5
79
19
20

219
250

Burnsville

N

0 SCALE   20   20
KILOMETERS   MILES

ROAD   HIGHWAY   STATE BOUNDARY

SIGHTSEEING HIGHLIGHTS

★★★★ MARSHALL COUNTY CHAMBER OF COMMERCE
522 Seventh St., Moundsville, 304/845-2773

Moundsville is named for its most famous landmark, the 69-foot-tall, 900-foot-around **Adena burial mound**, Grave Creek Mound State Park, 801 Jefferson Avenue, 304/843-1410. Built in 200 B.C., the huge mound is the largest of its kind in the Americas. Not the only unusual site in Moundsville, the **Palace of Gold**, Limestone Hill Road, 304/843-1600, is an elaborately detailed structure built by the New Vrindaban Spiritual Community. The Palace has been called "America's Taj Mahal" by the *New York Times*. The **West Virginia Penitentiary** (1866), 818 Jefferson Avenue, 304/845-6200, is an interesting and historic prison that has been restored and is open for tours. You can walk through virtually every area of the prison, including the Alamo Cell where the most vicious prisoners were kept, and view amazing murals painted by inmates.
Details: (2–4 hours)

★★★★ WHEELING CONVENTION AND VISITORS BUREAU
1401 Main St., Wheeling, 800/828-3097

Wheeling's early history was as an industrial and commercial center

---

SIGHTS
- **Ⓐ** Bethany/Wellsburg/ Weirton
- **Ⓑ** Clarksburg
- **Ⓒ** Fairmont/Mannington
- **Ⓓ** Fish Creek Covered Bridge
- **Ⓔ** Fort New Salem
- **Ⓕ** Morgantown
- **Ⓖ** Moundsville
- **Ⓗ** Sistersville
- **Ⓘ** West Virginia's Northern Railroad
- **Ⓙ** Wheeling

FOOD
- **Ⓕ** Back Bay
- **Ⓙ** Christopher's Cafeteria and Catering
- **Ⓖ** Glasshouse Grille
- **Ⓚ** Mehlman Cafeteria
- **Ⓑ** Minard's Spaghetti Inn
- **Ⓙ** Undo's
- **Ⓕ** West Virginia Brewing Co.
- **Ⓑ** Wonder Bar

LODGING
- **Ⓒ** Holiday Inn Fairmont
- **Ⓕ** Lakeview Resort and Conference Center
- **Ⓛ** Mountaineer Park and Gaming Resort
- **Ⓙ** Oglebay Resort and Conference Center

CAMPING
- **Ⓜ** Audra
- **Ⓐ** Six and Plum Campground
- **Ⓝ** Tomlinson State Parks
- **Ⓞ** Tygart

Note: Items with the same letter are located in the same place.

connecting east with west. After the Civil War, industry and business growth continued and today the city has made a mark for itself as an entertainment center.

The city's historic suspension bridge (1849) is the city's most recognizable landmark. Start your visit by stopping at **The Point Overlook Museum and Omni Center**, 989 Grandview Street, 304/232-3010, a visitors center and overlook of the area. From here, you can view two states, three counties, and 12 miles of river view.

In addition to a number of great live entertainment venues, the **Wheeling Downs Racetrack and Gaming Center**, 1 S. Stone Street, 304/232-5050, is the closest the Capital Region gets to Atlantic City–style excitement with greyhound racing, 700 video slot machines, video lottery poker, blackjack, and keno. The younger set will enjoy the *Challenger* **Learning Center**, 316 Washington Avenue, 304/243-4325, which was born out of the ill-fated *Challenger* space shuttle. The center is designed to educate and create interest in science, math, and space technology.

Kids of all ages will enjoy the **Good Children's Zoo** at Oglebay Resort, Route 88 N., 304/243-4000, which contains 65 acres of wildlife including bears, otters, bison, red wolves, ocelot, red pandas, and fish in a 3,000-gallon tank. Activities for kids include a 1 1/2-mile train ride, a hands-on Discovery Lab, theater/planetarium, and a petting zoo. The Waddington Gardens, located on the resort grounds, feature turn-of-the-century floral displays offering a different explosion of color from April through October. The **Oglebay Institute**, 1330 National Road, 304/242-7700, contains Wheeling artifacts, antiques, and art.

A **Victorian House Tour**, 800/SEE-1870, located in town, offers tours of five lovely homes all decorated in grand turn-of-the-century style. The **Eckhart House**, 810 Main Street, 304/232-5439, has "Tour, Tea and Confections" tours with an elegant Victorian buffet. The **Wymer's "General Store" Museum**, 1400 Main Street, 304/232-1810, is a collection of artifacts from Wheeling's history housed in an 1880s store. The **West Virginia Independence Hall**, 1528 Market Street, 304/238-1300, is a National Historic Landmark where West Virginia began its government after separating from Virginia after the Civil War.

Details: *(4–6 hours)*

★★★ GREATER MORGANTOWN CONVENTION AND VISITORS BUREAU

709 Beechurst Ave., Morgantown, 304/291-1354

In addition to the college, **University of West Virginia**, 304/293-0111, and its cultural arts offerings, Morgantown has a nice list of historical and cultural sites. Morgantown was a railroad boom town in the late 1800s. Of particular interest today is the **Metropolitan Theatre**, 371 High Street, 304/296-2900, (on the National Register of Historic Places), which was designed after the original Metropolitan Theatre in New York. Other particularly splendid buildings are the neoclassical **Old Post Office**, and some wonderful Queen Anne and colonial-revival mansions, especially in the post-Victorian neighborhood of **South Park**. The **Old Stone House**, 313 Chestnut Street, 304/296-7824, is one of the oldest stone dwellings in the state (circa 1795). Also notable is the **Easton Roller Mill**, 536 Harvard Avenue, 304/291-7226, with its antique steam engine, roller mills used in grinding wheat, and mill stones. As a striking contrast to the vintage architecture of the city is Morgantown's **Personal Rapid Transit System**, 304/293-5011, of above-ground streetcars which run without human operators. The computerized transit system is used primarily by students and its purpose is to serve as a national transportation research laboratory.

On the university campus, the **Cook-Hayman Pharmacy Museum**, 304/293-5101, displays antique tools, medicines, and typical nineteenth-century pharmacy furnishings. The college also features historic buildings and an acclaimed arts center, the **Creative Arts Center**, 304/293-4642, and the **West Virginia Public Theatre**, 304/598-1044. The **Core Arboretum**, 304/293-5201, is located on the Evansdale campus and offers study of a variety of species of plants, shrubs, and trees. If you have the chance, take a quick drive to the picturesque **Dent's Covered Bridge** on Highway 43 in Westover.

Details: Daily 8:30–5. (2–6 hours)

★★ MARION COUNTY CONVENTION AND VISITORS BUREAU

110 Adams St., Fairmont, 304/368-1123 or 800/834-7365

South of Morgantown, **Prickett's Fort State Park**, Route 3, Box 407, 304/363-3030, in Fairmont, is a recreated 1774 rustic log fort with living history interpreters demonstrating daily life. Here, you can watch pioneers forge metal, spin, weave, and make firearms. Other historic sites in Fairmont include the Beaux-Arts **Marion County Courthouse** (1897), 200 Jackson Street, 304/367-5400. There is also a **Miner's Memorial**, in Mary Lou Retton Park, which commemorates the 361 men who died in a 1907 mining disaster.

Details: *(2–4 hours)*

★★ FORT NEW SALEM
Salem, 304/782-5245

A 1790s Appalachian pioneer settlement has been reconstructed at Fort New Salem. Here, costumed interpreters demonstrate age-old crafts, festivals, daily life, and the practice of "putting by."

Details: *Memorial Day–Labor Day Wed–Sun 10–5. (1–2 hours)*

★★ WEST VIRGINIA'S NORTHERN RAILROAD
Kingwood, West Virginia, 800/253-1065 or 304/329-3333

This train excursion service takes travelers on a three-hour tour from Kingwood through the mountains of Preston County. The Northern Railroad also offers fall foliage tours in October.

Details: *May–Oct Sat–Sun and holidays 11 and 2; Fall foliage tours Oct noon. $12 adults, $6 children ages 3–12. (3 hours)*

★ BETHANY TOURISM
Main St., Bethany, (Bethany/Wellsburg/Weirton) 304/829-7285

Historic **Bethany College**, 800/922-7611, is located in the Scots-Irish–settled town of Bethany. Guided tours are offered for the 1793 home of the founder of the college and a striking Gothic tower completed in 1872. Nearby Wellsburg also has a historic district. Wellsburg rivaled Wheeling in commercial river travel and warehousing in the nineteenth century. The **Brooke County Historical Society Museum**, Sixth and Main Streets, 304/737-2787, houses some of the area's artifacts including furnishings, clothing, and toys. In Weirton, you can view a restored furnace (built 1790–1794), which produced cannonballs used in the War of 1812.

Details: *(1–2 hours)*

★ CLARKSBURG VISITORS BUREAU
109 Platinum Dr., Suite B, Clarksburg, 800/368-4324 or 304/842-7272

This historic town is the birthplace of **General Thomas "Stone-**

wall" Jackson. A 16-block district features restored historic buildings and homes. Nearby, the **Watters Smith Memorial State Park**, I-79, Lost Creek Exit, 304/745-3081, is a nineteenth-century farm museum that features a blacksmith's shop, bar, and smokehouse. **Philippi Covered Bridge**, U.S. 250, 304/457-3700, is the longest two-lane covered bridge still in use on a federal highway. Erected in 1852, it served as a barracks for Union troops during the first Civil War land battle in 1861.

    Details: Mon–Fri 9–5. (1–2 hours)

★ FISH CREEK COVERED BRIDGE
Route 13, Hundred

This 1881 covered bridge uses a single King Post Truss design and is 36 feet long. The bridge is located off U.S. 250 near Hundred on County 13.

    Details: (15 minutes)

★ SISTERSVILLE
800/752-4982

Located on the Ohio River, this oil and gas boom town has a nice restored historic district with Victorian buildings. The **Wells Inn**, 316 Charles Street, 304/652-1312, was built during the West Virginia oil boom of 1894 and has been elegantly refurbished.

    Details: (30 minutes)

FITNESS AND RECREATION

Some of the best white-water rafting/kayaking can be enjoyed along the **Cheat** and **Tygart Rivers**. Locals affectionately call the spring raft season, "Cheat Season." Class IV and V rapids are offered through outfitters including **American Whitewater Tours**, 800/624-8060; **Appalachian Wildwaters**, 800/624-8060; **Cheat River Outfitters**, 304/329-2024; **Laurel Highlands River Tours**, 800/472-3826; **Mountain Streams, Inc.**, 800/245-4090; and **White Water Adventurers**, 800/WWA-RAFT. The **Allegheny Trail** passes through the region making it a prime destination for hiking. Parks in the region include **Audra State Park**, Route 4, Box 564, Buckhannon, 304/457-1162, with 355 acres for swimming, hiking, picnicking, camping, and family recreation; **Cathedral State Park**, Route 1, Box 370, Aurora, 304/735-3771, with 132 acres of centuries-old forests for hiking and cross-country skiing; and **Coopers Rock State Forest**, Route 1, Box 270,

Bruceton Mills, 304/594-1651, with 12,700 acres of camping, fishing, hunting, picnic grounds, hiking trails, cross-country skiing, and amazing scenery. **Cheat Lake**, Route 12, Box 148, Morgantown, 304/291-1354, is a 1,730-acre lake with canoe, pontoon, power, and ski-boat rentals.

Tomlinson Run State Park, Box 97, in New Manchester, 304/564-3651, offers fishing, swimming, boating, camping, tennis, miniature golf, picnic areas, and a water slide. The **North Bend Rail Trail**, Harrisville, 304/643-2931, is one of the top rail trails in the country passing through quaint towns and containing 10 tunnels. Great fishing areas include **Cheat Lake**, Morgantown, 304/291-1354; **Pleasant Creek**, **Teter Creek**, Fairmont, 304/367-2720; and **Tygart Lake State Park**, Grafton, 304/265-3383; **Castlemans Run Lake**, Bethany, 304/829-7285; **Jug Wildlife Management Area**, Middlebourne, 304/420-4550; **Lewis Wetzel Wildlife Management Area**, Jacksonburg, 304/899-2233; and **Tomlinson Run State Park**, New Manchester, 304/564-3651.

Horseback riding, carriage/sleigh rides, hayrides, and overnight pack trips are offered by **Circle H Outfitters**, 304/594-3505, in Morgantown.

Golf Digest recently rated the Robert Trent Jones course at **Oglebay**, Route 88 N., 304/243-4000, as "One of America's 75 Best Public Golf Courses." The 18-hole championship course is designed to satisfy players at all levels. The Crispin Regulation Golf Course at Oglebay is also great for all player levels with 5,670 yards of play. Great golf can also be found at **Grand Vue Park**, 304/845-9810, in Moundsville.

FOOD

In Wheeling, in addition to Oglebay's, there are other notable spots to dine. **Undo's**, 1200 Market Street, 304/232-8817, is a family-owned eatery serving authentic Italian dishes. Huge portions of home-cooked food will make families happy at either **Mehlman Cafeteria**, U.S. Route 40, Clairsville, Ohio, 614/695-1000, or **Christopher's Cafeteria and Catering**, 10 Elm Grove Crossing, 304/242-4100.

The **Glasshouse Grille**, 709 Beechurst Avenue, Morgantown, 304/296-8460, serves delicious dishes like rainbow trout stuffed with crawfish dressing and smoked duck with pancetta. The restaurant is housed in the old Seneca Glass Works. Great seafood can be found at **Back Bay**, 1869 Mileground Road, Morgantown, 304/296-3027. Morgantown also has a microbrewery, the **West Virginia Brewing Co.**, 1291 University Avenue, 304/296-BREW, which offers brewery tours and serves great beers and a full lunch and dinner menu.

In Clarksburg, **Minard's Spaghetti Inn**, 813 E. Pike, 304/623-1711, has been serving up scrumptious Italian dishes and steaks since 1934. The **Wonder Bar**, Bridgeport Road, 304/622-1451, also offers quality steaks.

LODGING

Oglebay Resort and Conference Center, Route 88 N., in Wheeling, 800/624-6988, was originally the farm and summer estate of Colonel Earl W. Oglebay, a Cleveland industrialist. Oglebay later donated the farm to the city of Wheeling to use as a park and recreational area. The unique family recreational resort contains lodging, restaurants, and resort amenities including golf and tennis, a museum, meeting facilities, a small but wonderful zoo, shopping, and beautiful gardens.

During warmer months, the resort is an oasis of blooming floral creations and splashing fountains. In the winter months, Oglebay turns into a twinkling wonderland at the Festival of Lights, with its artistic light creations. Accommodations here include the Wilson Lodge with 204 comfortable rooms and amenities such as an indoor pool, Jacuzzi, and fitness center. There are also cottages for rent by the day, weekend, or week with fully equipped kitchens, large living rooms, and your choice of two to six bedrooms. The Ihlenfeld Dining Room in Wilson Lodge serves above-par American cuisine with views of the countryside. The resort also offers fishing, boating, and swimming in addition to its golf and tennis activities.

Lakeview Resort and Conference Center, 1 Lakeview Drive, Morgantown, 800/624-8300, offers resort amenities including 187 newly renovated guest rooms, 50 condominiums, two championship golf courses, and 1,729-acre Cheat Lake.

The **Mountaineer Park and Gaming Resort**, Route 2, Chester, 800/804-0468 or 304/387-2400, is located on the Northern Panhandle's northern tip. Here the resort offers video lottery and thoroughbred horse racing. The racetrack features a restaurant, accommodations, golf course, and two pools.

For affordable, family accommodations, the **Holiday Inn Fairmont**, Exit 137 off I-79 304/366-5500, has been newly renovated and features an outdoor swimming pool, restaurant, and lounge.

CAMPING

The **Six and Plum Campground**, Route 2, Box 114-8, Morgantown, 304/983-8585, features 50 campsites with boating and fishing on the

Monongahela River. Campgrounds are also located at **Tygart**, Grafton, 304/265-3383; **Audra**, Route 4, Box 564, Buckhannon, 304/457-1162; and **Tomlinson State Parks**, Box 97, New Manchester, 304/564-3651.

NIGHTLIFE

The center for musical entertainment in the state is the **Capitol Music Hall**, 1015 Main Street, in Wheeling, 304/234-2878, which has been home to the **Jamboree USA** live country music show since 1969. The Saturday night shows are broadcast live nationwide from WWVA Radio with nationally known artists. The **Victoria Vaudeville Theater**, 1228 Market Street, in Wheeling, 304/233-SING, also presents live entertainment in a mixture of country, gospel, bluegrass and fifties-style rock 'n' roll. The headline attraction is the *Memories of Elvis* extravaganza. More live music can be found in Fairmont at the **Sagebrush Round-Up**, Winfield Road, 304/366-4864.

During November and December, Wheeling is famous for its dazzling **Festival of Lights** display in the downtown area and at Oglebay Resort. Unusual light displays have a fantastical effect on the eyes at Oglebay where you can drive through a lit tunnel and see giant lit dinosaurs among other illuminated creations.

The **Wheeling Artisan Center**, 1400 Main Street, 304/232-1810, is a restored industrial building that contains a restaurant and brewery, and provides an arena for artisans to sell their crafts. The city also offers riverboat cruises aboard the **Valley Voyager** sternwheeler.

Feeling lucky? The **Wheeling Downs Racetrack and Gaming Center**, 1 S. Stone Street, Wheeling, 800/445-9475, or the **Mountaineer Gaming Park**, Route 2, Chester, 800/804-0468 or 304/387-2400, provide gaming opportunities of various types—from greyhound racing to video slot machines.

SHOPPING

The **L.G. Lamp Company**, 408 Boyers Avenue, Star City, 304/598-7558, sells hand-blown glass lamps, candy dishes, and vases. At **Brown's Creations In Clay, Inc.**, Route 10, Box 406, Morgantown, 304/296-6656, you can purchase handmade pottery and home-grown herbs. You can also buy goods made on site at the **Gentile Glass Co., Inc.**, 425 Industrial Avenue, Star City, 304/599-2750, which has an outlet shop selling specialty glass paperweights, hand-cut crystal tableware, and shades. The **Mountain People's Market Co-op**, 1400 University Avenue, Morgantown, 304/291-6131, offers natural foods, organic produce, organic bulk foods, herbs, and spices, books, candles, clothing, and more. You can bring your own containers to fill up with bulk peanut butter, oils, soy sauce, tofu, and more.

At the **Seneca Center**, 709 Beechurst Avenue, 304/291-3181, in Morgantown, a turn-of-the-century glass factory has been restored to contain upscale shops selling everything from antiques to clothing. South of Moundsville in Proctor, the **Thistle Dew Farm**, Route 89, Proctor Creek Road, 304/455-1728, sells bees-wax, honey, and other related products at a working honey farm. The **Homer Laughlin China Company**, Route 2, Newell, 304/387-1300, maker of the popular Fiesta Ware, is the largest manufacturer of dinnerware in the world.

At **Oglebay Resort and Conference Center**, Route 88 N., Wheeling, 304/243-4000, there are several upscale shops on site offering unusual goods including hand-crafted glassware at **Carriage House Glass**, 304/243-4058, holiday decorations, clothing, golf pro shop items, nature-themed items, herbs and plants, and collectibles.

14
WEST VIRGINIA HIGHLANDS

This is the West Virginia that the outdoor lover pictures in his or her mind's eye—sky-scraping peaks, rushing waterfalls, soaring cliffs, and an endless terrain of unspoiled forests. Rugged and isolated, the region contains a whopping 1.5 million acres of national parks and forests and a dozen state parks. Even the highest ranked ski resorts in the area make sure there is very little commercial presence. People often come to escape from telephones and fax machines, and to wind down. Here, they can cross-country ski, hike, or sit undisturbed by a fire in a rustic log cabin. People also come here to get an adrenaline rush—one that is achieved by rock climbing, mountain biking, and downhill skiing.

More and more families are getting back to nature as well. The Cass Scenic Railroad takes visitors up and down and around the state's second highest peak. Throughout the region there are family-oriented lodges, campsites, bed-and-breakfast inns, and cabins.

A PERFECT DAY IN THE WEST VIRGINIA HIGHLANDS

Begin at the Cranberry Glades Visitor Center and hike down to see the cranberry bogs and wildlife. Then enter the Highland Scenic Byway directly across from the entrance to Cranberry Glades. Continue north on I-219 and east onto Route 66 to the state-owned railroad town of Cass. Take a two-hour steam

WEST VIRGINIA HIGHLANDS

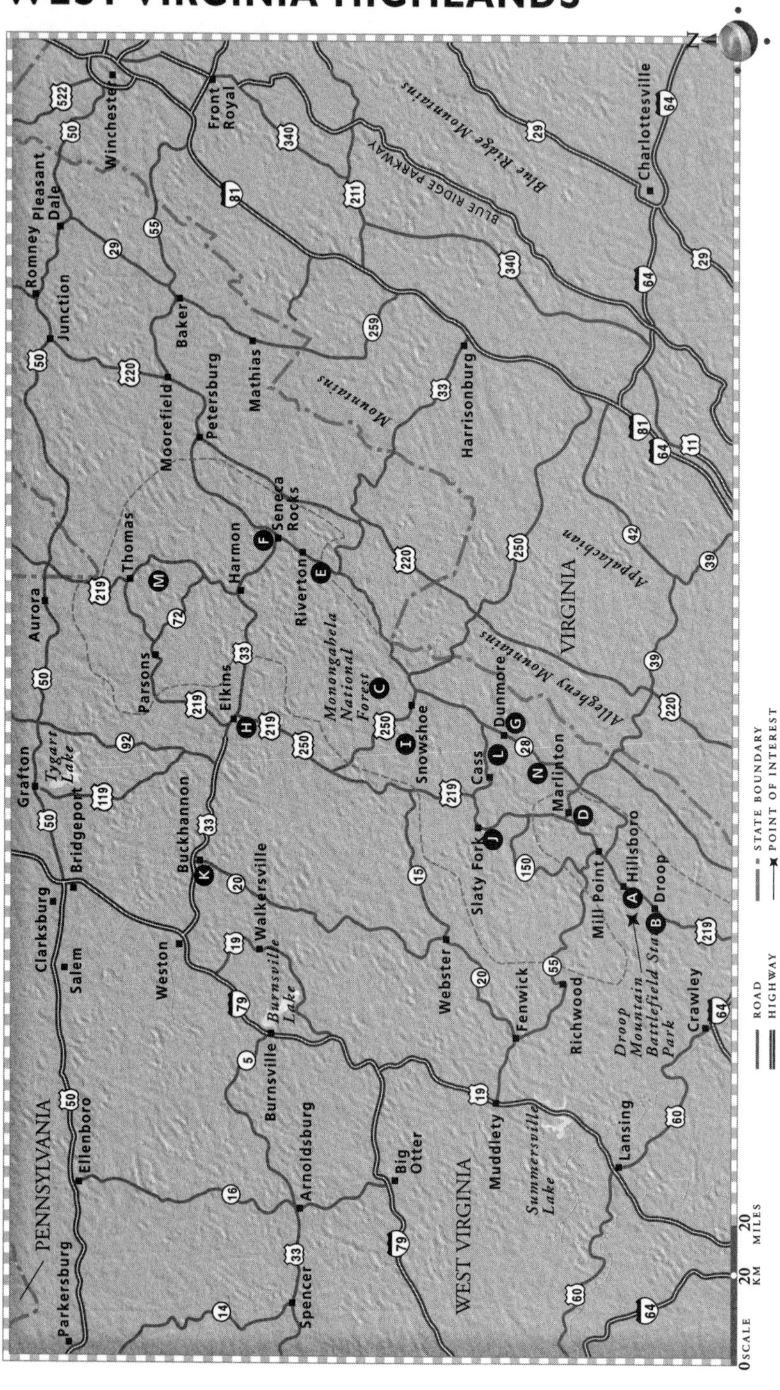

PENNSYLVANIA

WEST VIRGINIA

VIRGINIA

Parkersburg
Ellenboro
Spencer
Arnoldsburg
Big Otter
Burnsville
Burnsville Lake
Weston
Salem
Clarksburg
Grafton
Bridgeport Lake
Tygart Lake
Aurora
Thomas
Parsons
Elkins
Buckhannon
Walkersville
Webster
Muddlety
Summersville Lake
Fenwick
Richwood
Lansing
Crawley
Mill Point
Hillsboro
Droop
Droop Mountain Battlefield State Park
Slaty Fork
Cass
Marlinton
Dunmore
Snowshoe
Monongabela National Forest
Riverton
Harmon
Seneca Rocks
Petersburg
Moorefield
Baker
Mathias
Harrisonburg
Charlottesville
Junction
Romney
Pleasant Dale
Winchester
Front Royal

Blue Ridge Mountains
BLUE RIDGE PARKWAY
Mountains
Appalachian Mountains
Allegheny Mountains

A
B
C
D
E
F
G
H
I
J
K
L
M
N

SCALE
0   20   KM
0   20   MILES

STATE BOUNDARY
POINT OF INTEREST
ROAD
HIGHWAY

train ride to Whitaker Station or spend a half-day on board and travel to Bald Knob. Continue on Route 66 to the Green Bank Country Store for lunch, homemade ice cream, and browsing. Just a few miles down the road is the National Radio Astronomy Observatory where you can take a guided bus tour of one of four facilities in the world that listens for signs of life from space. Take 28 north to Seneca Rocks Park for unbelievable scenery. Retrace your route back to I-219 and head for Snowshoe for an impeccable dining experience at the Red Fox Restaurant.

SIGHTSEEING HIGHLIGHTS

★★★★ MONONGAHELA NATIONAL FOREST
Cranberry Mountain Visitor Center, Elkins, 304/636-1800
This nationally preserved forest sprawls out over 901,000 acres in the region. It is here that the state's highest peak is located, Spruce Knob, at 4,861 feet. The awe-inspiring vantage point of the surrounding forest land is accessible only by a gravel road off WV 28. Once you ascend to the top, there's an observation tower and interpretive trails. The forest also includes 121 miles of the famed Allegheny Trail, so naturally it is a favorite of hikers. **Dolly Sods** is a high plateau on Allegheny Mountain with a similar climate and plant life to Canada. The Highland Scenic Highway is a breathtaking roadway extending 43

SIGHTS
- **A** Beartown State Park
- **B** Droop Mountain Battlefield State Park
- **C** Monongahela National Forest
- **D** National Radio Astronomy Observatory
- **A** Pearl S. Buck Birthplace Museum
- **E** Seneca Caverns
- **E** Seneca Rocks
- **F** Seneca State Forest
- **G** Smoke Hole Caverns

FOOD
- **H** C.J. Maggie's American Grill
- **D** French's Diner
- **I** Red Fox Restaurant
- **J** Restaurant at Elk River
- **B** River Place Restaurant

LODGING
- **K** Deer Park Country Inn
- **L** Erehwon Cabins
- **H** Graceland Inn & Conference Center
- **D** Jerico Bed & Breakfast

CAMPING
- **M** Blackwater Falls State Park
- **N** Seneca State Forest
- **F** Yokum's Vacationland

Note: Items with the same letter are located in the same place.

miles from Richwood to Route 219. **Cranberry Glades Botanical Area** is located at the junction of Rt. 150 and Rt. 39/55 at one end of the Highland Scenic Highway. Here you can view audio-visual programs, get information, and arrange for tours of the cranberry bogs. West of the visitors center are the **Falls of Hills Creek**, accessible by a trail down a steep gorge. The series of three falls cascade 20 feet, then 45 feet, and finally 65 feet. Monongahela also contains some amazing hunting, fishing, and wilderness trails. There are few places like this left on the East Coast.

Details: Memorial Day–Labor Day daily 9–5, Jan–Apr & Nov daily 10–4, Sep–Oct Fri–Sun 9–5. (2–8 hours)

★★★★ NATIONAL RADIO ASTRONOMY OBSERVATORY
Rte. 92/28, Green Bank, northeast of Marlinton
304/456-2011

For anyone who has ever wondered about those remote observatories in the movies, this is your chance to get an up-close look. The Green Bank observatory is nestled in a valley surrounded by mountains and very few buildings, protected against unwanted, man-made interference. Once inside the observatory you discover that these telescopes, often thought to listen only for alien messages, are used annually by more than 250 scientists for various reasons. The observatory was created in 1958 to provide the world's finest scientists with state-of-the-art equipment for exploring the universe. The recently completed Green Bank Telescope dwarfs its other giant 140-foot telescope and is the largest fully steerable radio telescope in the world. It will be used as the primary instrument for pioneering research over a much greater band of radio wavelengths than any telescope of comparable size. The group known as "Search for Extra-Terrestrial Intelligence" (SETI) was founded at this observatory and is a major presence here today. Plans are underway for a new visitors center and exhibition space. The facility features guided tours, some exhibits, audio visual show, and demonstrations at the current Tour Center.

Details: Tours daily mid-June–Labor Day and weekends Memorial Day weekend–mid-June and Sep–Oct; off-season group tours are available by reservation only, 9–4. Free. (2 hours)

★★★★ SENECA ROCKS
Rte. 55/28, 304/567-2827 or 304/257-4488

Indian legend says that young warriors wishing to marry the daughter of a great Seneca Chief had to scale this mighty cliff to win her hand. The young Seneca princess, Snow Bird, had been climbing the rock since her childhood. Rock climbers immediately recognize this 900-foot-high strata of Tuscarora sandstone that towers over the Monon-gahela National Forest. Many believe this is the most challenging climb in the East. Most of us will choose to view its dramatic architecture from a safe distance or take on the Granny Trail instead. The view from the top is spectacular and well worth getting winded. Professional climbing schools offer lessons in the art of the climb. At the visitors center, a presentation is available on the history of the site with information on how to hike to its top.

Details: Guided hikes and climbs by the Seneca Rocks Climbing School average $225/person for a two-day class, reservations 800/548-0108. (2–4 hours depends on climbing/hiking choice)

★★★ PEARL S. BUCK BIRTHPLACE MUSEUM
U.S. 219, Hillsboro, 304/653-4430

Buck's *The Good Earth* was required reading for most schoolchildren in America not too long ago. The first American woman to win both a Pulitzer and Nobel Prize for Literature, she was awarded a Pulitzer for *The Good Earth* in 1932 and the Nobel Prize in 1938 for the high quality of her literary work. She was born on this site in 1892 and her birthplace is today a memorial to her life. The white-frame house, restored in 1958, sits nestled in the hills of the Appalachian Mountains and contains many of her original furnishings and a lifetime of memorabilia. Costumed guides give tours on demand.

Details: Daily May–Oct. $4 adults, $1 children. (30-minute tours)

★★★ BEARTOWN STATE PARK
HC 64, Hillsboro, off Rte. 219 southwest of Hillsboro
800/CALL WVA or 304/653-4254

During the Pennsylvanian Age, wind and rain created the deep crevices and walls of Droop (or Pottsville) Sandstone in this hilltop. The result is an eerie monument to nature that was named "Beartown" because locals thought that the many cavelike openings in the rocks made ideal winter dens for the black bears in the area and that the streetlike network of crevices looked like a town from above. There is a short, but easy walk to the rock formations from the parking area.

Details: *Dawn–dusk. (1 hour)*

★★ DROOP MOUNTAIN BATTLEFIELD STATE PARK
South of Hillsboro off Rte. 219, 304/653-4254

Further south off Route 219, Droop Mountain is a spectacular park site on which West Virginia's largest Civil War battle was fought on November 6, 1863. The 285-acre park features interpretive exhibits, Confederate earthworks, and a small museum with artifacts from the battle. The views here are second to none.

Details: *Dawn–dusk. (1 hour)*

★★ SENECA STATE FOREST
Rte. 1, Dunmore, 800/CALL WVA or 304/799-6213

West Virginia's oldest state forest features rustic log guest cabins near a four-acre lake with trout, bass, and bluegill. The park's 11,684 acres of woodlands feature hiking trails, hunting, and wildlife. The furnished cabins were built in the 1930s by the Civilian Conservation Corps and feature stone fireplaces, gas-powered lights, wood-burning stoves, and refrigerators. With no running water, guests must hand-pump their water nearby.

Details: *Dawn–dusk. (2–8 hours)*

★ SENECA CAVERNS
3 miles southwest of Riverton on Rte. 33/28
304/567-2691

Seneca boasts being West Virginia's largest caverns. Seneca has a romantic legend that the Seneca Indian Princess, Snow Bird, married a young brave in its Great Ballroom. A sideline to the caverns is Seneca's gemstone mining operation, which is the only one of its kind in the state.

Details: *Memorial Day–Labor Day daily 8–7, Apr–May and Sep–Oct 9–5. $7.50 adults, $3.75 children ages 6–11. (45-minute tours)*

★ SMOKE HOLE CAVERNS
Seneca Rocks, Rte. 55/28, 800/828-8478

Located near Seneca Rocks, Smoke Hole is famous for the longest ribbon stalactite in the world. At Smoke Hole some features include a room of a million stalactites and a trout-filled pool in the Crystal Cave.

Details: Memorial Day–Labor Day daily 8:30–7:30, remainder of year 9–5. $7.50 adults, $5 children ages 5–12. (45-minute tours)

COVERED BRIDGES

Walkersville Covered Bridge, U.S. 19 to Walkersville, south one mile, crosses the right fork of the West Fork River and is a 39-foot structure built in 1903. At the **Locust Creek Covered Bridge**, three miles off U.S. 219 on Locust Creek Road, 800/336-7009, you can view a rare Warren Double Intersection truss design (circa 1870) on the 130-foot bridge.

SCENIC RAILROADS

During the spring, the **Cass Scenic Railroad State Park** scenic steam-train tours depart from the old Cass depot to the top of Cheat Mountain. The park's headquarters are located at State Route 28/92 between Dunmore and Green Bank, 800/CALL WVA or 304/456-4300. Tours are either half a day to the towering Bald Knob, or two hours to Whitaker Station. Cass also offers Saturday evening dinner train tours during the summer. During the fall, the trains offer spectacular views of the vibrant foliage. The tiny railroad logging town of Cass has been purchased by the state and its rows of white-frame cottages function as overnight accommodations year-round.

The little town of Moorefield, located off Route 55, 30 miles north of Seneca Rocks, was established in 1777 and is listed on the National Register of Historic Places. It hosts a few good antique shops and the Old Stone Tavern.

One of the best-preserved logging towns in the country, Cass also contains an Old General Store and a few other specialty shops. The cottages are within walking distance to the Greenbrier River Trail and the Cass Scenic Railroad Tours.

The new **Durbin and Green-brier Valley Railroad**, P.O. Box 44, E. Main Street, 304/456-4935, offers scenic rides aboard charming open-air trains. The 45-minute excursions take travelers between Durbin and Cass along a portion of railway once used heavily for logging purposes. The tours are short, but delightful, especially to children who will love the open-air cars and 1930s wooden caboose.

A little further north in Romney, the **Potomac Eagle Scenic Railroad**, 800/22-EAGLE or 304/822-7464, promises that guests will spot rare bald eagles on 90 percent of their excursions. The trains travel through The Trough of the remote South Branch Valley. The town of Romney has some quaint antique shops and a country store to pass time until the next tour.

FITNESS AND RECREATION

In addition to great skiing, the area's treacherous terrain is enticing to hikers and mountain bikers. At **Elk River Touring Center**, Slatyfork, 304/572-3771, adventurers can check in at the lodge and then head for off-road mountain bike, cross-country ski, and snowshoe tours. At the end of the day guests can come back for a nap and a great meal at the lodge. The **White Grass Ski Touring Center**, Route 1, Box 299, Davis, 304/866-4114, in Canaan Valley, also offers cross-country skiing and showshoeing with 50 kilometers of trails and 25 kilometers of machine-groomed trails. Lessons and rentals are available at both outfitters.

From the solitude of fishing and boating in mountain streams and lakes to the white-knuckle adrenaline of rock climbing on Seneca Rocks, there's an activity for every type of outdoorsperson.

One favorite outdoor spot is the **Summersville Dam**, part of the Gauley River National Recreation Area and the second highest rock-filled dam in the

BIKING NEAR SENECA ROCKS

West Virginia Tourism Department

eastern U.S. **Stonewall Jackson Lake State Park** features a 26-mile-wide lake with 82 miles of shoreline. Here, you can cruise the lake aboard a paddlewheeler, in addition to fishing, boating, hunting, and camping.

Watoga State Park, Star Route 1, Box 252, Marlinton, 800/CALL WVA or 304/799-4087, is West Virginia's largest state park. It features modern or log-constructed cabins, two campgrounds, miles of picturesque hiking trails, access to the Greenbrier River, horseback trail rides, and recreational facilities including swimming, boating, and game court for activities like tennis and volleyball. The park's visitors center features a restaurant and commissary with groceries and supplies.

Other significant outdoor recreation sites include **Burnsville Lake and Wildlife Management Area**, Burnsville, 304/853-2371, with its 968-acre lake; **Stonecoal Lake Wildlife Management Area**, Horner, 304/924-6211, with its excellent deer hunting and warm water fishing; **Summersville Lake and Wildlife Management Area**, Summersville, 304/872-5809, which offers warm water fishing and scuba diving; **Sutton Lake**, Sutton, 304/765-2705, brags plenty of bass, muskie, and pike fishing; **Kumbrabow State Forest**, Huttonsville, 304/335-2219, offering rustic cabins; and the **Lost River State Park and Stables**, Mathias, 304/897-5372, which features beautiful horseback riding trails with wonderful views. Great trout fishing locations include **Elk River Wildlife Management Area**, Sutton, 304/765-7837; **Holly River State Park**, Hacker Valley, 304/493-6353; and the **Elk River Trout Ranch**, Monterville, 304/339-6455.

There are numerous wildlife refuges including the **Canaan Valley National Wildlife Refuge**, Davis, 304/637-7321. More than 746 acres are managed by the U.S. Fish and Wildlife Service, which offers seasonal interpretive hikes. Hunting is also offered at the **Short Mountain Wildlife Management Area**, Kirby, 304/822-3551; and **Springfield Wildlife Management Area**, Springfield, 304/822-3551. Deer, elk, black bear, buffalo, mountain lion, bobcat, fox, bald eagle, wild boar, and river otter all thrive in a natural habitat at the **West Virginia State Wildlife Center**, French Creek, 304/924-6211.

If that's not enough, there's also cave exploration, wildflower tours, hot-air balloon tours, white-water rafting, canoeing—and to top it all off, you can dive off the New River Bridge on Bridge Day to say you've done it all.

FOOD

When Brian and Margaret Ann Ball opened the **Red Fox Restaurant**, Whistlepunk Village, Snowshoe Ski Resort, 304/572-1111, nearly a decade ago, one visit would have convinced you that this place would be a permanent fixture. Worth a drive in a snowstorm to the top of Snowshoe's 4,800-foot peak, the lush decor, seamless service, and the freshest and most inspired menu you could imagine are a stark contrast to the wild, untamed wilderness of West Virginia. Ingredients that are native to the area, such as local trout, pheasant, and quail, are used. The menu includes dishes like Rack of Seneca Venison with Lobster and Tender Young Hen and Wild Boar Sausage. For dessert there's homemade Pumpkin Creme Caramel or a concoction created by Thomas Jefferson called Blueberry Grunt. Reservations are suggested.

There's hearty but healthy fare at the **Restaurant at Elk River**, U.S. 219, Slatyfork, 304/572-3771. The restaurant has a laid-back, fire-warmed atmosphere with live music on some nights. Entrées include the freshest Elk River Trout, good quality steaks, chicken dishes, and a few vegetarian items.

The retro **French's Diner**, on the corner of Main Street, Marlinton, 304/799-9910, has been the talk of numerous travel articles in recent years making it especially popular with tourists to the chagrin of the locals. Hearty breakfasts and traditional diner fare are done with panache in this restored diner. Just down the street at the **River Place Restaurant**, First Avenue, 304/799-7233. Locals have been packing this place for years where country cooking, great sandwiches, and homemade desserts are what's cookin'.

In Elkins, locals and ski bums alike frequent **C.J. Maggie's American Grill**, 5 Main Street, 304/472-2490, for fajitas, Tex-Mex, burgers, nachos, and wood-fired pizza.

LODGING

At **Erehwon Cabins**, ("nowhere" spelled backwards), HC 61, Box 76, Cass, 24927, 304/572-5140, the owners have built four of the most elegant (though remote) log cabins you'll ever find. Each cabin is located on its own piece of two-acre heaven with dramatic views of the surrounding mountains. All cabins feature a stone fireplace, TV with VCR and direct TV, washer and dryer, gas grill, and a fully equipped kitchen. Rates average $150 per night depending on length of stay and the time of the year.

In Marlinton, the **Jerico Bed & Breakfast**, Jerico Road, Marinton, 304/799-624, is typical of the inns in the area with wonderful Victorian architecture and a mixture of antiques and country style. The Jerico features some restored 1800s log cabins in addition to rooms in the house. Breakfasts consist of homemade breads, egg dishes, and fresh fruit. Average rates are $40 during the summer and $65 during busy times such as ski season.

The **Graceland Inn & Conference Center**, 100 Campus Drive, Elkins, 800/624-3157, is on the National Register of Historic Places. The stately mansion sits on a hilltop above the small town on the campus of Davis and Elkins College. The house was built in 1893 by one of the state's wealthiest coal and railroad barons. The 13 guest rooms are furnished with period pieces and each has its own bath, climate control, and computer access. There are also three luxurious suites and 26 additional guest rooms in the adjacent conference center. Rates are approximately $40 to $70 in the conference center and $65 to $135 for rooms/suites in the mansion.

One of the more unusual country inns in the region is **Deer Park Country Inn**, P.O. Box 817, Buckhannon, 800/296-8430. The 1800s farmhouse and adjacent 1770s log cabin are in a tranquil setting. The rooms are cozy and antique filled and the meals delicious at a notable restaurant where the chef is superb. Rates average $100 a night for a two-person stay.

SKI RESORTS

Picture, if you will, a rustic mountaintop ski village with timbered and fieldstone lodges, luxury spa, five-star restaurants, and one-of-a-kind shops. The slopes have been groomed with the most state-of-the-art equipment available. Horse-drawn sleighs travel through the village streets. New England–quality skiing is served up here with Southern hospitality. This is the vision of Intrawest Resorts, which has dedicated $160 million in the **Snowshoe/Silver Creek Resort**, Box 10, 304/572-5252, to make it a premier skiing destination. Snowshoe already has some of the highest rated slopes on the East Coast. Those who know skiing, know that it was Intrawest that in just five short years, transformed Whistler/Blackcomb, British Columbia, into the highest rated ski resort in North America.

To date, Intrawest has installed ultra-modern chair lifts, massively upgraded snowmaking facilities and opened the new Ruckus Ridge snow-tubing park. By 1999, Intrawest plans to have completed its second phase which includes the construction of the Rimfire Lodge, the cornerstone of the new village. By 2003, Intrawest plans to have completed an entire village at the top of Cheat Mountain (Snowshoe's peak) that will rival the world's finest ski resorts and will also be transformed into a four seasons destination with superior golfing and warm weather amenities.

Currently there are 54 slopes and trails (41 percent easier, 41 percent more difficult, 18 percent most difficult) with a 1,500-foot vertical drop; the longest run is 1.5 miles. Snowshoe has 180 inches of snow annually and 100-percent snowmaking capacity. The resort's elevation at the top of the mountain is 4,848

JACKSON'S MILL HISTORIC DISTRICT

Located in Weston, 304/269-5100 or 800/287-8206, at the junction of Route 33 and Route 19, is the site of the boyhood home of General Stonewall Jackson. The **Jackson's Mill Historic District** features several historic sites including his family's original gristmill (circa 1837) and the restored **Blaker Mill** with its unusual horizontal waterwheel. Jackson's family cabin has been reconstructed, and there is a cemetery on site. Adjacent to the mill site is a **Genealogical and Historical Library and Museum**, Route 33 and Abbott Run Road, Horner, 304/269-7091, with archives, library, and historic artifacts.

feet. The resort offers night skiing and snow tubing, and there is a state-of-the-art terrain park with halfpipe, lights, music, and more. Currently, 1,500 rooms are near or at the resort. A 12-acre slope is used solely for lessons at various levels by experienced instructors.

Canaan Valley Resort, Route 32 N., Davis, 304/866-4121, is situated at an elevation of 4,280 feet with great snow conditions throughout the season for day and night skiing and snowboarding. It has 34 slopes (30 percent beginner, 40 percent intermediate, 30 percent advanced) with a longest run of 6,000 feet and a vertical drop of 850 feet. Snowmaking capacity is at 85 percent. The resort has recently added a tubing and terrain park. Canaan has a family feel with outdoor ice skating, great children's ski programs, and nice, comfortable lodging at the main Canaan Valley Lodge and Mountain Cottages in particular. There is also a modern health club with an indoor heated pool, exercise room, whirlpool, and saunas.

Deerfield Village Resort in Canaan Valley, 304/866-4698, is an AAA three-diamond property with four seasons of amenities including great golf. Lift tickets for Canaan are available here as are equipment rentals. For fun, drive nearby to the little towns of Davis and Thomas. In Thomas, visit **Sweet's Body and Soul Café Mountain Store**, 21 Main Street, 304/463-4458, for mountain storytelling, stacks of used books, and goodies like home-baked bread and big-city coffee. The town of Davis nearby has become the center of commerce for the Canaan Valley's outdoor visitors with shops and restaurants.

Timberline Four Season Resort, Davis, 304/866-4801, has a top elevation of 4,268 feet and an impressive vertical drop of 1,000 feet. With 94 percent snowmaking capacity, there are 35 slopes and trails (34 percent beginner, 32 percent intermediate, 34 percent advanced) and a longest run of two miles—"Salamander"—the longest in the South. Two of the most scenic runs here are "Almost Heaven" and "Dew Drop," and for hard-core skiers, "The Drop" and "Off The Wall" should satisfy. Nearly one-third of the mountain is lit for night skiing. The main lodge features a cafeteria, pub, and live entertainment on weekends.

CAMPING

Most state parks and forests have campsites available, many with RV hookups and amenities such as showers and laundry facilities. **Blackwater Falls State Park**, from Davis, 1/2-mile southwest off SR 32 (follow signs), 304/259-5117 or 800/CALL WVA, has beautiful sites. Waters from the Blackwater River cut a deep canyon in the park with a plunge of five stories for a remarkable vista. There is a 55-room lodge, cabins, and campsites in the park. Activities include cross-country skiing, boating, hiking, horseback riding, and nature programs.

At **Seneca State Forest**, cabins are available April through early December; $50 to $75 per night depending on the size of the cabin, camping $7 per site per night. Even though you'll have to leave your blow dryer at home, linens, dishes, and towels are provided along with a rowing canoe.

Kitschy **Yokum's Vacationland** near Seneca Rocks has lots of amenities and even a reproduction of an Indian village with tepees. Call 800/CALL WVA for a complete list of campgrounds and state park camping information. Two other commercial campgrounds in the area are Beaver Creek and Riverside.

NIGHTLIFE

Nightlife in this untamed part of the country is mostly geared toward entertaining folks who've spent the day barreling down a mountain or plunging over rapids. There are many easygoing clubs at the area's ski resorts and outfitters. Some of the best known hangouts include the **White Grass Café** at the White Grass Touring Center, 304/866-4114, and **The Connection Center**, at Snowshoe, 304/572-5252. There's also a comedy club at Snowshoe called the **Comedy Cellar**, 304/572-5252.

In Petersburg, the **Country Store Opry**, Box 787, 304/257-1743, calls itself "The Country Music Capital of the Potomac Highlands" and presents live shows every first, third, and fifth Saturday night, April through December. There are also live performances at the **McCoy-McMechen Theatre**, Main Street, Moorefield, 304/538-6685.

Highland National Scenic Highway

Take Route 39/55 east from Richwood to the Highlands National Scenic Highway (Route 150) across from the **Cranberry Mountain Visitor Center**. Drive the 43-mile mountaintop roadway, stopping along the way at any or all of four overlooks. Along the route you'll find the **Cranberry Glades Botanical Area**, where you can view unique cranberry bogs. Three lovely waterfalls are located at the **Hills Creek Scenic Area** as well. The road climbs 2,200 feet for spectacular vistas of the West Virginia terrain. You'll depart Route 150 via U.S. 219 at the **Elk Mountain Summit**. From here take U.S. 219 north through **Slatyfork** and **Snowshoe**, past sparkling mountain streams, cattle farms, and more hilly vistas. The views are well worth the strain on your brake pads. End your journey in the quaint railroad town of **Cass** along the Greenbriar River.

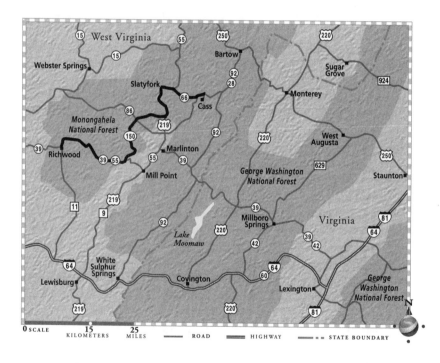

15
NEW RIVER/ GREENBRIER VALLEY

Anyone fond of white-knuckling his or her way down wild rivers will immediately recognize this part of West Virginia as rafting country. In the past two decades savvy entrepreneurs have taken advantage of the growing interest in adventure/environmental travel and turned the New River National Gorge and Greenbrier Rivers into world-class white-water rafting destinations. Towns such as the formerly sleepy Fayetteville are now anchors for many river runners with wonderful dining, shopping, and entertainment venues. West Virginia has become a formidable player in the white-water industry.

The same substance that feverishly hurtles a raft through miles of untamed wilderness is also responsible for feeding the area's gently flowing mineral springs famous for their curative powers. For more than a century visitors seeking rejuvenation from the healing waters of mineral springs have headed for the Greenbrier Valley. Just a few miles away is another highly recognizable landmark, the New River Gorge Bridge. Towering 876 feet over the New River's foaming white waters, it is the longest single-arch steel bridge in the world.

A PERFECT DAY IN NEW RIVER/ GREENBRIER VALLEY
Much of the New River/Greenbrier Valley is hilly, and the roads wind around dramatic slopes, through covered bridges, and beneath towering forests.

NEW RIVER/GREENBRIER VALLEY

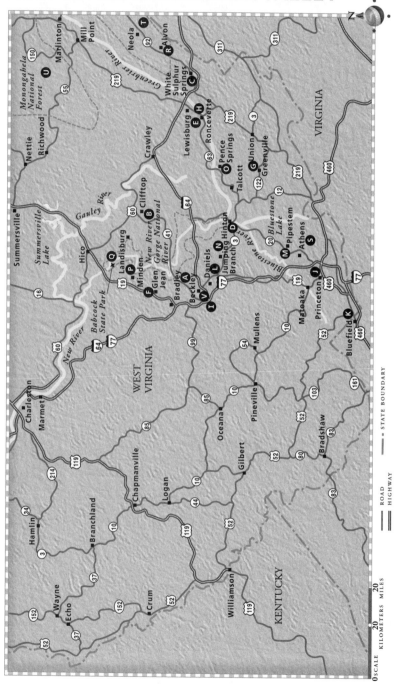

During the winter months, you will need a four-wheel-drive vehicle to traverse secondary roads and get to out-of-the-way natural sites. If you're visiting anytime from spring through fall, be adventurous and take one of the white-water rafting trips along the New or Greenbrier Rivers. Not only is rafting great fun, but it is a wonderful way to explore the terrain of the region. Raft guides are a wealth of information and are known for their colorful stories. If you decide against braving the white water, there are other wonderful experiences to be had.

Head to Bluefield and drive past gilded-age homes of West Virginia's coal barons, then head north on I-77 to Beckley and visit the Exhibition Coal Mine (open during warm months). Take I-77/64 to Tamarack to get a glimpse of West Virginia's rich arts and crafts industry. Have lunch at Tamarack's fantastic restaurant, which is operated by the Greenbrier Resort. Take Route 19 into Fayetteville and onto the Canyon Rim Visitors Center to get a magnificent view of the New River Gorge Bridge. Take Route 60 to Lewisburg for a walking tour of the town's historic district.

Finally, continue on Route 60 to either stay at or tour the Greenbrier Resort, one of the finest resort hotels in the world.

SIGHTS

- **A** Beckley Exhibition Coal Mine
- **B** Glade Creek Grist Mill
- **C** Greenbrier Resort
- **D** Hinton's Historic District
- **E** Lost World Caverns
- **F** New River Gorge Bridge
- **G** The Old Mill
- **H** Organ Cave
- **I** Tamarack

FOOD

- **J** Bobby Joe's Café
- **K** David's
- **E** General Lewis Inn
- **L** Glade Springs Resort

FOOD (continued)

- **C** Greenbrier Resort
- **J** Johnston's Restaurant
- **E** Julian's
- **K** Monabeth's
- **M** Oak Supper Club

LODGING

- **N** Foxwood Bed and Breakfast
- **E** General Lewis Lodge
- **N** Glade Springs Resort
- **C** Greenbrier Resort
- **J** Hale House Bed and Breakfast
- **O** Pence Springs Hotel
- **E** Swift Level Farm

CAMPING

- **P** Ace Adventure Center
- **Q** Babcock State Park
- **R** Blue Bend Recreation Area
- **D** Bluestone State Park/Bluestone Lake and Wildlife Management Area
- **S** Grandfather Hollow Wilderness Campground
- **T** Lake Sherwood
- **U** Monongahela National Forest
- **M** Pipestem Resort State Park and Equestrian Center
- **V** Twin Falls Resort State Park

Note: Items with the same letter are located in the same place.

SIGHTSEEING HIGHLIGHTS

★★★★ GREENBRIER RESORT
300 W. Main St., White Sulphur Springs, 800/624-6070
The finest hotel in the state is also a wonderful destination for touring. It all began when the healing mineral springs that feed the resort's spa were discovered in 1778. This prompted the opening of The Old White resort in the 1800s. It was renamed The Greenbrier in 1910. The hotel served as a military hospital during World War II and was redecorated between 1946 and 1948. It reopened as a hotel in 1948 and has maintained its status as a premier resort hotel ever since.

The hotel offers guided behind-the-scenes, history and grounds tours. The behind-the-scenes tours are especially fun because they show what goes into the dinner preparations. One tour not to be missed is of the underground bunkers, which were intended for congressional continuity in times of nuclear war. The former Government Relocation Facility (code name: Greek Island) was a top secret of the Cold War. Planned by the Eisenhower Administration, it was designed to accommodate both Senate and House members. The 32-year-secret was always kept in a state of constant readiness by a small group of government employees. Sparse and military in appearance, the facility was exposed by the *Washington Post* in 1992 and phased out in 1995. You'll never forget the enormous boom of closing 25-ton steel doors, the empty dormitory beds, and the meeting rooms meant for government business in times of great war.

Details: *Tours average $15. (1–2 hours)*

★★★ BECKLEY EXHIBITION COAL MINE
Follow signs from Beckley to New River Park
304/256-1747
The town of Beckley was once a center for coal mining. At the Beckley Exhibition Coal Mine, you can hop aboard remodeled mine cars with former miners as guides and descend 1,500 feet underground into a former working coal mine for a 45-minute tour. The **Wildwood House Museum**, 304/252-8614, adjacent to the tours, features artifacts, photos, and displays. An original, three-room furnished coal company house from the turn of the century, a mine superintendent's home, and authentic coal camp houses are also on the property.

Details: *Early Apr–Nov | 10–6, underground tours 10–5:30. $5 adults, $4 children ages 4–12. (2 hours)*

★★★ TAMARACK
1 Tamarack Park, I-77 Exit 45, 88-TAMARACK or 304/256-6702

With its striking red crown-like roof jutting out against the blue West Virginia sky, Tamarack is a tribute, showcase, and marketplace for the state's craftspeople. The harsh climate and isolation of West Virginia forced early pioneers to develop skills in a diverse range of areas—textiles, glass-making, metalwork, woodworking, pottery, toy- and jewelry-making, basket-weaving, etc. Carrying on traditions passed on from generation to generation, artists and craftspeople continue these trades today in a thriving cottage industry. At Tamarack, you can buy handmade quilts, paintings, sculptures, furniture, flower arrangements, clothing, pottery, and more. If you're just passing through the area and don't have time to scour the countryside for handmade goods, this is the place for you.

There are also five craft demonstration studios, a theater for live performances and films, galleries, gardens, and a nature trail on the property. Homemade food items are available as well and, if you get hungry while shopping, there's "A Taste of West Virginia" food court. The facility also serves as a state visitors center with brochures, maps, and travel counselors.

Details: *Daily 9–9, closed Christmas Day only. Free. (2 hours)*

★★ GLADE CREEK GRIST MILL
Rte. 41, Clifftop, 304/438-3003

Located in Babcock State Park, this mill is one of the most photographed sites in West Virginia. Although the basic structure of the fully operable mill dates from 1890, this is a replica constructed in 1976 from portions of several old mills in the state. Freshly ground cornmeal and buckwheat flour are available for sale.

Details: *(1 hour)*

★★ HINTON'S HISTORIC DISTRICT
Hinton Visitor Center, State Rte. 20, 304/466-5420

Walking tours are available if you would like to view this quaint little town developed by the C&O Railroad from the 1870s until the early

1900s. Adventurous types can rent from numerous outfitters in the area to hike, camp, fish, rock climb, mountain bike, and canoe. Views along the river are nothing short of breathtaking.

Details: *(2–8 hours)*

★★ LOST WORLD CAVERNS
1¹/₂ miles north of Lewisburg, 304/645-6677

Perhaps a true spelunker would balk at the notion of visiting a commercial cavern or cave, but for the rest of us it is certainly nice to have lighting, safety roping, and guides to help us make our way through the underworld. The enormous caverns are a registered natural landmark and contain amazing rooms measuring nearly 1,000 by 75 feet. Discovered by Virginia Polytechnic Institute in 1942, are waterfalls, terraced stalagmites, and stone formations. You'll see commercial signs for these caverns that are located north of Lewisburg.

Details: *May–Labor Day daily 9–7, rest of the year daily 9–5. $7 adults, $4 children ages 6–12. (1–2 hours)*

★★ NEW RIVER GORGE BRIDGE
P.O. Box 246, Glen Jean, West Virginia, 304/465-0508

West Virginia's New River is the second oldest river in the world. Its waters provide opportunities for rafting, hiking trails along its banks, canoeing, and nature observation. Just north of the tiny railroad town of Hinton, the New River takes on the waters of the Greenbrier River and plunges into a 1,000-foot-deep gorge. Here, 53 miles of its course were designated in 1978 as the New River Gorge National River in order to protect its free-flowing waters. The park system encompasses nearly 63,000 acres of stunning landscape along the river between Hinton and Fayetteville. This is also the heart of the state's rafting industry with commercial outfitters offering Class I through Class V raft trips. Also in the park area, Grandview Park is home to the famous outdoor dramas *Hatfields and McCoys* and *Honey in the Rock*, as well as other performances.

This bridge is the park's crowning attraction. It is the second highest bridge in the U.S. and the longest single-arch steel bridge in the world. The best spot to view the 876-foot-tall bridge is the Canyon Rim Visitors Center on U.S. 19 at Fayetteville. Park near the Hinton Visitor Center to view the lovely Sandstone Falls.

Details: *(1 hour)*

★ ORGAN CAVE
417 Masters Rd., Ronceverte, 304/645-7600
The Organ Cave is named for its 40-foot-tall formation that looks like a pipe organ. This is an access point for one of the country's largest limestone cave networks.
  Details: Daily 9–5:30. $10 adults, $5 children ages 6–12. (1–2 hours)

★ THE OLD MILL
Rte.122, Greenville, 304/772-3003
Located in Greenville, this mill was erected as Cook's Mill in 1867 on the site of the original mill dating back to the late 1700s. The current structure has been heavily restored and features demonstrations and numerous special events.
  Details: (1 hour)

COVERED BRIDGES
The roster of covered bridges in this region includes the **Herns Mill Covered Bridge** near Lewisburg, (U.S. 60 in Lewisburg, go left onto County 60/11, left on County 40, Muddy Creek Mountain Road, 2.6 miles to bridge, 304/645-1000), a 54-foot bridge over Milligan Creek built in 1884. Also near Lewisburg, **Hokes Mill Covered Bridge**, (from Ronceverte south of Lewisburg take Route 219 south and turn left at County 48 3.6 miles to County 62, then south to the bridge, 304/252-2244), is more than 81 feet long over Second Creek and was built in the 1890s for $700.

Big Bend Tunnels is an overlook on Route 3 in Talcott that features a monument to John Henry, the "steel-drivin' man." You can also view the 6,500-foot-long twin C&O Railroad tunnels in which Henry reputedly worked in 1873. For more information call 800/CALL WVA.

Near Salt Sulphur Springs, six miles south of Union just of I-219, 304/252-2244, the **Indian Creek Covered Bridge** was built in 1903 and was restored in 1965 using materials and methods of its original builders. From Salt Sulphur Springs, the **Laurel Creek Covered Bridge** is only a few miles away. From US 219 take County 219/7 to Lillydale, turn right on County 219/11 to the bridge. The smallest covered bridge in the state, more than 24 feet long, the Laurel Creek Bridge was built in 1911.

FITNESS AND RECREATION

The New River offers Class I through Class V white-water rafting with more than 20 qualified commercial outfitters to guide you. The Upper New River is known for milder rapids focusing on surrounding wildlife and nature, and the Lower New is world-renowned for wild Class IV and V white water. The average cost for a one-day excursion ranges from $50 to more than $75. You can also traverse the New River and see the New River Gorge Bridge via jetboat or canopied boat tour. For a list of outfits offering everything from mild family-oriented trips to more challenging runs, call 888/RAFT WVA.

Throughout the region are a multitude of hiking and biking trails of varying levels. While only 12 miles of the famous Appalachian Trail go through the area, the **Allegheny Trail** follows the crest of Peters Mountain northeastward offering challenging and scenic hiking (especially at Hanging Rock Observatory). The **Greenbrier River Trail**, N. Caldwell-Cass, 304/799-4087, is a fantastic way to see the area. The trail stretches 76 miles through small towns, over 35 bridges, and through two tunnels, and connects with Greenbrier and Seneca state forests and Watoga and Cass Scenic Railroad state parks.

At **Blue Bend Recreational Area**, Alvon, 304/536-1440, are numerous opportunities for fishing, hunting, lake boating, rock climbing, horseback riding, spelunking, camping, golfing, and skiing.

The **Greenbrier's**, White Sulphur Springs, 304/536-1110, world-class golf course was built in 1924 by George O'Neil and redesigned by Jack Nicklaus in 1979. Sam Snead, born and raised in nearby Hot Springs, Virginia, is the golf professional emeritus at the resort. To play during high season (April-October), 18 holes will cost you $125. The golf course at **Glade Springs**, 200 Lake Drive, Daniels, 800/634-5233, is ranked next in line statewide to the course at the Greenbrier and features a George Cobb layout.

FOOD

Even if you're not overnighting at the famed **Greenbrier Resort**, 300 W. Main Street, 800/624-6070, in White Sulphur Springs, dinner is an absolute must if you're in the area. The elegant dining room presents wonderful cuisine from a team of chefs, many of whom have been trained at the Greenbrier Culinary Apprenticeship Program, which the hotel instituted in the 1950s to ensure an ample supply of quality chefs. Don't forget to order the Greenbrier Bread Pudding for dessert. Service is attentive, but not overbearing. Meals at the new Sam Snead Golf Club are also memorable. Allowing you to sneak a taste of the Greenbrier without actually going there, Tamarack offers some select cuisine at the "Taste of West Virginia" food court.

The cozy **General Lewis Inn**, 301 E. Washington Street, 304/645-2600, in Lewisburg serves delicious inexpensive fare for breakfast, lunch, and dinner in historic surroundings. Breakfast entrées are under $4 and lunch isn't much more averaging $5 per item. Dinner is still a bargain at around $7 an entrée. For breakfast and lunch there's standard fare; at night the kitchen serves up made-from-scratch country cooking like fried chicken and biscuits.

Also in Lewisburg, **Julian's,** 102 S. Lafayette Street, 304/645-4145, is consistently rated as one of the state's finest restaurants. Fare includes prime beef and fresh seafood and is priced affordably at an average of $15 for a dinner entrée.

Glade Springs Resort, 200 Lake Drive, Daniels, 800/634-5233, offers fresh beef, seafood, and pasta dishes with a glorious view of the surrounding mountains in its clubhouse. Dinner entrées are moderately priced at an average of $14. Near Pipestem, the **Oak Supper Club**, Route 20, 304/466-4800, is one of the few true fine dining options in the region.

In Bluefield, at **Monabeth's**, 1416 Bland Street, 304/325-3520, lunch is mostly light sandwiches and dinner is epicurean with great beef, seafood, and chicken dishes. **David's**, located in the old Municipal Building, 304/325-9291, has great sandwiches and light fare.

In nearby Princeton, **Bobby Joe's Café** on Mercer Street, 304/487-1073, is a local favorite, as is the country cookin' at **Johnston's Restaurant**, on Oakville Road, 304/425-7591.

LODGING

One glance at the "Quiet please. It's sleepy time down South." signs along the stately corridors of the **Greenbrier Resort**, 300 W. Main Street, White Sulphur Springs, 800/624-6070, and you come to a calming realization. The simple reason that this hotel is one of the finest in the world is its legendary manners, breeding, and graciousness. It doesn't hurt that its interior features some of the most beautifully decorated public rooms to be found anywhere. The resort is currently an AAA five-diamond property and is a member of the "Leading Hotels of the World."

Here, soft voices fill the cavernous lobby area with its museum-quality antiques, historic paintings, and enormous roaring fireplace. Tastefully dressed guests wander in and out of upscale shops on the lower level eyeing the latest in St. John and Ralph Lauren. In the $7-million spa, guests treat themselves to European treatments using fresh, natural mineral waters. Facilities here include private walk-in whirlpool baths, Swiss showers, Scotch spray, steam, sauna, and therapy rooms for massage and body wraps. There is also a gorgeous

Olympic-size indoor swimming pool, ice-skating rink, trap and skeet shooting, bowling alley, carriage/sleigh rides, croquet and training with live falcons, to name a few activities offered. Guest rooms, suites, and cottages are tastefully decorated and luxuriously appointed with all the comforts imaginable. Rates for double occupancy average about $180 to $200 during low season (winter months) and $250 to $330 during high season (April through October). Rates are the Modified American Plan rate and include breakfast daily in the Main Dining Room and dinner nightly in the Main Dining Room or Sam Snead's Golf Club.

Another great golf resort is **Glade Springs Resort**, 200 Lake Drive, Daniels, 800/634-5233, which offers a variety of accommodations and amenities. Executive suites are nicely decorated and feature living rooms, wet bar and Jacuzzi tubs. The manor houses are even more luxurious with spacious bedrooms, cavernous baths, and common rooms that include living room area with fireplace, conference room, and full kitchens. There are golf, an Olympic-size heated pool, kids' playground, racquet club, horseback riding, and skiing at its sister Winterplace Ski Resort. The property is currently going through growing pains after merging with Winterplace to truly become a four-season resort. Rates average $125 per night during golf season, 3000 Lake Drive, Daniels, 800/634-5233.

The **General Lewis Lodge**, 301 E. Washington Street, Lewisburg, 304/645-2600, is an antique-filled inn featuring 26 bedrooms with private baths. All guest rooms have 100-year-old beds and antiques along with modern amenities such as telephones, cable television, and air conditioning. Rooms here are comfortable and charming but not overly plush, (i.e. bare hardwood floors, simple walls, few accents.) Rates average $80 to $100 a night depending on the room.

The **Pence Springs Hotel**, Box 90, Spence Springs, 304/445-2606, has undergone numerous transformations over the years. Originally a mineral spa, the hotel has been built and rebuilt three times during its history. The current Georgian/colonial-style building was built in 1918 and was frequented by rail travelers as a Prohibition-era speakeasy. Later, the hotel served as a women's prison from 1947 to 1984. Since then, owners have taken great care in bringing back the hotel's original luster with fine furnishings, antiques, and pleasant dining facilities. Rates are affordable at $85 to $95 a night.

Most bed-and-breakfast inns in the area are comfortably decorated with turn-of-the-century antiques mixed with country flair. The **Hale House Bed and Breakfast**, 209 Hale Avenue, in Princeton, 304/487-6783, is located in a striking wisteria-draped mansion in a quiet residential area. The rooms contain lovely mahogany or wrought-iron beds and some have private baths that are nicely appointed. Rates average $60 to $70 a night including breakfast and afternoon tea. The **Foxwood Bed and Breakfast**, Ellison Ridge Road, Jumping Branch, 304/466-5514, near Winterplace Ski Resort, features five comfortable suites and two additional guest rooms all with private baths. Guests can take advantage of the inn's 250-acre mountain setting. Rates average $80 to $100. **Swift Level Farm**, Route 2, Box 269-A, 304/645-1155, in Lewisburg, is ideal for horseback riders. It is an 1827 farmhouse that offers lots of riding opportunities on its 150-acre active horse farm. Rates range from $50 per room to $150 for a private log cabin or $160 for the entire house.

SKI RESORTS

Winterplace, I-77 south of Beckley to exit 28, 800/607-SNOW or 304/787-3221, was purchased in 1992 by Bright Resorts and since that time has invested in improving the resort. Winterplace has added new ski slopes, upgraded its snowmaking equipment, built a new lodge with four new restaurants/clubs, expanded the ski shop, acquired more and improved the quality of rental equipment, and completed a new cafeteria. There are several lodging options here including the usual crate furniture–feel condos. Accommodations range from $36 for basic to $200 for more luxurious amenities. **Glade Springs Resort**, 200 Lake Drive, Daniels, 800/634-5233, qualifies as being one of the more luxurious. Some economical chains include the **Sleep Inn**, 1124 Airport Road, Beaver, 304/255-4222, and **Hampton Inn**, 110 Harper Park Drive, Beckley, 304/252-2121. Winterplace has a total of seven beginner level, 13 intermediate, and four expert trails available making it ideal for average skiers. Snowboarding and ski lessons are available for a variety of skill levels.

CAMPING

The New River/Greenbrier Valley's state parks offer exceptional camping facilities along with spectacular scenery and outdoor activities. **Babcock State Park**, Clifftop, 304/438-3004, contains one of the country's most famous gristmills and borders the New River Gorge National River. It offers camping facilities and cabins. **Pipestem Resort State Park and Equestrian Center**, Route 20, Pipestem, 800/CALL WVA, features traditional camping at the Bluestone Gorge, lodges with fireplaces and cabins. Camping at **Twin Falls Resort State Park**, Beckley, 304/394-4000, you'll find an 18-hole golf course, cottages, and a nineteenth-century pioneer farm. Anglers will appreciate the facilities at **Bluestone State Park/Bluestone Lake and Wildlife Management Area**, Hinton, 304/466-2805, on a more than 2,000-acre lake.

The **Blue Bend Recreation Area**, Alvon, 304/536-1440, and **Lake Sherwood**, Neola, 304/280-2267, are located in the **Monongahela National Forest** and offer rustic camping in a beautiful undisturbed setting.

The **Grandfather Hollow Wilderness Campground**, Athens, 304/384-9736, features a black bear habitat and other wildlife programs, as well as horseback riding, fishing, petting zoo, and cabins, in addition to campsites and RV hookups. The **Ace Adventure Center**, Concho Road, Minden, 304/469-2651, is located directly adjacent to the New River Gorge National River and contains a variety of facilities from tent sites to A-frame chalets.

NIGHTLIFE

The white-water town of Lansing has a great local bar, the **Red Dog Saloon**, Box 39, Lansing, 800/879-7483. Here, tired rafters turn up a few and spin yarns of high adventure.

PERFORMING ARTS

The New River/Greenbrier Valley has a few intimate clubs entertaining tired skiers at Winterplace and tired rafters in Fayetteville, good quality national-level performances at Carnegie Hall in Lewisburg, and homespun festivals and special events throughout the region. For something truly unique, see one of the region's outdoor dramas at **Grandview Park** on the New River Gorge National River. The *Hatfields and McCoys* start their feuding every summer with a cast of more than 100 locals. Other productions include *Honey in the Rock*, and *Anything Goes*, Theatre West Virginia, 800/666-9142 or 304/256-6800.

SHOPPING

In Lewisburg, **Robert's Antiques**, 120 E. Washington Street, 304/647-3404, is of particular interest with its wacky antique electronics exhibit (the mannequin in the electric chair is something you don't see everyday), and wonderful early-American and primitive antique furnishings, paintings, books, and collectibles.

16
WEST VIRGINIA'S
CAPITAL REGION

The western portion of West Virginia is the state's commercial and legislative hub. Here, in the state's capital city of Charleston and surrounding cities of Huntington and Parkersburg reside the majority of the state's residents. The region offers more commercial shopping and dining and more tall buildings than other parts of the state, but is also comprised of many parks, peaks, and waterways so important to the state's identity and appeal. Here, visitors will be able to enjoy some of the comforts and conveniences of big-city life and still gain a better understanding of the pioneer spirit that forged a nation. Charleston, in particular, has done an especially fine job of reviving its historic downtown, with lovely renovated buildings, housing shops, restaurants, and businesses.

A PERFECT DAY IN WEST VIRGINIA'S CAPITAL REGION

Begin your tour of the region at Blennerhassett Island State Park and visit the home connected with scandal and intrigue surrounding Aaron Burr and resident Harman Blennerhassett. Before leaving the area, stop in at the Allegheny Bookstore in Parkersburg and choose from 50,000 new and used book in an ornate library built by Andrew Carnegie. Take I-77 south to Charleston and take a tour of the gold-domed State Capitol. Stop in at Cabin Creek Quilts and choose from some of the most exquisite handmade quilts available today. Take

WEST VIRGINIA'S CAPITAL REGION

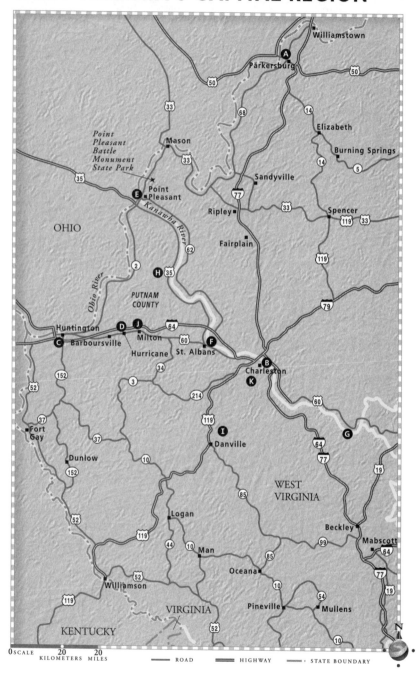

Williamstown

A Parkersburg

50

33

68

14

Elizabeth

Point
Pleasant
Battle
Monument
State Park

Mason

33

Burning Springs

14

5

Sandyville

35

77

Spencer

119   33

E Point
Pleasant

Kanawha River

Ripley

33

OHIO

Ohio River

Fairplain

62

119

2

H 35

119

PUTNAM
COUNTY

79

Huntington

D **J** 64

C Barboursville   Milton

60

F

B

K Charleston

Hurricane   St. Albans

152

34

60

52

3

214

G

37

119

I

64

Fort
Gay

Danville

77

37

WEST
VIRGINIA

19

Dunlow

10

152

85

52

Logan

Beckley

119

Mabscott

44   10   Man

99

64

52

85

77

Williamson

Oceana

10

19

119

54

VIRGINIA

Pineville

Mullens

KENTUCKY

52

10

N

0 SCALE   20   20
KILOMETERS MILES

—— ROAD   ━━ HIGHWAY   ⋯ STATE BOUNDARY

I-64 to Huntington and end your day at a turn-of-the-century amusement park on the Ohio River.

CHARLESTON SIGHTSEEING HIGHLIGHTS

The state's capital city has a definite small-town feel with a small high-rise area and the scenic Kanawha River running through the town. The old downtown area has been carefully restored and now contains some lovely refurbished buildings home with offices, shopping, and dining. The nation's largest enclosed downtown mall is situated in the restored area enticing suburbanites to come downtown to be entertained. The Haddad Riverfront Park has also recently opened featuring a 2,000-seat amphitheater and boat pier where the PA Denny sternwheeler is docked.

★ CAPITOL COMPLEX
Charleston, 304/558-3809
This complex contains the striking **Capitol Building**, 1900 Washington Street E., 304/558-3809, with a glimmering 293-foot gold-leaf dome. This building was completed in 1932 and features dazzling antiques and fixtures including a 10,080-piece Czechoslovakian

SIGHTS

- **A** Blennerhassett Island Historical State Park
- **B** Capitol Complex
- **B** East End District
- **C** Heritage Village
- **C** Huntington Museum of Art
- **D** Main Street Gallery of Fine Arts and Crafts
- **C** Museum of Radio and Technology
- **E** Point Pleasant Battle Monument State Park
- **D** Waves of Fun Water Park
- **E** West Virginia State Farm Museum

FOOD

- **F** Chilton House
- **A** Harman's Restaurant
- **A** Point of View Restaurant
- **C** Rebels and Redcoats Tavern
- **C** Station at Huntington's Heritage Village
- **A** Third Street Deli
- **B** Window's on the River
- **F** Wren's Nest

LODGING

- **B** Blennerhassett Hotel
- **B** Brass Pineapple
- **B** Charleston Marriott Towne Center

LODGING (continued)

- **A** Comfort Suites
- **B** Embassy Suites Charleston
- **G** Glen Ferris Inn

CAMPING

- **C** Beech Fork State Park
- **C** Cabwaylingo State Forest
- **H** Chief Cornstalk Wildlife Management Area
- **C** Chief Logan State Park
- **I** Fork Creek Wildlife Management Area
- **J** Fox Fire Resort
- **K** Kanawha State Forest

Note: Items with the same letter are located in the same town or area.

crystal chandelier. The **Governor's Mansion**, 1716 Kanawha Boulevard E., 304/558-3809, built in 1925, and the **West Virginia Cultural Center**, 1900 Washington Street E., 304/558-0162, (a museum of the state's history.) The cultural center houses various artifacts exploring pioneer life, industrial success, and ancient history. A theater is also located on the site which offers a variety of live performances including *Mountain Stage*, a weekly show broadcast live on National Public Radio of jazz, folk, blues, rock, and classical music.
Details: Mon–Fri 8–4. (4 hours)

★ **EAST END DISTRICT**
Charleston Convention and Visitors Bureau, 200 Civic Center Dr., Charleston, 800/733-5469 or 304/344-5075
This historic district (bordered by Bradford, Quarrier, and Michigan Streets) is home to many refurbished nineteenth-century homes of varying architectural styles. In the East End Historic District there is the **Sunrise Museum**, 746 Myrtle Road, 304/344-8035, featuring art galleries, children's museum, planetarium and 16 acres of gardens, trails, and wooded hillside. **Booker T. Washington** spent his boyhood in neighboring Malden. A monument to the famous educator is located in the Capitol Complex and his home is being recreated a few miles away. One of the city's most picturesque parks contains the **Craik-Patton House**, 2809 Kanawha Boulevard, 304/925-5341, a restored Greek Revival home built in 1834 by the grandson of George Washington's personal physician.
Details: (full day)

HUNTINGTON SIGHTSEEING HIGHLIGHTS

The city of Huntington is a turn-of-the-century railroad town with wide, sprawling lanes and grand Victorian mansions reflecting the wealth of the town's first residents. Named for a railroad baron and resident, the town is situated between the Ohio River and contains a large park extending nearly the length of the city. Huntington is home to Marshall University, which is the second largest university in the state.

★★★★ **HERITAGE VILLAGE**
210 11th St., 304/696-5954
You can get a taste of the city's history and flavor in downtown Huntington's former B&O Railway Station. The building complex

---

features authentic train cars and locomotives, unique shops, fine restaurant, the city's first bank (once robbed by the Jesse James Gang), and a memorial to the city's founder.

Details: Daily 11–6. (4 hours)

★ HUNTINGTON MUSEUM OF ART
2033 McCoy Rd., 304/529-2701

This museum is the state's largest art museum and houses a collection of English, French, and American paintings, historical glass, and Georgian silver. The museum is located on a hilltop among 50 picturesque acres and contains a reference library, studio workshops, a 300-seat auditorium, an amphitheater, a museum gift shop, nature trails, and a sculpture garden. The museum's nationally acclaimed 3,000-square-foot plant conservatory houses subtropical plants, shrubs, ground covers, and seasonal flowers.

Details: Tue–Sat 10–5, Sun noon–5. Donations accepted. (2 hours)

★ MUSEUM OF RADIO AND TECHNOLOGY
304/525-8890

At this museum you can see hundreds of antique radios from the 1920s to the 1950s. There are also numerous places to watch glass blowers and artisans practice their craft as well as to purchase fine glass objects, especially in nearby Milton. (See Shopping)

Details: Sat 10–4, Sun 1–4. Call for tour reservations. (2 hours)

HURRICANE/PUTNAM COUNTY SIGHTSEEING HIGHLIGHTS

The tiny town of Hurricane boasts an impressive collection of arts and crafts shops and galleries. Hurricane also features some historic homes and buildings and a small history museum pertaining to the area.

★★ MAIN STREET GALLERY OF FINE ARTS AND CRAFTS
City of Hurricane, 2801 Virginia Ave., 304/562-5896

The gallery contains a crafts cooperative of 25 artisans and includes wooden crafts, dolls, ceramics, toys, baby gifts, clothing, floral art, baskets, holiday decorations, jewelry, and souvenirs. This gallery allows visitors to watch craftspersons in action, as well as purchase the goods.

Details: (2 hours)

★ WAVES OF FUN WATER PARK
1 Valley Dr., Hurricane, 304/562-0518
Another amusement park in the area, Waves of Fun has the state's largest wave pool, as well as three water slides, concession area, fitness trail, aquatube, volleyball court, swimming, sunbathing, and picnic areas.
Details: *Memorial–Labor Day Mon–Sat 11–7. $6.50 adults, $5 children ages 5–11. (2–4 hours)*

PARKERSBURG SIGHTSEEING HIGHLIGHTS

The town's first residents were pioneers in the 1780s. Many years later in 1957, Parkersburg had the dubious honor of being called "the Savings Bond Capital of America" when the U.S. Department's Bureau of Public Debt moved here. Some of the buildings containing historical or architectural significance include the two-story Henry Cooper Log House (1910) and federal-style Cook House (1825–1829). The Julia-Ann Square Historic District is a late nineteenth- and early twentieth-century residential neighborhood where some of the town's most prominent families once lived. The region's ties to the oil and gas industry can be reviewed at the Oil and Gas Museum on Third Street. The museum presents the story of the industry through video and artifacts.

★ BLENNERHASSETT ISLAND HISTORICAL STATE PARK
Parkersburg/Wood County Convention and Visitors Bureau, 350 7th St., 800/752-4982 or 304/428-1130
This historical park is perhaps the most notable historical attraction in the area. Visitors can take **Rubie's Sternwheelers** over to the island to see where Aaron Burr and Harman Blennerhassett attempted to establish a Southwest empire. They plotted to take Mexico from Spanish rule, causing President Thomas Jefferson to arrest them on suspicion of treason. Tours of the eighteenth-century mansion, craft village, and grounds are available.
Details: *(3 hours)*

POINT PLEASANT SIGHTSEEING HIGHLIGHTS

★★ POINT PLEASANT BATTLE MONUMENT STATE PARK
Point Pleasant Battle Monument State Park
800/CALL WVA or 304/675-0869

A monument and museum stands in this state park commemorating, what many recognize as, the first battle of the American Revolution. The fighting took place between frontiersmen and Shawnee Chief Cornstalk.

Details: *(2 hours)*

★ **WEST VIRGINIA STATE FARM MUSEUM**
Rte. 1, 304/675-5737
One of the state's largest living pioneer farms, this state farm encompasses 50 acres with 31 reconstructed buildings.
Details: *Apr–Nov Tue–Sat 9–5, Sun 1–5. Free. (1–2 hours)*

SCENIC TOWNS

The town of **Barboursville** offers a walking tour of its historic district which contains 36 homes and buildings. The town was founded in 1813 and became a political center for the county after the railroads were completed. The walking tour's highlights include an 1800s store, homes, log cabins, and pre–Civil War cemetery.

In Milton, a lovely restored covered bridge, the **Mud River Covered Bridge** (1876), Highway 25, has a span of 112 feet over the Mud River.

The turn-of-the-century **Camden Park**, U.S. Route 60 W., 304/429-4321, an amusement area on the Ohio River, contains 26 acres of old-fashioned fun including a wooden roller coaster, log flume ride, kiddieland, and the all-important corn dogs and cotton candy. Another entertainment venue is the **Tri-State Greyhound Park**, 1 Greyhound Drive, Cross Lanes, 304/776-1000 or 800/224-9683, with year-round greyhound racing. The greyhound racing arena also has video slot machines and a family-style restaurant on the premises. The area also offers riverboat cruises aboard the *Jewel City* sternwheeler riverboat, Camden Park, U.S. Route 60 W., 304/429-4321, railway excursions, and interactive mystery dinner theater aboard a train. **New River Train Excursions**, 429 Chestnut Street, Kenova, 304/453-1641, in the fall takes passengers along the Kanawha and New Rivers for an all-day tour, which stops in the Charleston area and travels through the New River Gorge to Hinton in the Alleghenies. The train also occasionally travels to The Greenbrier, Pence Springs Hotel, and other destinations throughout the year.

The town of Williamstown contains an interesting historic district. The mid-1800s buildings and homes include a grand Italianate villa-style home filled with its original furnishings.

Other than Parkersburg, the Mid-Ohio Valley is chiefly residential. There is a fair amount of farmland with a few historic pioneer towns that contain some restored public buildings and homes. In Burning Springs, a restored log church (**Ruble Log Church**), Chestnut Run Road, 304/275-3846, is one of the oldest buildings in the Little Kanawha River Valley. There are also two covered bridges in the area of note. The 1887 **Staats Mill Covered Bridge**, 304/275-3846, was moved from its original site in 1982 to Fairplain. The 1889 **Sarvis Fork Covered Bridge**, U.S. 21, was moved from Carnahan's Ford to Sandyville in 1924.

FITNESS AND RECREATION

The western portion of the state has an abundance of outdoor activities for sportsmen. Some of the region's most popular fishing spots include **Beech Fork Lake**, Lavalette, 304/525-4831; **Beech Fork State Park**, Barboursville, 304/522-0303; **East Lynn Lake**, East Lynn, 304/696-5500; and **Laurel Lake**, Lenore, 304/475-2923.

Hunters are especially fond of **Big Ugly Wildlife Management Area**, Leet, 304/675-0871, with its rugged terrain and abundance of white-tail deer and small game. Another favorite hunting and fishing park is the **Chief Cornstalk Wildlife Management Area**, Arlee, 304/675-0871, which also has rustic camping and a rifle range. **Fork Creek Wildlife Management Area**, Nellis, 304/675-0871, offers 9,000 acres of camping and hunting for deer and small game. **McClintic Wildlife Station**, Point Pleasant, 304/675-0871; **Mill Creek Wildlife Management Area**, Milton, 304/675-0871; and **Hughes River Wildlife Management Area**, Cisco, 304/ 420-4550, also offer hunting for deer and small game.

Kanawha State Forest, Charleston, 304/558-3500, near Charleston, is a 9,302-acre forest touting excellent camping, swimming, hiking, cross-country skiing, horseback riding, picnic areas, playgrounds, fishing, and hunting. **Beech Fork State Park**, Barboursville, 304/522-0303, also offers camping at 275 campsites, hiking trails, picnic facilities, game courts, and wildlife programs.

The **Mountain State Rails to Rivers and Trails Train**, Huntington/ Charleston, 304/529-6412, takes passengers to the **New River Gorge National River** for white-water rafting, skiing, hiking, mountain biking, or horseback riding. **Cabwaylingo State Forest**, Dunlow, 304/385-4255, offers 8,123 acres of forest land with cabins, camping, swimming, hunting, hiking, and picnic areas. In addition to the outdoor historical drama, *The Aracoma Story*, **Chief Logan State Park**, Logan, 304/792-7125, has camping, hiking, and picnic facilities.

Canoe excursions are offered by **Coal River Livery**, South Charleston,

800/CANOE-11, and include fishing and camping. Mountain biking on 2,000 acres of specially designed mountain biking trails is available at **Charles Fork Lake**, Spencer, 304/927-1780. The **North Bend Rail Trail**, Cairo, 304/643-2931, also runs through the region. The scenic 71-mile hiking, biking, and horseback riding trail has been rated one of the finest trails in the country.

Hikers and bikers will enjoy the history and scenery along the **Kanawha Trace**, Huntington, 304/523-3408, stretching from Barboursville to Fraziers Bottom on the Kanawha River. A guidebook with details is available by calling 304/523-3408. There are also many trails in and around Charleston and Huntington. **Little Creek Park**, South Charleston, 304/744-4731, and **Ritter Park**, Huntington, 304/696-5954, are two of my favorite areas.

One of the outdoor amenities in and around the city of Charleston is **Coonskin Park**, 304/341-8000, which features a swimming pool, par 3 golf course, miniature golf, paddleboat lake, tennis and restaurant. There's also NASCAR racing at **West Virginia Motor Speedway**, Mineral Wells, 304/489-1889, near Parkersburg.

FOOD

One of the best-loved restaurants in the area is **Chilton House**, 26th Avenue, St. Alban west of Charleston, 304/722-2918. The restaurant is located in an 1849 historic building on the National Register and offers three-star continental cuisine. **Window's on the River**, 600 Kanawha Boulevard E., 304/344-4092, is a romantic spot atop the Charleston House Holiday Inn with spectacular views of the Kanawha River. For reasonably priced home-style food, the **Wren's Nest**, Coal River Road in St. Albans, 304/727-3224, is a log cabin roadside supper club from the 1940s.

In Huntington, **Rebels and Redcoats Tavern**, 412 Seventh Avenue, West, 304/523-8829, is located in an eighteenth-century colonial tavern with Blenko stained-glass windows. Dishes are classic and well-prepared like châteaubriand, rack of spring lamb, and Rebels Red Snapper. The **Station at Huntington's Heritage Village**, Veterans Memorial Boulevard and 11th Avenue, 304/523-6373, is a great family spot in a historic setting serving incredible ribs, burgers, and steaks.

In Parkersburg, the **Point of View Restaurant**, River Hill Road, 304/863-3366, has spectacular views and serves fresh seafood, great steaks, and prime rib. **Harman's Restaurant**, 320 Market Street, 304/422-3131, in the Blennerhassett Hotel, is a fine dining spot serving continental cuisine. For lunch here, a great choice is the **Third Street Deli**, 430 Third Street, 304/422-0003, for delicious sandwiches, soups, salads, and desserts.

LODGING

Charleston has a strong convention and meeting industry and, therefore, has garnered several modern hotels offering comfortable accommodations. The new **Embassy Suites**, 300 Court Street, 800/668-7637, is located downtown near the shopping and restored districts and features restaurant, lounge, indoor pool, fitness center, and whirlpool. Rates are $99 to $149. The **Charleston Marriott Towne Center**, 200 Lee Street, East, 304/345-6500, offers modern, nicely decorated rooms near all of downtown's sites at $114 to $134 a night.

There are also several fine bed-and-breakfast inns in the area including the **Brass Pineapple**, 1611 Virginia Street, East, Charleston, 304/344-0748. The cozy inn has six beautifully decorated guest rooms and serves a hearty breakfast in the richly detailed dining room with stained glass windows. The rooms are comfortable, yet have especially nice touches like down comforters and individual televisions. Rates are $70 to $95.

The **Blennerhassett Hotel**, 320 Market Street, 304/422-3131, is a 107-year-old National Historic Landmark hotel which has been restored and features 104 nicely appointed rooms.

In Parkersburg, the **Comfort Suites**, I-77 and State Route 14, 800/228-5150, has comfortable suites that are clean and well-appointed—many with Jacuzzi tubs. The hotel offers complimentary breakfast, indoor/outdoor pool, whirlpool, sauna, nautilus fitness room, and suites with TV/VCR, microwaves, refrigerator, and wet bar.

The **Glen Ferris Inn**, P.O. Box 119, Glen Ferris, 304/632-1111, is located 42 miles east of Charleston and overlooks the Kanawha Falls. The federal-style mansion (1839) was formerly a stagecoach stop and today contains 15 comfortable and pretty guest rooms from Victorian to Shaker styles. Rates are affordable at $60 to $130 a night.

CAMPING

Kanawha State Forest, is a favorite campsite near Charleston. Near Huntington, **Beech Fork State Park**, offers camping at 275 campsites. Other parks that offer camping include **Cabwaylingo State Forest** and **Chief Logan State Park**. Call 800/CALL WVA to make reservations in these state facilities. In Milton, **Fox Fire Resort**, 304/743-5622, is a full-service campground offering water park, swimming, paddleboats, canoes, miniature golf, and hot-air balloon rides. Rustic camping can be enjoyed at **Chief Cornstalk Wildlife Management Area**, Arlee, 304/675-0871, and **Fork Creek Wildlife Management Area**, Nellis, 304/675-0871.

NIGHTLIFE

At the **Mountaineer Opry House**, 1247 Hillview Drive, Milton, 304/733-2721, bluegrass and gospel performers appear Friday and Saturday nights, October through May.

PERFORMING ARTS

In Parkersburg, the **Actors Guild**, Eighth and Market Streets, 304/485-1300, presents a variety of stage productions and has won critical acclaim on a national level. The **Smoot Theatre**, 213 Smith Street, Parkersburg, 304/422-7529, was a vaudeville theater built in 1926. Today, special programs and live entertainment play regularly at the historic theater.

SHOPPING

There are tons of places in the region to find handmade items such as hand-blown glass, quilts, and pottery. Whether you are looking for unique glass ornaments at **C.A.S. Art Glass**, 100 Main Street, 304/869-3336, in Ellenboro, (hours vary, so call ahead), or Amish goods at the **Pleasant Valley Trading Company**, Route 2, in Walker, 304/679-3919, you will find some truly unusual venues to choose from.

Some other notable glass companies that offer tours and observation, as well as fine glass for sale, include the famous **Fenton Art Glass Gift Shop**, 420 Caroline Avenue, 304/375-7772, in Williamstown, where tours are available on request; **Mid-Atlantic Glass of West Virginia**, Old U.S. Route 50, 304/869-3351, in Ellenboro; the **Blenko Glass Company's Visitor Center**, Fairgrounds Road, 304/743-9081, in Milton; and **Pilgrim Glass**, Airport Road, 304/453-3553, in Ceredo.

For a slice of Americana, **Berdines 5 & Dime**, 106 North Court Street, 304/643-2217, in Harrisville east of Parkersburg, is the oldest dime store in the country. West Virginia's largest country store is in Parkersburg at the more than 5,500-square-foot **Mulberry Lane**, 4009 Emerson Avenue, 304/428-1949. In Parkersburg, Andrew Carnegie built the library-now-bookstore (**Trans Allegheny Book Store**, 1904–1905), 304/422-4499, where you can shop among 50,000 titles both new and used.

Arts and crafts are also plentiful in the region. Some notable craft shops include the **Berry House**, 318 Norway Avenue, 304/529-1132, in Huntington; **Little Kanawhah Crafthouse**, 304/485-3149, in Parkersburg; and the **Cedar Lakes Crafts Center**, HC 88, 304/372-7873, in Ripley.

APPENDIX

Consider this appendix your travel tool box. Use it along with the material in the Planning Your Trip chapter to craft the trip you want. Here are the tools you'll find inside:

1. **Planning Map.** Make copies of this map and plot out various trip possibilities. Once you've decided on your route, you can write it on the original map and refer to it as you're traveling.

2. **Mileage Chart.** This chart shows the driving distances (in miles) between various destinations throughout the state/region. Use it in conjunction with the Planning Map.

3. **Special Interest Tours.** If you'd like to plan a trip around a certain theme—such as nature, history, or art—one of these tours may work for you.

4. **Calendar of Events.** Here you'll find a month-by-month listing of major area events.

5. **Resources.** This guide lists various regional chambers of commerce and visitors bureaus, state offices, bed-and-breakfast registries, and other useful sources of information.

PLANNING MAP: Virginias

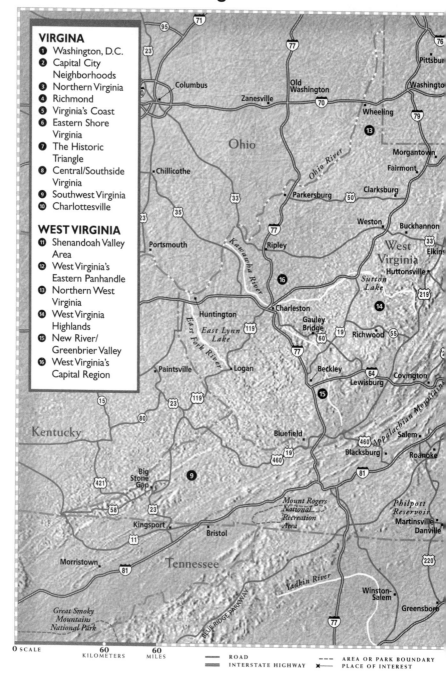

VIRGINA
- ❶ Washington, D.C.
- ❷ Capital City Neighborhoods
- ❸ Northern Virginia
- ❹ Richmond
- ❺ Virginia's Coast
- ❻ Eastern Shore Virginia
- ❼ The Historic Triangle
- ❽ Central/Southside Virginia
- ❾ Southwest Virginia
- ❿ Charlottesville

WEST VIRGINIA
- ⓫ Shenandoah Valley Area
- ⓬ West Virginia's Eastern Panhandle
- ⓭ Northern West Virginia
- ⓮ West Virginia Highlands
- ⓯ New River/ Greenbrier Valley
- ⓰ West Virginia's Capital Region

0 SCALE
60 KILOMETERS
60 MILES

━━━ ROAD
━━━ INTERSTATE HIGHWAY
╴╴╴ AREA OR PARK BOUNDARY
✕ PLACE OF INTEREST

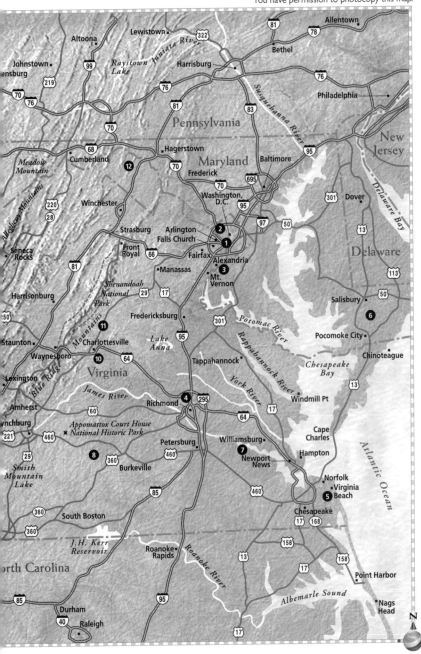

	Abingdon, VA	Alexandria, VA	Arlington, VA	Charles City, VA	Charleston, WV	Charlottesville, VA	Fayetteville, WV	Fredericksburg, VA	Jamestown, VA	Norfolk, VA	Petersburg, VA	Richmond, VA	Roanoke, VA	Virginia Beach, VA	Washington, D.C.	Williamsburg, VA
Alexandria, VA	363															
Arlington, VA	355	8														
Chaarles City, VA	339	130	134													
Charleston, WV	183	371	362	346												
Charlottesville, VA	240	120	112	101	247											
Fayetteville, WV	143	332	324	307	68	208										
Fredericksburg, VA	312	52	55	86	319	74	280									
Jamestown, VA	369	161	164	32	377	131	338	116								
Norfolk, VA	398	189	193	66	405	160	366	145	51							
Petersburg, VA	331	127	131	25	338	93	299	83	77	105						
Richmond, VA	306	103	106	33	314	68	275	58	63	92	25					
Roanoke, VA	132	244	236	220	179	121	140	193	250	279	212	187				
Virginia Beach, VA	413	204	208	81	420	175	381	160	66	18	120	107	294			
Washington, D.C.	361	8	7	135	363	118	330	56	166	194	132	108	242	209		
Williamsburg, VA	358	150	153	24	366	120	326	105	10	44	65	52	239	59	155	
Winchester, VA	298	83	69	163	306	130	267	84	193	222	159	135	179	237	75	182

SPECIAL INTEREST TOURS

With *Virginias Travel•Smart* guidebook you can plan a trip of any length—a one-day excursion, a getaway weekend, or a three-week vacation—around any special interest. To get you started, the following pages contain six tours geared toward a variety of interests. For more information, refer to the chapters listed—chapter names are bolded and chapter numbers appear inside black bullets. You can follow a tour in its entirety, or shorten, lengthen, or combine parts of each, depending on your starting and ending points.

Discuss alternative routes and schedules with your travel companions—it's a great way to have fun, even before you leave home. And remember: don't hesitate to change your itinerary once you're on the road. Careful study and planning ahead of time will help you make informed decisions as you go, but spontaneity is the extra ingredient that will make your trip memorable.

BEST OF CAPITAL REGION

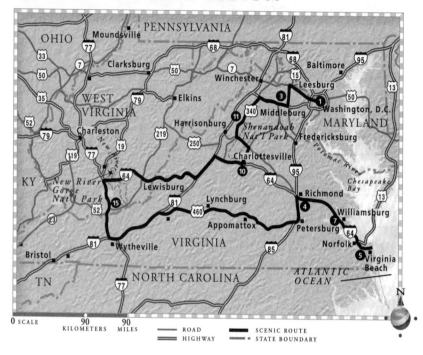

If you only have two weeks in the Capital Region this itinerary will allow you to see the variety of landscapes, attractions, and culture.

- ❶ **Washington, D.C.** (Lincoln Memorial, United States Capitol)
- ❸ **Northern Virginia** (Leesburg/Middleburg)
- ⓫ **Shenandoah Valley Area** (Skyline Drive)
- ❿ **Charlottesville** (Monticello)
- ⓯ **New River/Greenbrier Valley** (Fayetteville)
- ❹ **Richmond** (St. John's Church, Maymont, Monument Avenue/The Fan)
- ❼ **Historic Triangle** (Williamsburg)
- ❺ **Virginia's Coast** (Virginia Beach)

Time needed: one to two weeks

NATURE LOVERS' TOUR

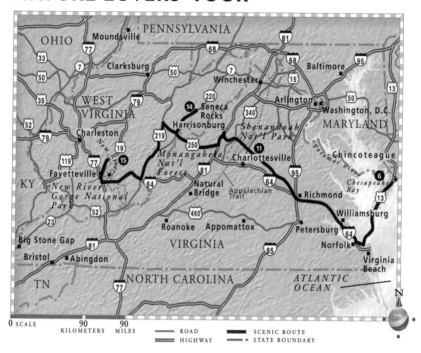

This route will give you the best scenery, activities, and wildlife of the region. It will truly take two weeks to enjoy this list of outdoor delights, however, you can customize to fit your travel plans.

- ❻ **Eastern Shore** (Chincoteague)
- ⓫ **Shenandoah Valley Area** (Appalachian Trail, Natural Bridge, Shenandoah National Park)
- ⓮ **West Virginia Highlands** (Seneca, Snowshoe Resort)
- ⓯ **New River/Greenbrier Valley** (New River Gorge National Park, Fayetteville/white-water rafting)

Time needed: two weeks

ARTS AND CULTURE TOUR

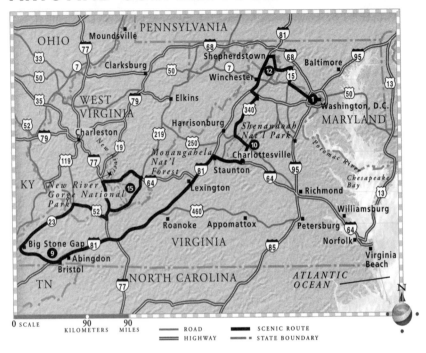

From bluegrass to opera, the Capital Region's diverse mix of arts and culture make it a fascinating destination for entertainment.

- ❶ **Washington, D.C.** (the Smithsonian Institution)
- ⓬ **West Virginia's Eastern Panhandle** (Shepherdstown, art theater)
- ❿ **Charlottesville** (University of Virginia, Ash Lawn-Highland)
- ❾ **Southwest Virginia** (Abingdon, Barter Theatre, Bristol/Big Stone Gap—bluegrass/outdoor theater)
- ⓯ **New River/Greenbrier Valley** (Tamarack, folk art/crafts)

Time needed: two weeks

FAMILY FUN TOUR

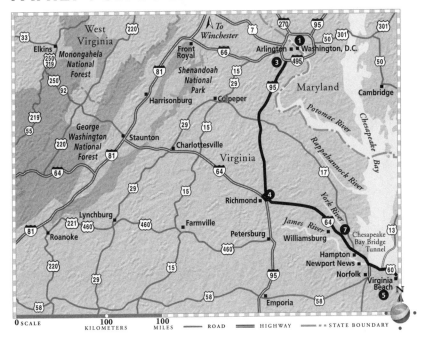

Families visiting the region will find something to keep virtually every age entertained. From great theme parks to fascinating museums, the region is a family vacation paradise. Spend most of your time between Washington and the beach area in Virginia for the highest concentration of attractions that will appeal to kids (of all ages that is).

- **❶ Washington, D.C.** (the Smithsonian Institution, White House and White House Visitor Center)
- **❸ Northern Virginia** (Arlington, Newseum)
- **❹ Richmond** (Paramount's Kings Dominion, milder white-water rafting)
- **❼ Historic Triangle** (Colonial Williamsburg, Busch Gardens, Water Country USA)
- **❺ Virginia's Coast** (Virginia Beach, beach and Virginia Marine Science Museum)

Time needed: one to two weeks

CIVIL WAR HISTORY TOUR

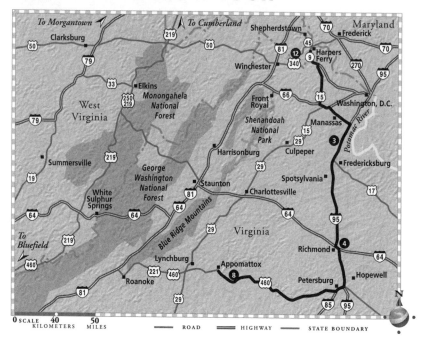

The nice folks in Virginia have made it easy for you to visit the region's many Civil War battlefields and sites. Virginia's Civil War Trails are marked with red, white, and blue road signs pertaining to various campaigns—the 1862 Peninsula Campaign, Shenandoah Valley Campaign, 1861–1865 Northern Virginia Campaign, the 1864 Overland Campaign, and Lee's Retreat. For brochures and detailed routes of the campaigns call 888/CIVIL WAR. This route will take those who have limited time to some of the most important sites in the country.

- **①② West Virginia's Eastern Panhandle** (Harper's Ferry)
- **③ Northern Virginia** (Manassas, Fredericksburg)
- **④ Richmond** (Virginia's State Capitol, Museum and White House of the Confederacy)
- **⑧ Central Southside** (Appomattox, Petersburg, Hopewell)

Time needed: one week

ROMANTIC GETAWAY TOUR

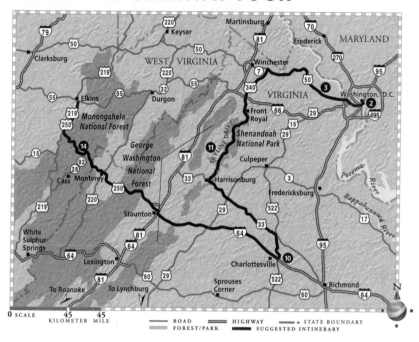

Virginia and West Virginia provide an excellent getaway with romantic inns, wonderful restaurants, and spectacular scenery. Although there are plenty of cozy spots along the coast as well, there's just something romantic about a crackling fire and a mountain sunset.

- ❷ **Washington, D.C.** (Inn at Little Washington)
- ❸ **Northern Virginia** (Virginia's Hunt Country)
- ⓫ **Shenandoah Valley Area** (Skyline Drive)
- ❿ **Charlottesville** (hot-air balloon rides, wineries)
- ⓮ **West Virginia Highlands** (West Virginia Mountains, Greenbrier, Erehwon Cabins)

Time needed: one week

RESOURCES

Virginia Tourism Corporation, 901 E. Byrd St., Richmond, 23219, 800/VISIT VA, www.virginia.com

Washington, D.C., Convention and Visitors Assn., 1212 New York Ave., NW, Suite 600, 20005-3992, 202/789-7099, www.washington.org

West Virginia Division of Tourism, 2101 Washington St., E., Charleston, 25305, 800/CALL WVA, www.westvirginia.com

Virginia Division of State Parks, 203 Governor St., Richmond, 23219, 800/933-7275

West Virginia Division of State Parks, Capitol Complex, Charleston, 25305, 800/CALL WVA

U.S. Fish and Wildlife Service, Dept. of Interior, 413/253-8322

Shenandoah National Park, 540/999-2243

Washington National Forest, 540/564-8300

Monongahela National Forest, 304/636-1800

Jefferson National Forest, 540/265-6054

Lodging Chain Reservation Numbers

Best Western, 800/528-1234

Clarion Inn, 800/CLARION

Comfort Inn, 800/228-5150

Days Inn, 800/325-2525

Econolodge, 800/55 ECONO

Hilton, 800/HILTON 7

Holiday Inn, 800/465-4329

Hyatt, 800/233-1234

Marriott, 800/228-9290

Motel 6, 800/4 MOTEL 6

Omni, 800/843-6664

Quality Inn, 800/228-5151

Radisson, 800/333-3333

Ramada, 800/2 RAMADA

Sheraton, 800/325-3535

Sleep Inn, 800/SLEEP IN

Super 8, 800/800-8000

Travelodge, 800/578-7878

Hampton Visitor Center, 710 Settlers Landing Road, Hampton; 800/800-2202 or 757/727-1102. Daily 9–5.

Norfolk Convention and Visitors Bureau, 232 Virginia Beach Boulevard,
   Norfolk, 23510, 757/664-6620 or 800/368-3097.
Norfolk Visitor Center, I-64 (Exit 273), Fourth View Street, Norfolk,
   757/441-1852 or 800/368-3097.

*There are four visitor centers in the Richmond area offering assistance with maps,
directions, hints on where to go and offering discounts off hotel reservations if
made from a visitor center.*
Main Visitor Center, 1710 Robin Hood Road, Exit 78 off I-95/I-64,
   804/358-5511. Memorial Day–Labor Day daily 9–7, rest of the year 9–5.
Airport Visitor Center, Richmond International Airport, Exit 197 off I-64,
   804/236-3260. Mon–Sat 9:30–5:30, Sun noon–5.
Downtown Visitor Center, Bell Tower on Capitol Square, 804/648-3146.
   Daily 9–4.
Hanover Visitor Center (north of Richmond), Ashland, Exit 92B off I-95,
   804/752-6755.

Newport News Visitor Information Center, 13560 Jefferson Avenue,
   Newport News, 23603, 757/886-7777, 888/4WE-R-FUN. Daily 9–5.
Gray Line Tours; 757/853-6480; reservations made by 4 p.m. for next day
   tours.
Norfolk Trolley Tour, departs from front of Waterside Festival Marketplace,
   757/640-6300; May–Labor Day. 10:30 a.m., noon, 1:30, and 3 p.m.; Sept
   noon, 1:30 p.m. and 3 p.m.; $3.50 adults, $1.75 children under age
   12/seniors/handicapped.

INDEX

Map Index